IMAGES
of America

WESTBROOK

ON THE PRESUMPSCOT

IMAGES
of America

WESTBROOK

ON THE PRESUMPSCOT

The Westbrook History 2000 Committee
and Dianne LeConte

ARCADIA
PUBLISHING

ISBN 978-0-7385-8969-5

Published by Arcadia Publishing
Charleston, South Carolina

Printed in the United States of America

Library of Congress Catalog Card Number:

For all general information contact Arcadia Publishing at:
Telephone 843-853-2070
Fax 843-853-0044
E-mail sales@arcadiapublishing.com
For customer service and orders:
Toll-Free 1-888-313-2665

Visit us on the Internet at www.arcadiapublishing.com

Contents

Acknowledgments

Westbrook History 2000 Committee:

Vaun Born, Betty Brown, Ethelyn Chase, Grace Curtis, Newton Curtis Jr., Lillian Dyhrberg, Lori Hawkes, William Jacobs, Wayne Kimball, Kathleen King, John LaPointe, Patricia Larrabee, Philip LaViolette, Dianne LeConte, Betty Morabito, Bill Robertson, Michael Sanphy, Ellie Saunders, and Joseph Thibault.

Special thanks to:

Beverly Canales for nights and weekends and William Kahler for technical work.

Introduction

The Rockameecocks and Aucocisco people were among the Abenakis, Native Americans who planted corn along the banks of the Presumpscot and fished its waters. For the early European settlers and their families, the river would remain a source of food and a water highway, as they harnessed its power for industry and travel.

In 1729, the foundation was laid for what would become a lumber business in Saccarappa, a hamlet of Stroudwater. Several years later in 1737, Joseph Conant traveled by canoe up the river with his family to build a home and a mill to support them. By February of 1814, Stroudwater seceded from Falmouth and by June of that year, it changed its name to Westbrook. The villages comprising Westbrook—Saccarappa, Congin, and Duck Pond—had developed small manufacturing. The tax assessor's list of 1814 contained the following: Saccarappa was listed with nine saw mills, two grist mills, and three carding and fulling mills. Congin (now Cumberland Mills) had three saw mills and one grist mill, and Duck Pond and Duck Pond Brook were home to five saw mills and one grist mill. In the 1830s, a mill was built in Saccarappa that would become the Westbrook Manufacturing Company. This building was later purchased by the Dana Warp Company, founded in 1866.

The Congin Paper Mill opened its doors in 1854. Two years later, the mill was purchased by Samuel D. Warren and Otis Warren, who founded the S. D. Warren Company. Since that time, members of the Warren family have been well-known for their philanthropy: Cornelia for her involvement in the Settlement House Movement, Ned for the acquisition of art and antiquities that have become the cornerstone of the classical collections at the Boston Museum of Fine Art and the Bowdoin College Museum, and Fisk for his involvement in social issues. Their philanthropy was made possible by the labor of Westbrook workers.

The descendants of the early English settlers were joined by Irish day laborers who dug the Cumberland & Oxford Canal. Scottish workers, and later French workers from Quebec, northern Maine, and the Maritimes, arrived in Westbrook to work in the textile mills. Danish farmers, by way of New Denmark, New Brunswick, became paper workers in this area.

Religious life was first organized by the Congregationalists. By the late eighteenth century, Wesleyan circuit preachers gathered a group that would become the nucleus for the local Methodist Church. Universalists built their first church in 1840. Catholics were numerous enough that by 1879, St. Hyacinthe Parish was formed. Soon after, the Lutheran Church was formed in 1882.

On June 20, 1794, Robert Blair from County Armagh, Ireland, arrived in Portland. Ten days later, he began teaching students from Saccarappa, Congin, and Rocky Hill. From this modest beginning, the Westbrook School System began to develop.

With the spread of industry, new housing was built on Brown Street and Walker Street for the workers at the Dana Warp Mill and the Haskell Silk Mill. The Warrens hired Portland architect John Calvin Stevens to design the houses on Cottage Place and the Queen Anne-style cottages on Brown Street. Henry George, author of *Poverty and Progress*, was popular by the 1880s in the United States and Britain; and Fisk Warren, with others, developed Halidon Village as a single-tax colony.

Strong in the face of a challenge, the people of Westbrook patiently rebuilt dams and bridges washed out by river floods and ice jams. They celebrated centennials and anniversaries in both the good and the hard times. They embraced the advent of the daguerreotype and were enthusiastic about the development of photography. In the 1891 city directory, the photographer H. E. Wight advertised that "Any person wanting Photographs, Pastels, Crayons, Waters Colors, will serve their own interests in visiting my studio. A High Novelty I am offering now in Glace Photography, which for beauty and durability are not excelled anywhere. Come and see them." The photographic narrative that follows here is not exhaustive, but it is rather a rich sample of Westbrook images.

John LaPointe

One

Mills

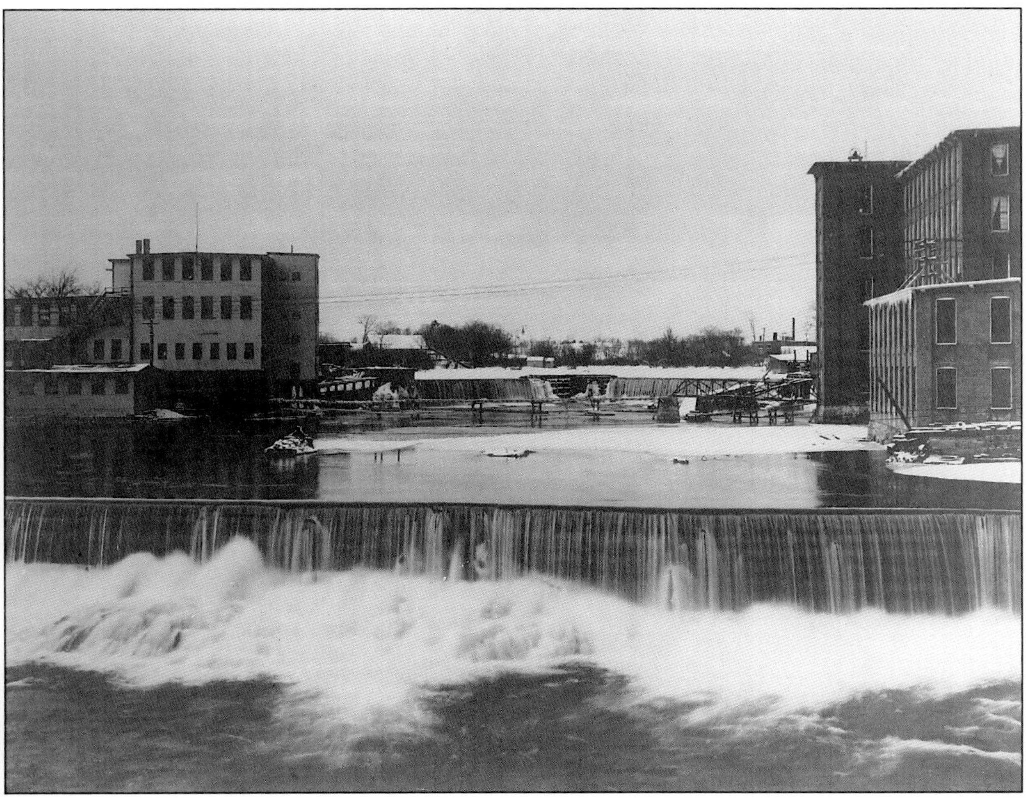

Presumpscot Falls, with a view of some of Westbrook's mill buildings.

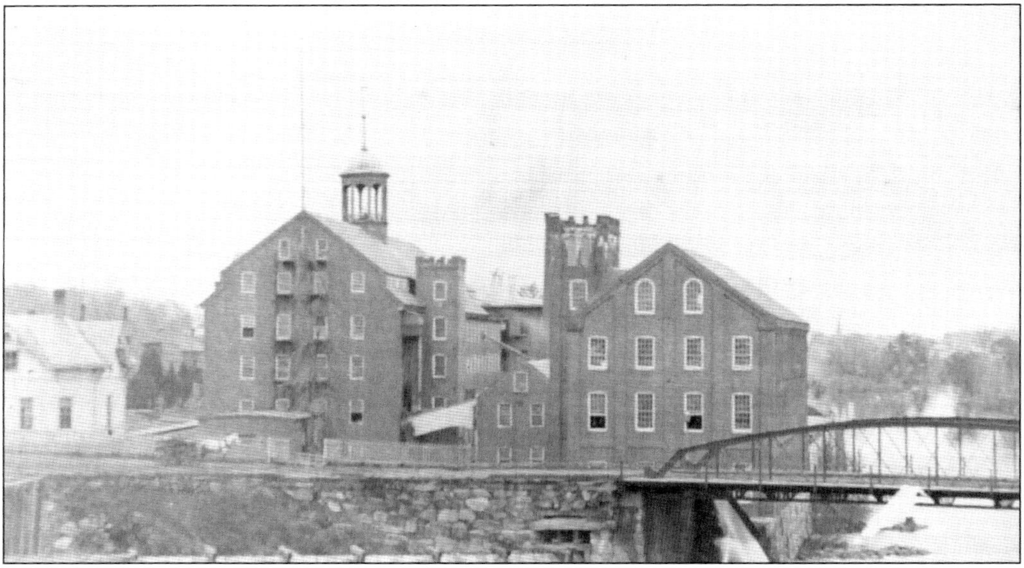

The Westbrook Manufacturing Company, c. 1874. "Duck" or heavy canvas used for making sails and tents was manufactured here. Atop its four stories, Mill No. 2 housed a belfry that contained the mill bell. The iron bridge crosses the river at Bridge Street.

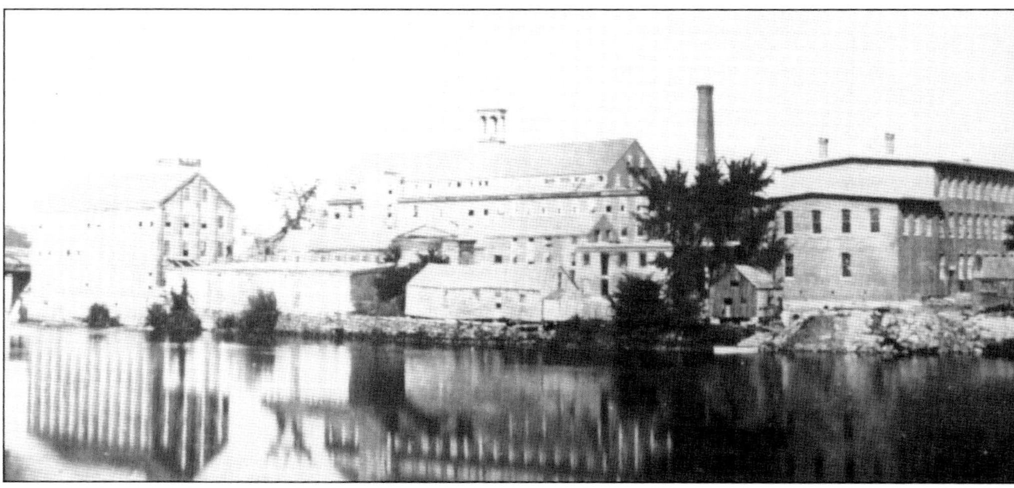

Rear view of the Westbrook Manufacturing Company, c. 1874. The small wooden building seen below the chimney is M. V. Knight, blacksmith.

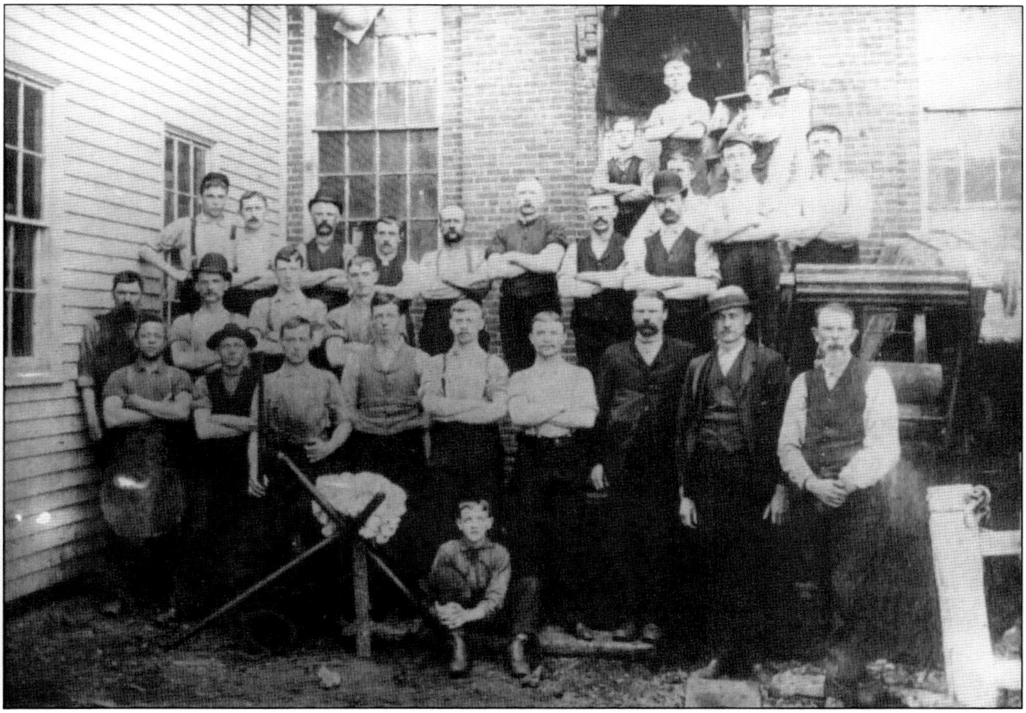

An unidentified crew of workers from the Westbrook Manufacturing Company pose outside in the late 1800s.

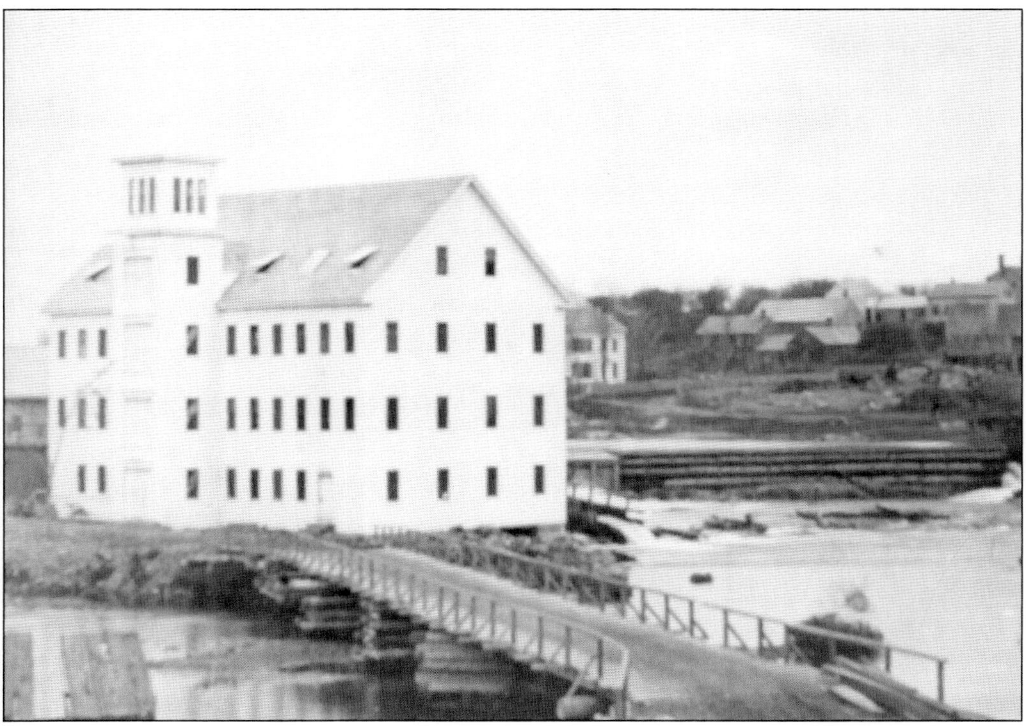

Dana Warp Mill in 1882. When the company first opened, it used the building on the "island" originally built by the Westbrook Manufacturing Company.

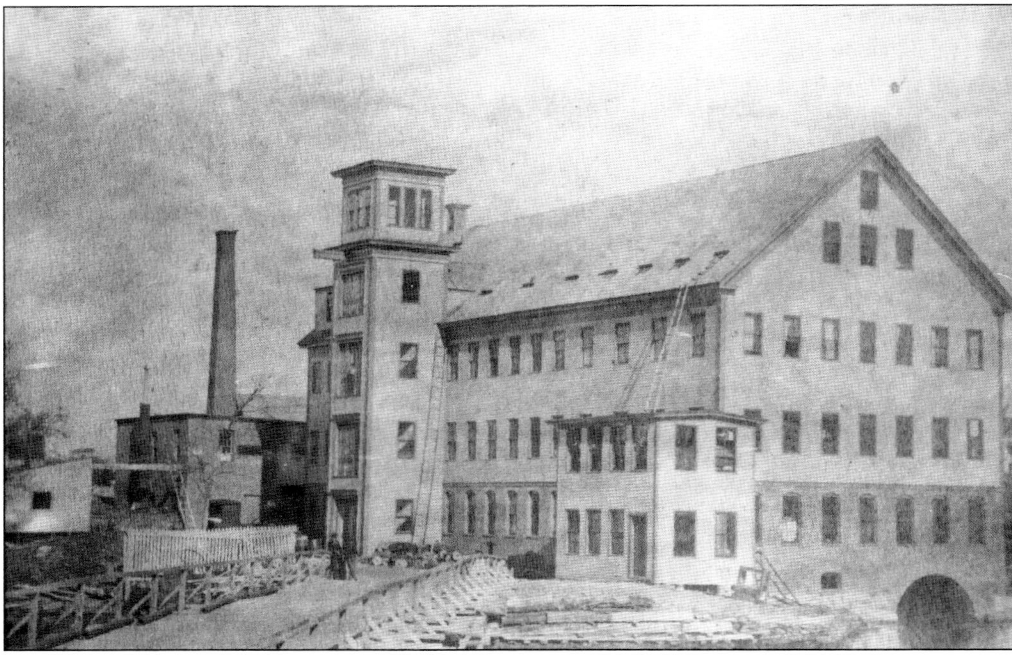

Another view of the Dana Warp Mill in 1882.

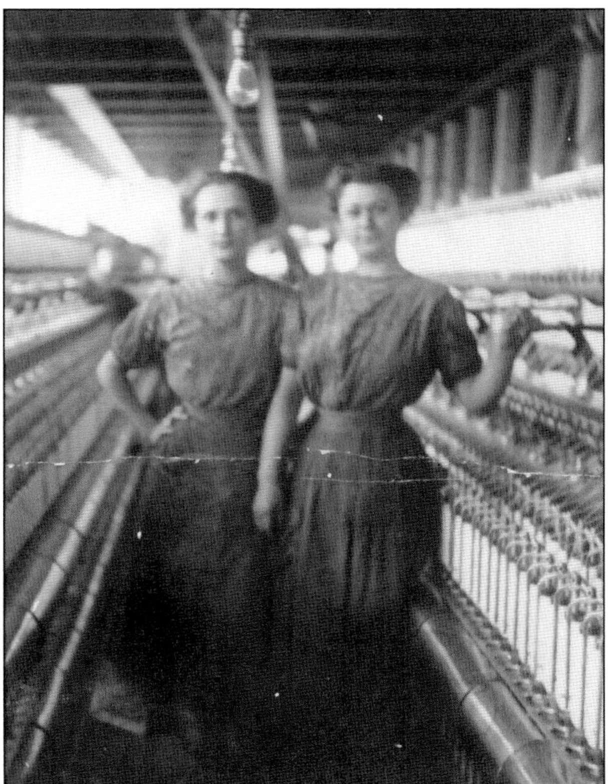

Dana Warp Mill "girls," 1910. On the left is Antonia LeConte, who later married Cecil McAloney. On the right is Lottie Landry, who later married Henry Pedneault. (Curtis Collection.)

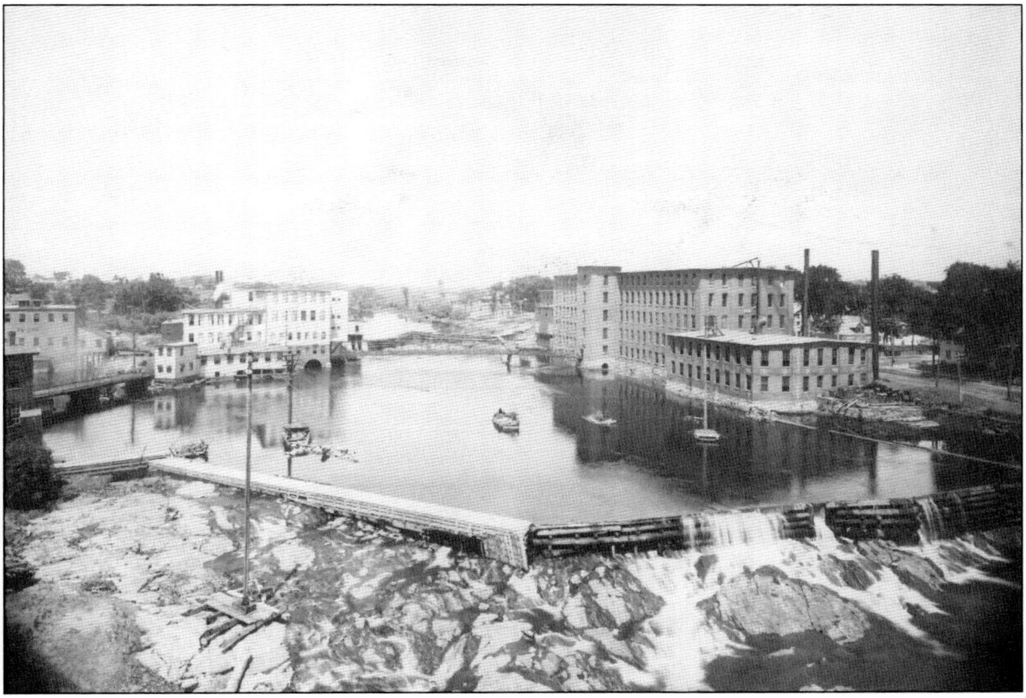

Dana Warp Mills, Numbers 1 and 2. The old power house can be seen on the left. Note the bridge (center) which connects the two mills. Bridge Street is on the far right.

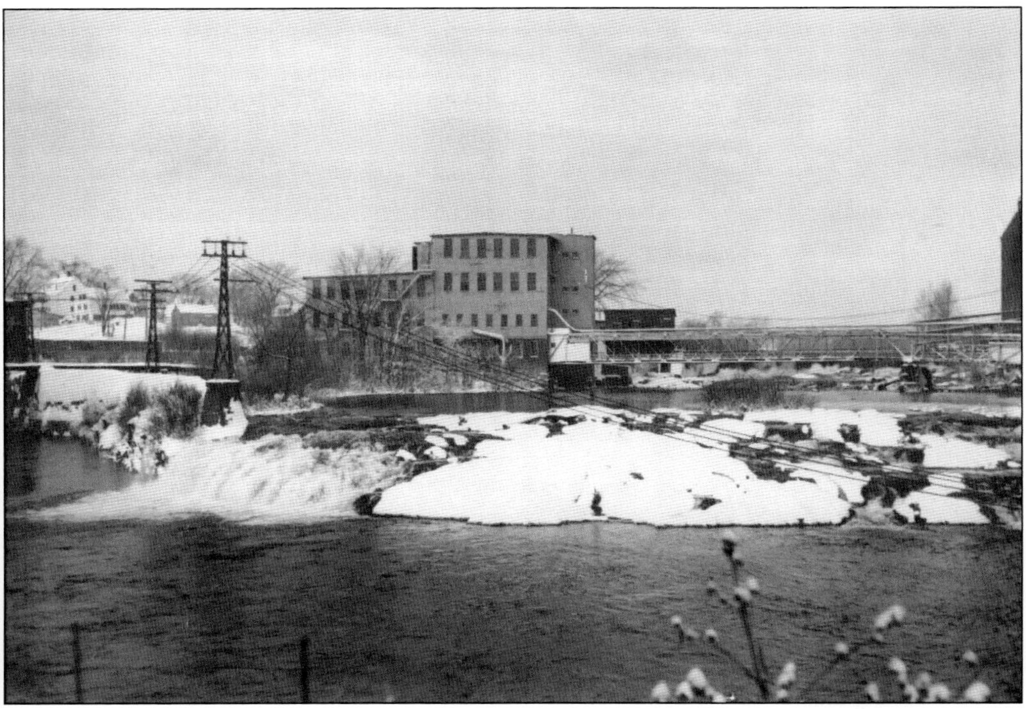

Dana Warp Mill No. 1 on the island, giving a good view of the connecting bridge between the two mills.

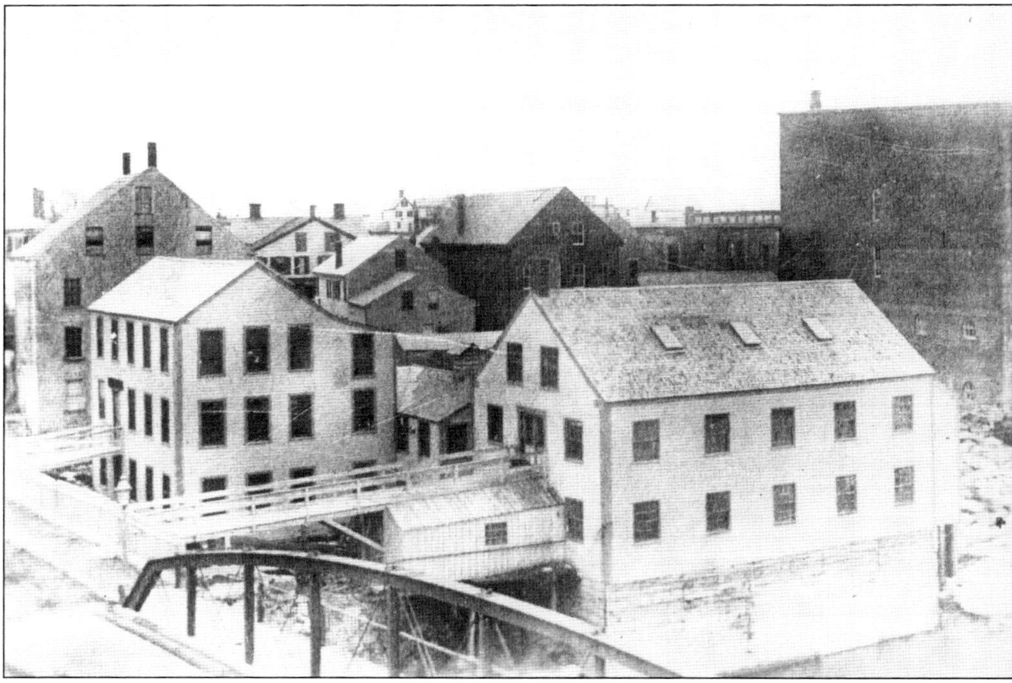

Tenement house on Bridge Street housing the first silk mill (No. 1), *c.* 1865. This mill, owned by Mr. Vogel, was located on the west side of Bridge Street, next to the bridge. It was eventually bought by Mr. Haskell.

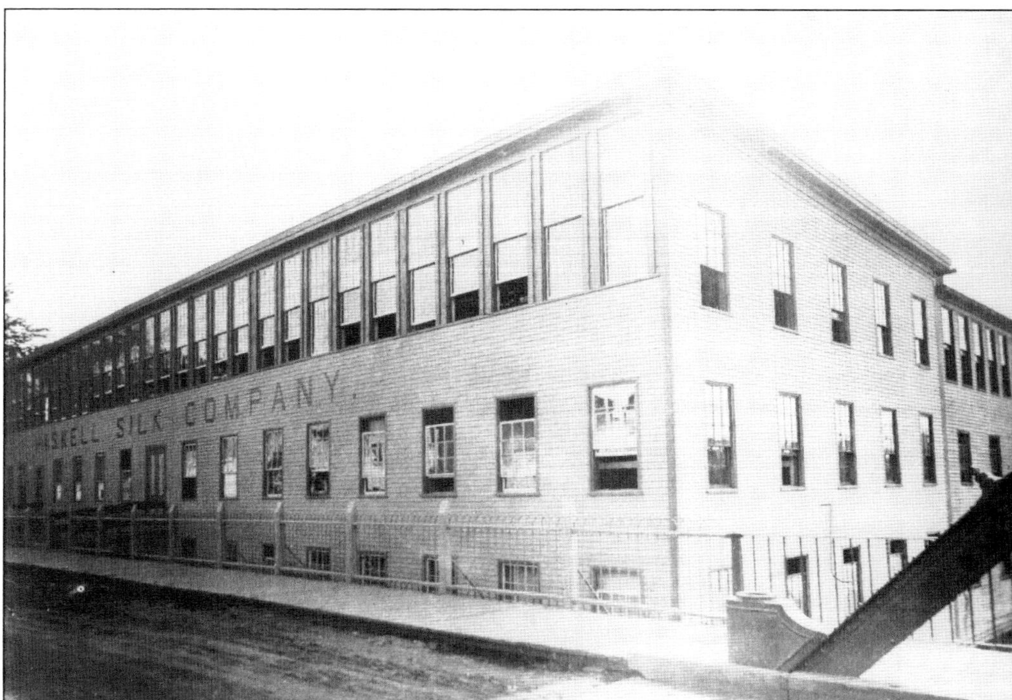

Haskell Silk Mill, located on Bridge Street, just before it was torn down in 1900.

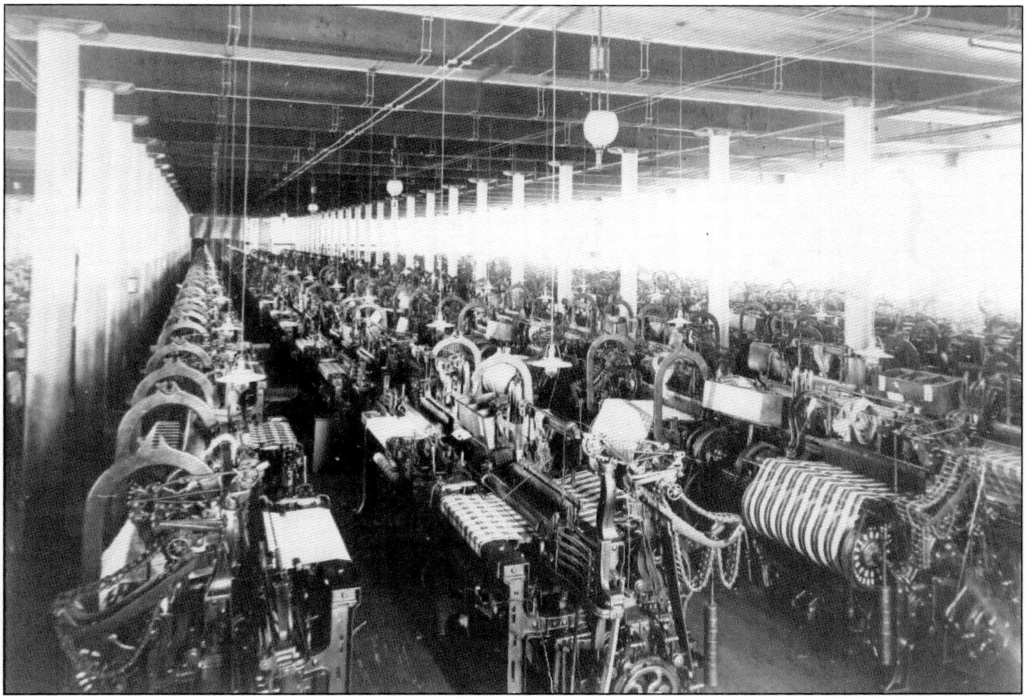

A view of the interior of the Haskell Silk Mill, showing the machinery and various silk patterns being manufactured.

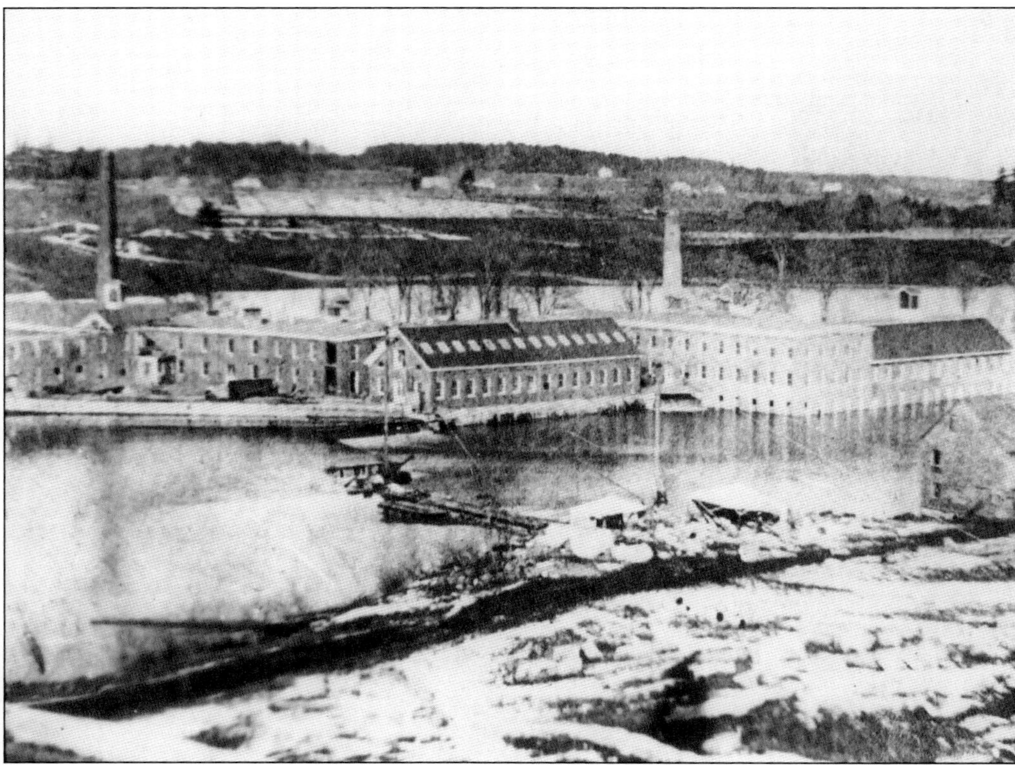

The S. D. Warren Paper Mill, 1879.

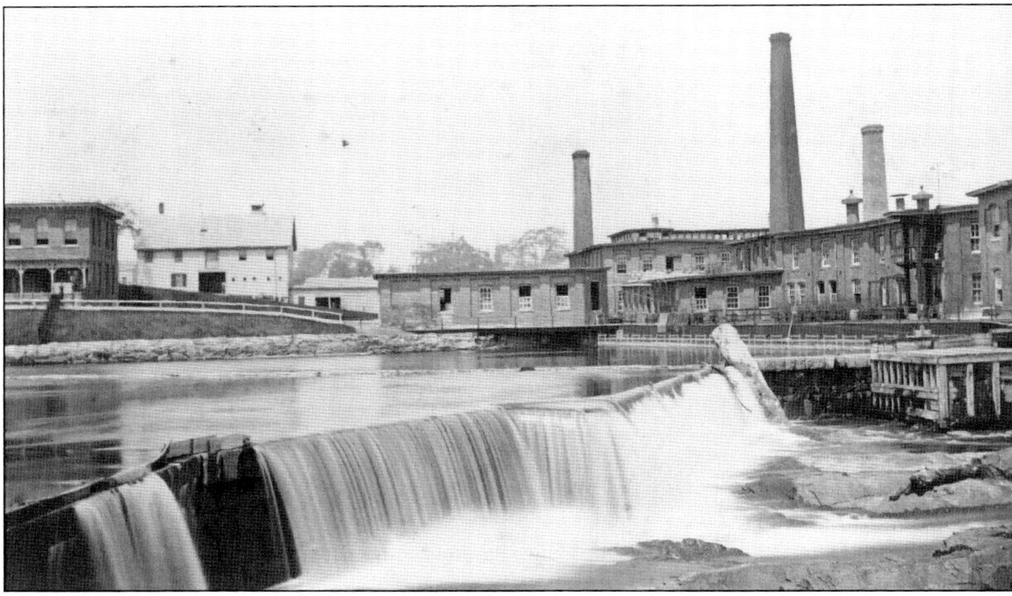

Another view of the S. D. Warren Paper Mill (also called the Cumberland Mills), 1884.

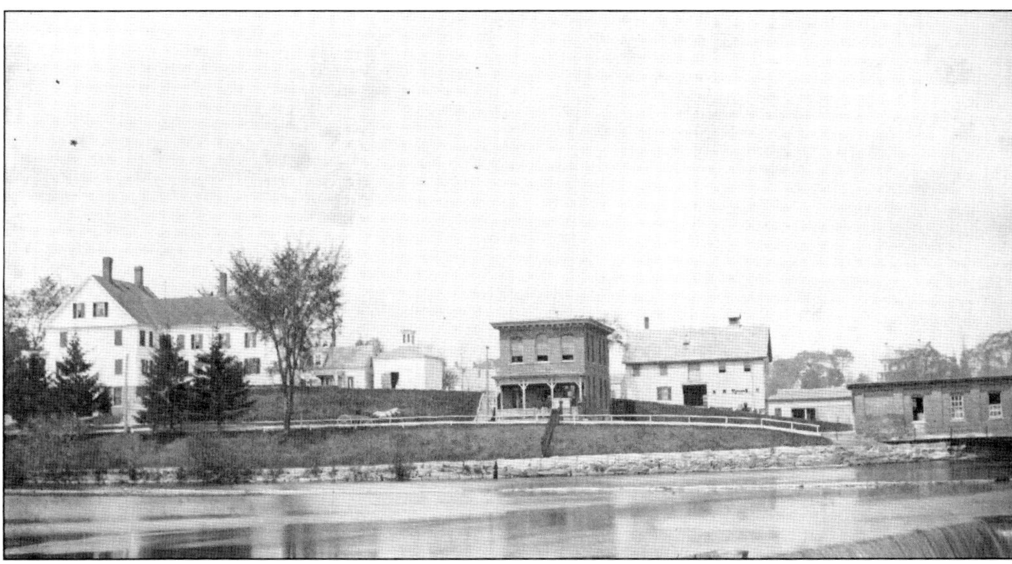

The brick office and stables of the S. D. Warren Paper Company, *c.* 1885.

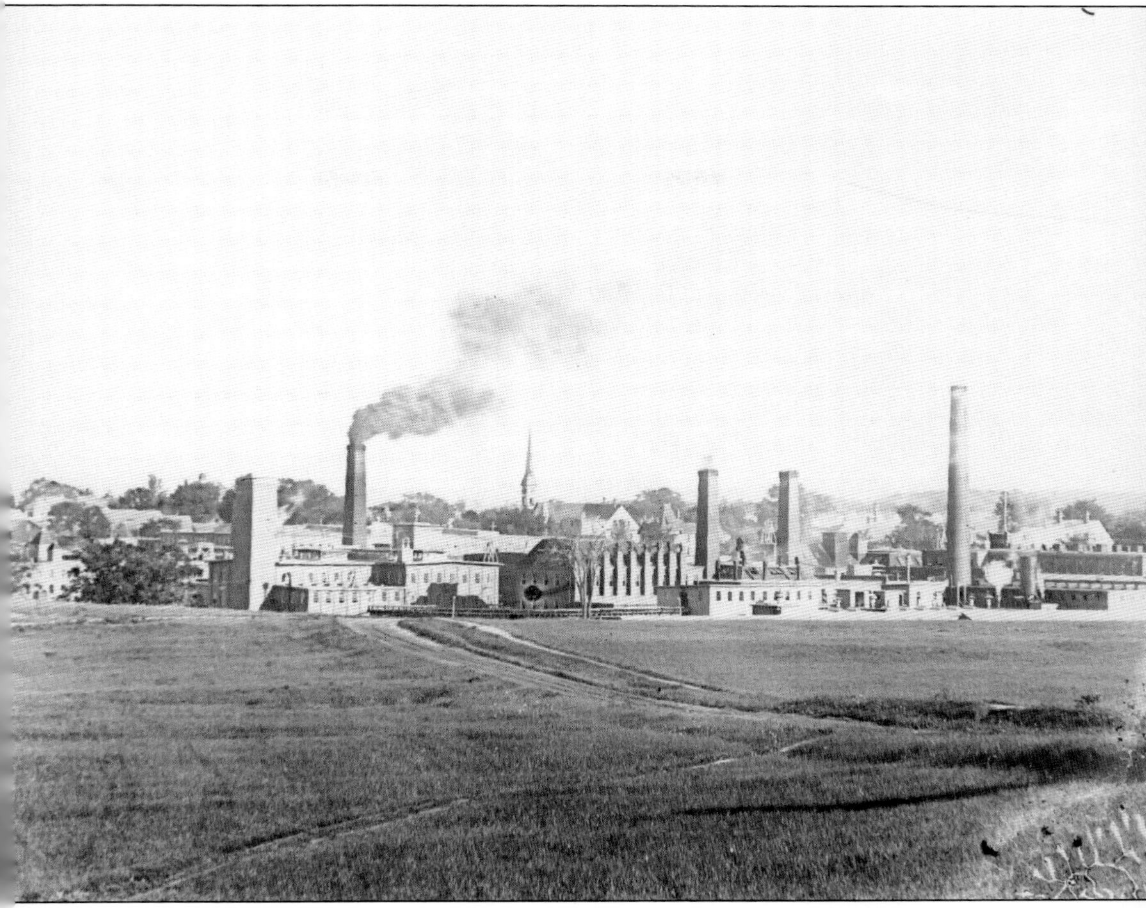

Rear view of the S. D. Warren Paper Mill, c. 1885. The steeple of the Warren Congregational Church can be seen in the center background. When Samuel Dennis Warren purchased the mill with other partners in 1854, it was the Cumberland Mills. Eventually, the other partners withdrew and Mr. Warren carried on the Cumberland Mills until re-organization in 1918 when the name changed to S. D. Warren Company. Although Mr. Warren resided in Boston, where the firm's offices were, he and his successors were always generous to the people of Westbrook, through their donations of buildings, churches, and a swimming pool—to name a few benefits in addition to the employment of many. The Warrens prospered because of the river and Westbrook people prospered because of the mills.

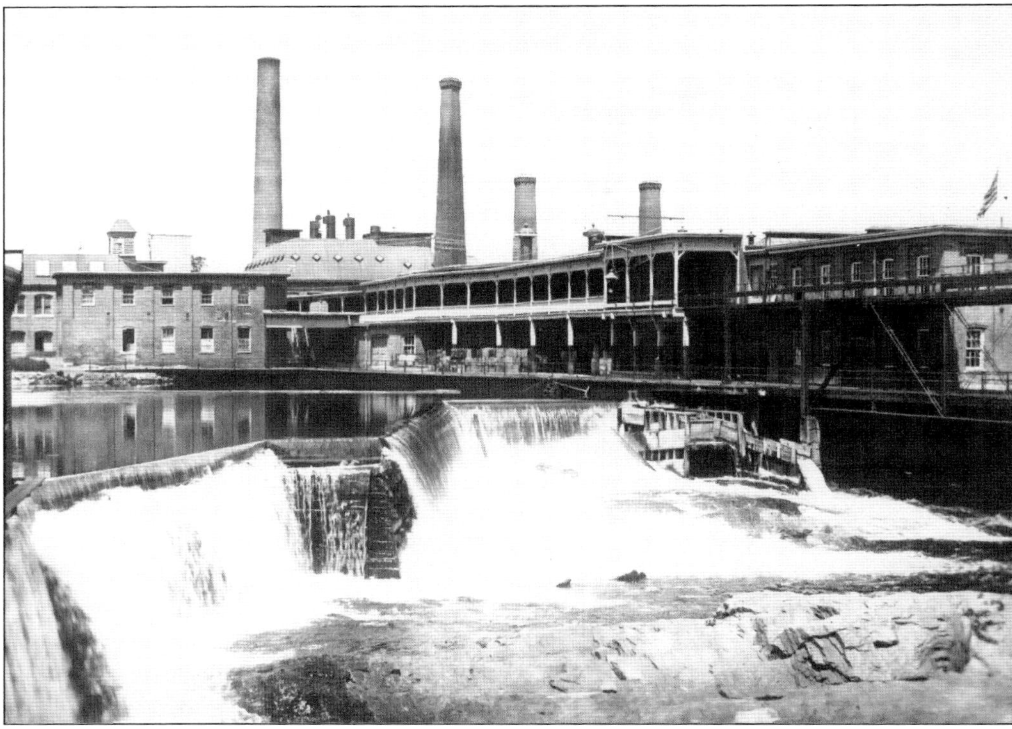

A view of the S. D. Warren Company showing the falls, 1890.

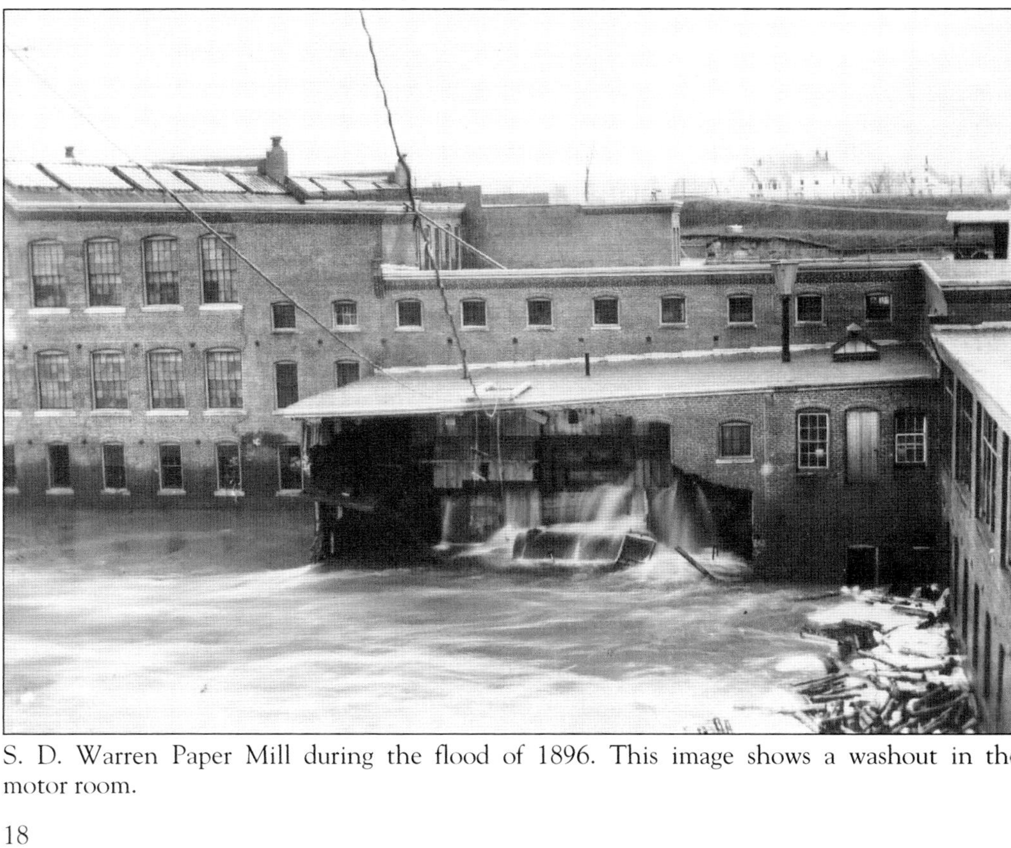

S. D. Warren Paper Mill during the flood of 1896. This image shows a washout in the motor room.

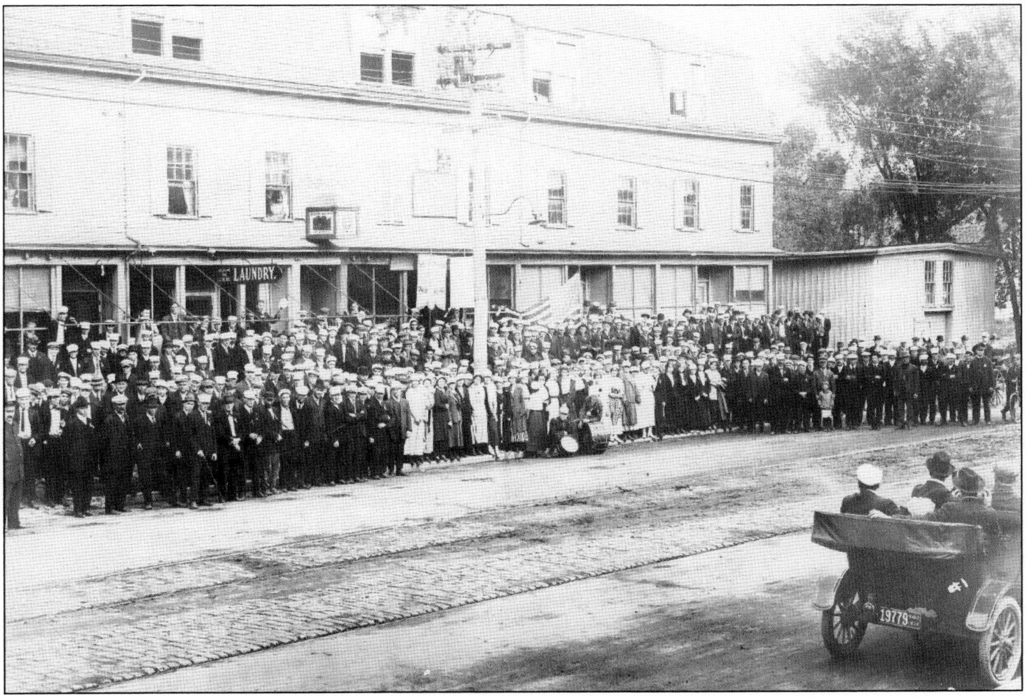

Strikers of the Warren Paper Mills, 1916. This picture was taken from the front of what is now the Warren Memorial Library.

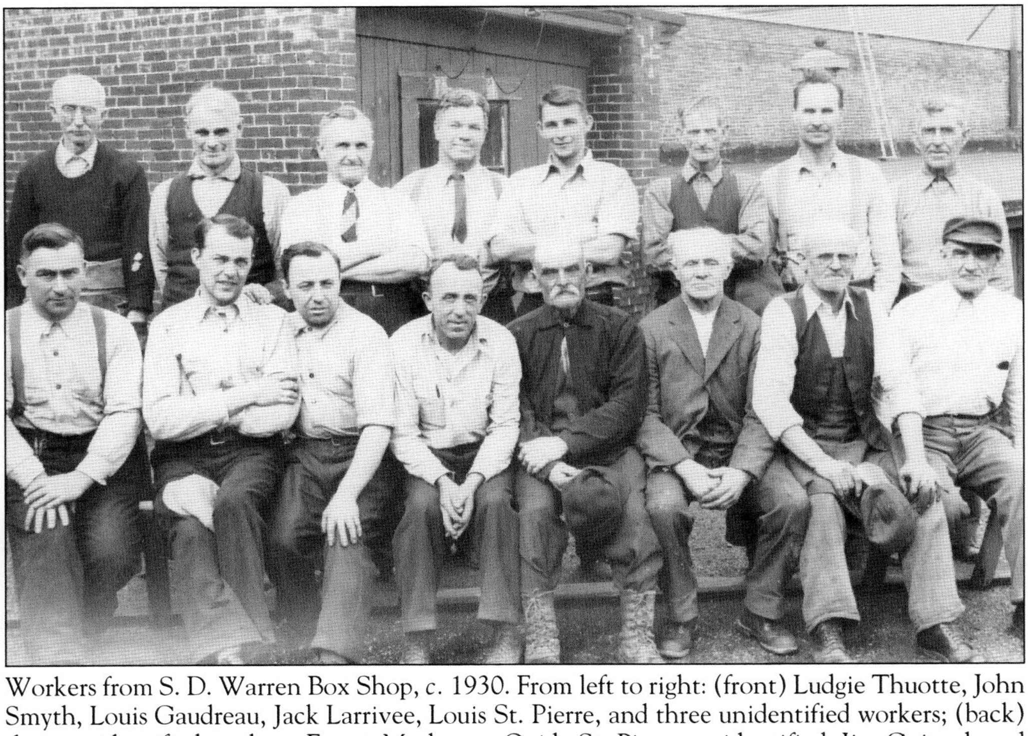

Workers from S. D. Warren Box Shop, c. 1930. From left to right: (front) Ludgie Thuotte, John Smyth, Louis Gaudreau, Jack Larrivee, Louis St. Pierre, and three unidentified workers; (back) three unidentified workers, Ernest Mushreau, Ovide St. Pierre, unidentified, Jim Guitard, and Emery Labreque.

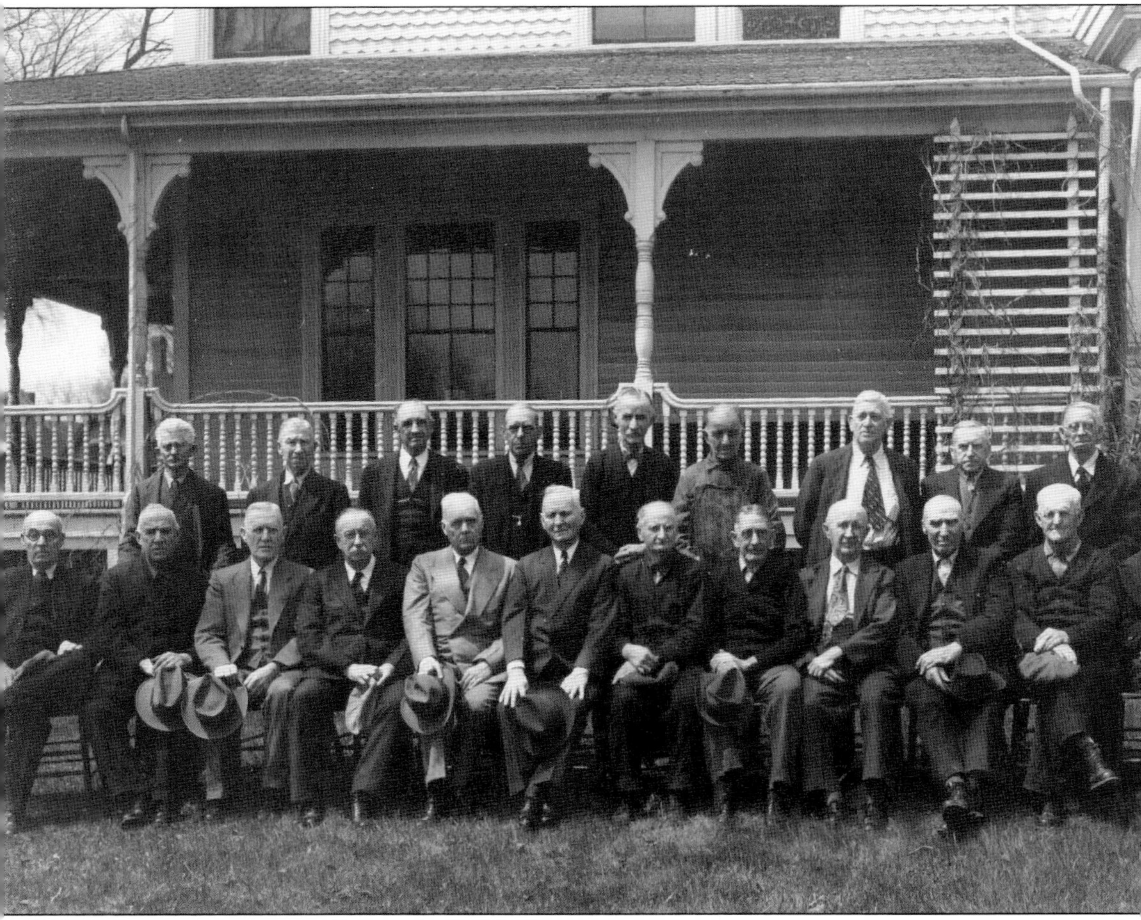

S. D. Warren Fifty-Year Club, May 7, 1943. From left to right: (front). George H. Naylor, Jacob A. Bancroft, Patrick Welch, Edwin L. Brown, Joseph A. Warren, George W. Conant, Archelaus Lewis, Herbert E. Lord, Loton M. Hill, Joseph Blake, George H. Lord, Alvin A. Barbour; (back) Neils H. Smith, Thomas Meehan, Henry L. Hendrickson, Harry L. Pride, Oscar Libby, Moses Doucet, Andrew C. Kelley, C. Roy Wyer, Perley L. Babbidge, and Samuel A. Guimond. Not pictured: Roger D. Smith, Nelson Libby, and Horatio N. Harriman. Mr. Archelaus Lewis had been with the company for sixty years on this date. All others had completed at least fifty years of employment with S .D. Warren.

Two

Businesses

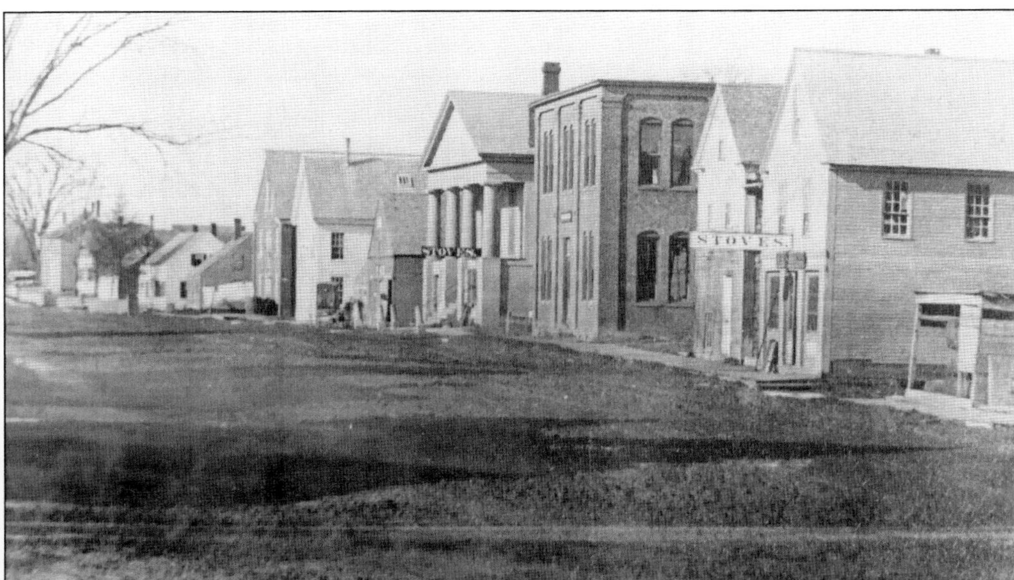

Main Street, c. 1850. With the development of the textile mills at the upper falls and the paper mill at the lower falls, employment rose and population began to grow. Business began to increase to accommodate this influx. This photograph shows the old Universalist church in the center, which later became the Foster and Brown Machine Shop.

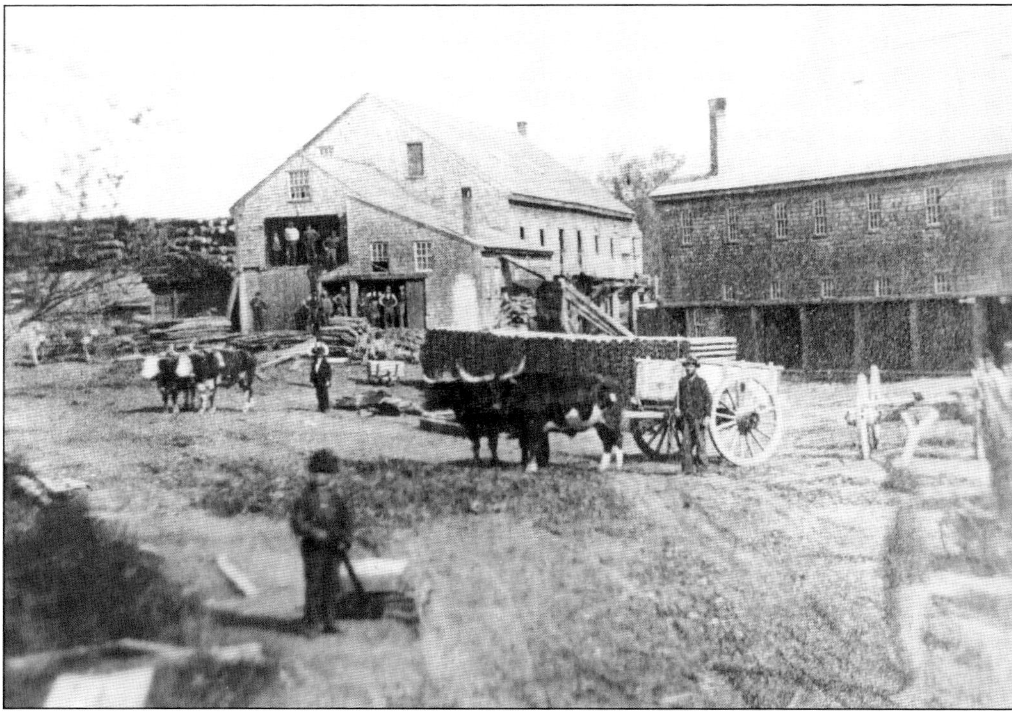

The old saw mill located on "Pork Hill," 1878.

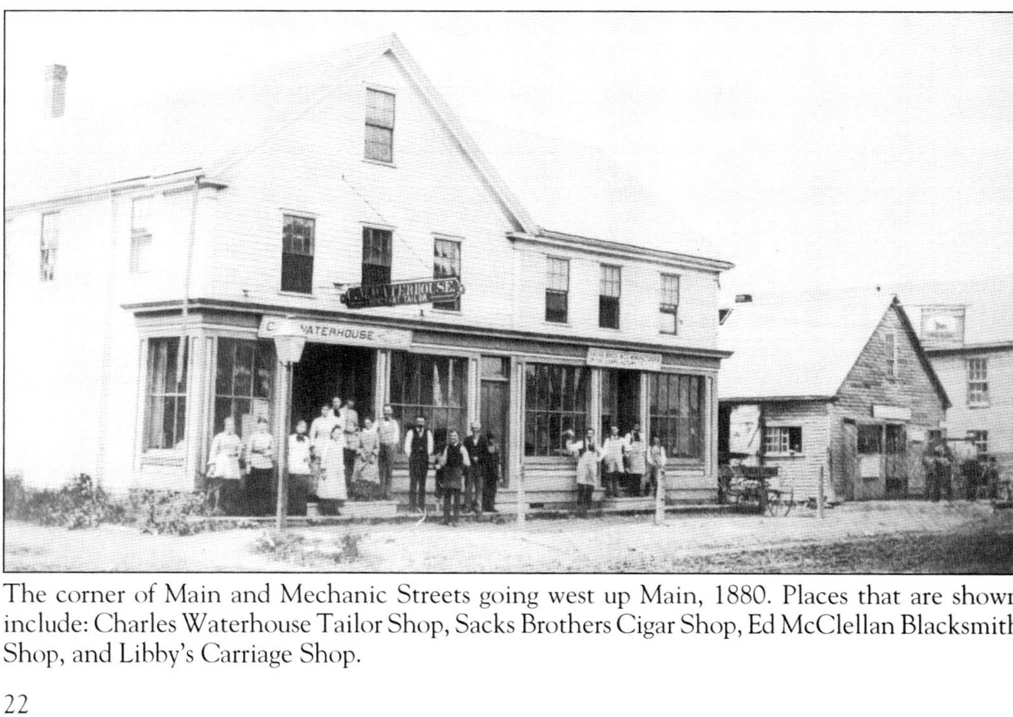

The corner of Main and Mechanic Streets going west up Main, 1880. Places that are shown include: Charles Waterhouse Tailor Shop, Sacks Brothers Cigar Shop, Ed McClellan Blacksmith Shop, and Libby's Carriage Shop.

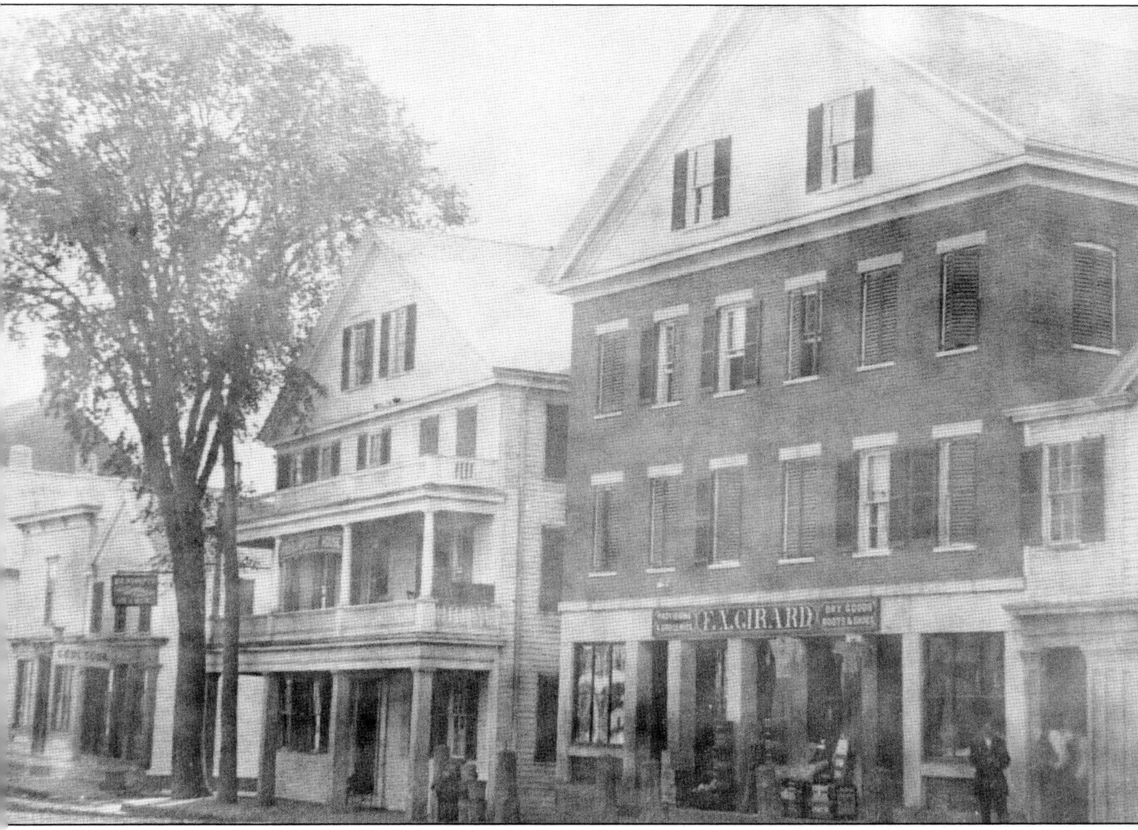

At the square, c. 1880. On the right is F. X. Girard, Groceries Etc. at 75 Main St., Saccarappa (before the numbering system was changed). At the center is Presumpscot House, a hotel and boarding house. On the left is the old post office.

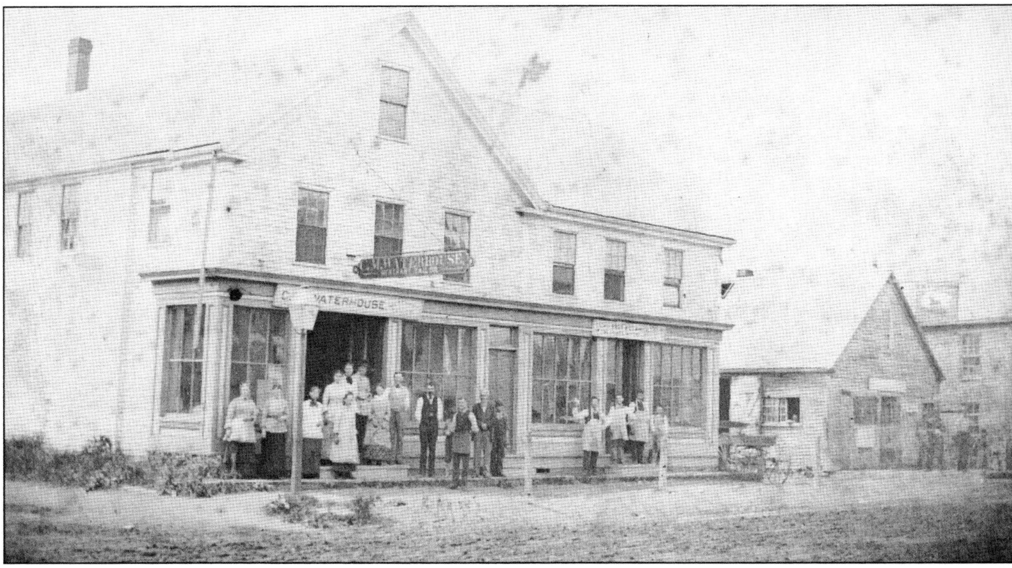

C. M. Waterhouse and crew, 1880. This shop was at the corner of Main and Mechanic Streets. Sacks Fine Cigars is at the center and the Henry McLellan Blacksmith Shop is on the right. (Westbrook Historical Society Collection.)

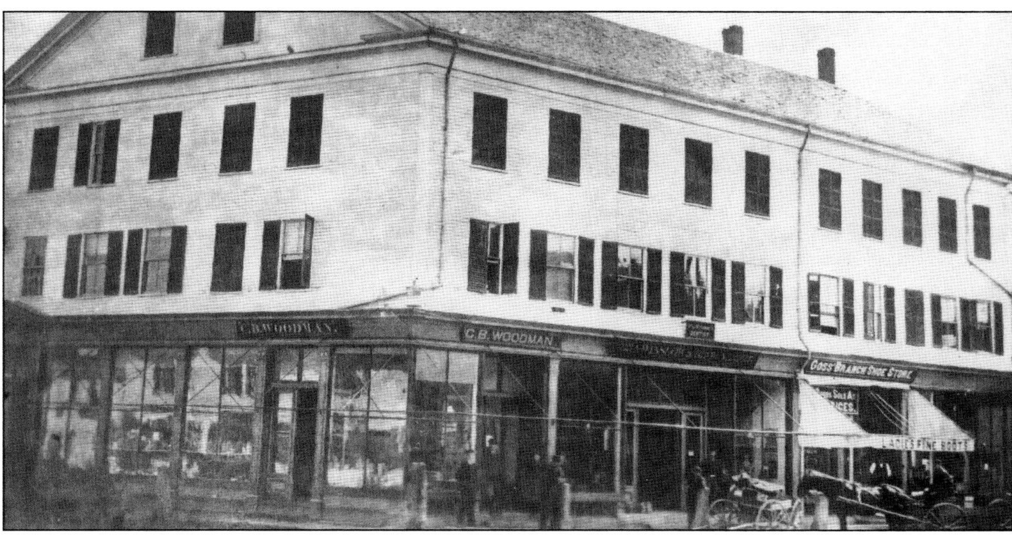

Corner of Bridge and Main Streets at the square, 1883. C. B. Woodman Store and McCann's Shoe Store can be seen.

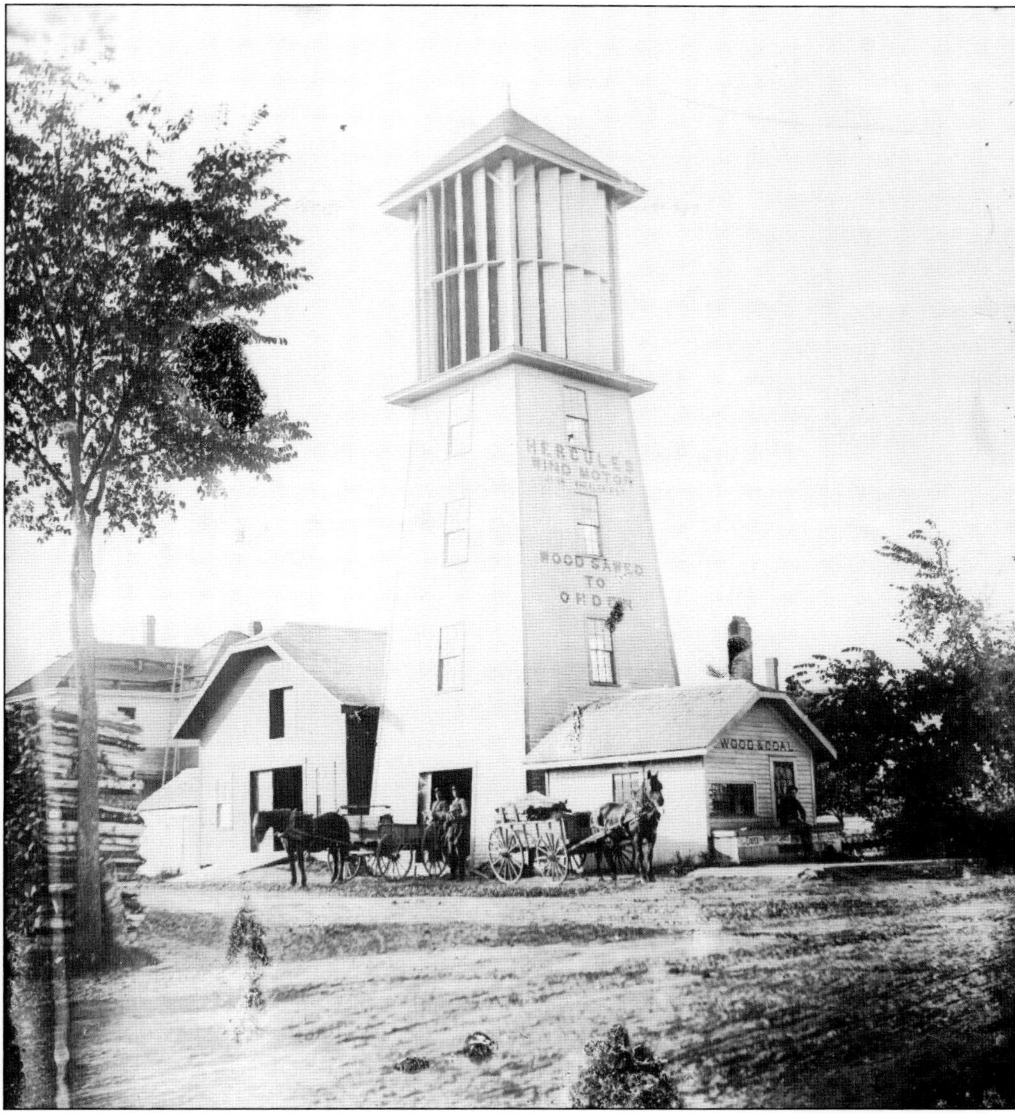

John Wheeler's coal and wood office and windmill at the corner of Main and Haskell Streets, *c.* 1885.

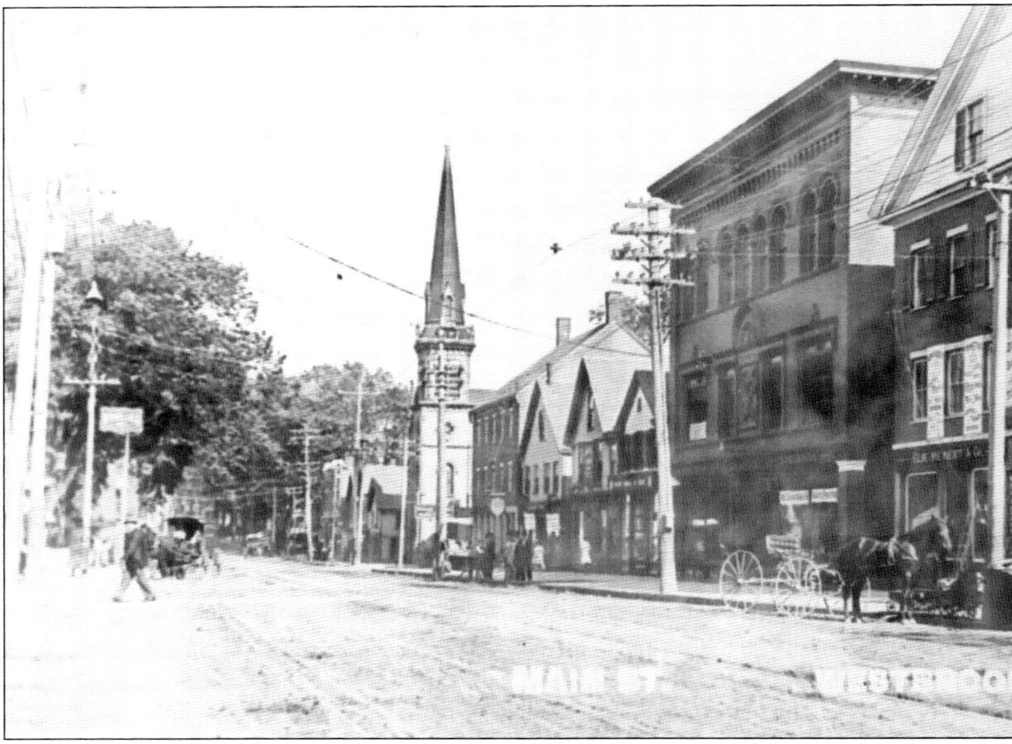

Main Street, looking east in the late 1800s. Westbrook Congregational Church is in the center.

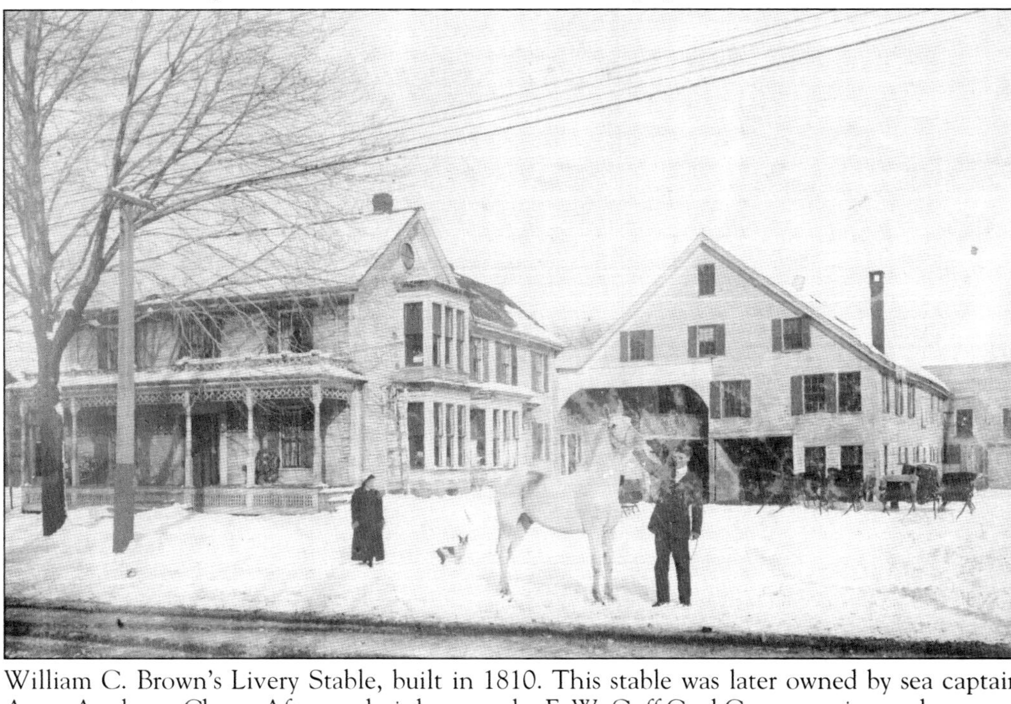

William C. Brown's Livery Stable, built in 1810. This stable was later owned by sea captain Amos Appleton Chase. Afterwards, it became the F. W. Goff Coal Co., operating at the corner of Main Street and Warren Avenue. This is the present site of the S. D. Warren Credit Union. (Ethelyn Chase Collection.)

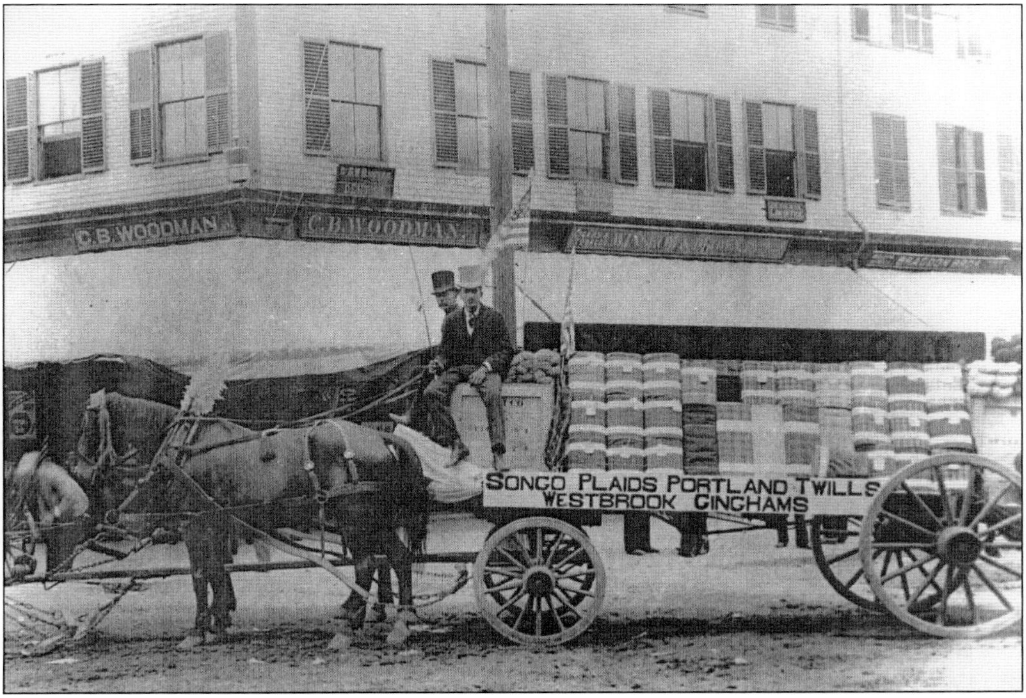

Vallee Square in the 1890s. This wagonload of goods is from the Gingham Mill .

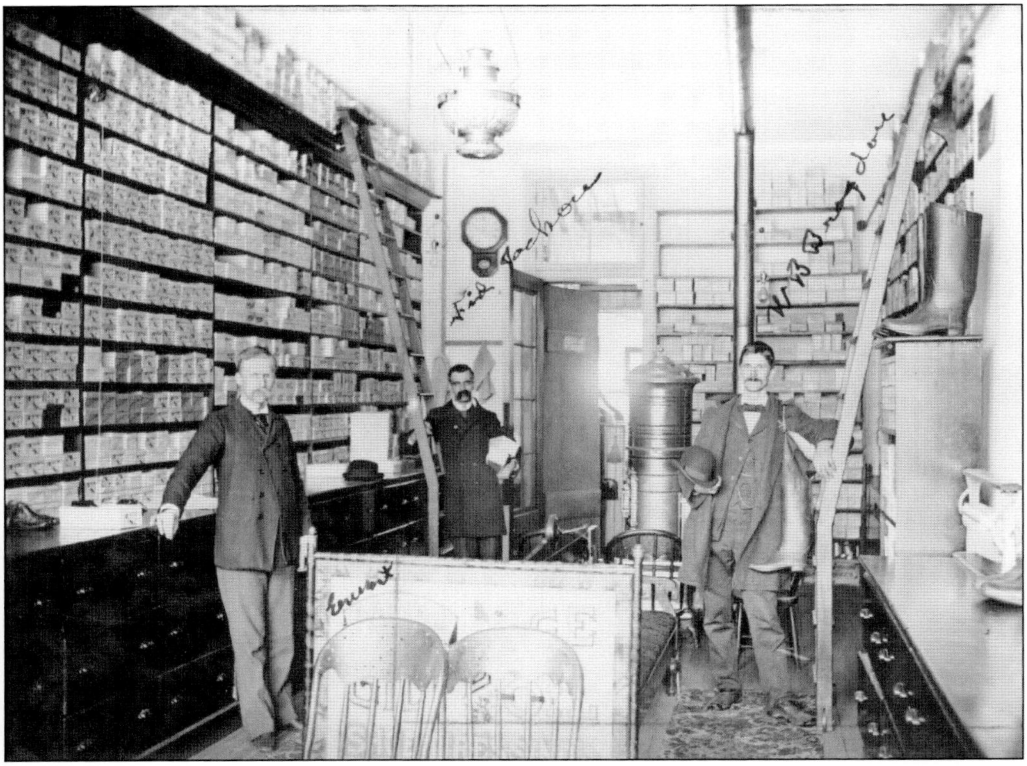
Bragdon Shoe Store at 663 Main Street, 1898. Pictured from left to right: ? Ernest, Fred Jackson, and W. B. Bragdon.

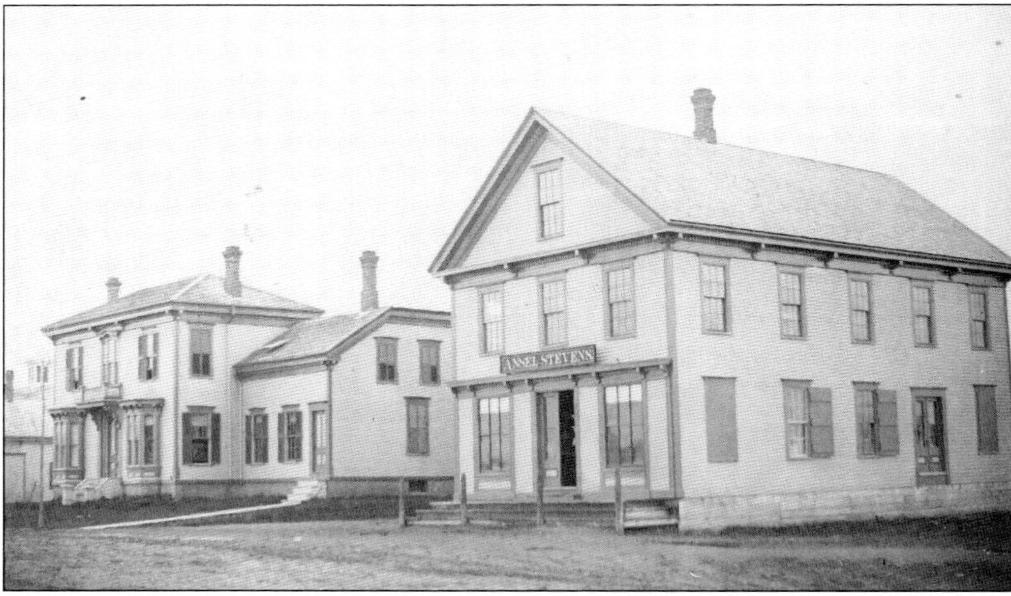

Old Westbrook Hospital (left), located on the north side of Main Street, just above Rochester Street. The building was once owned by Ansel Stevens. (Westbrook Historical Society Collection.)

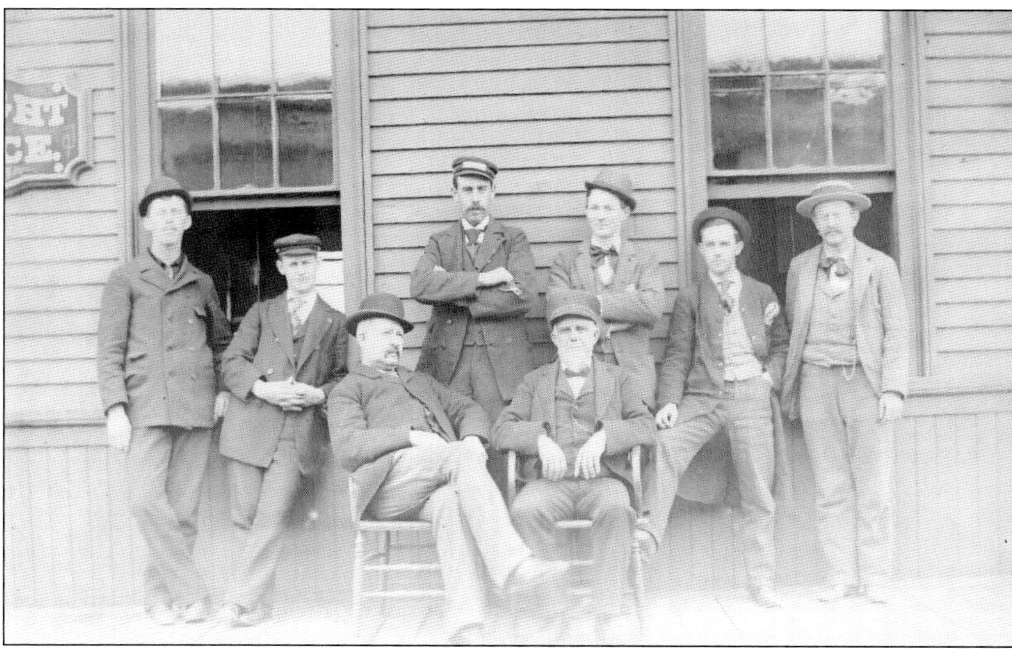

Work crew from the Maine Central Railroad Station, Cumberland Mills, 1894.

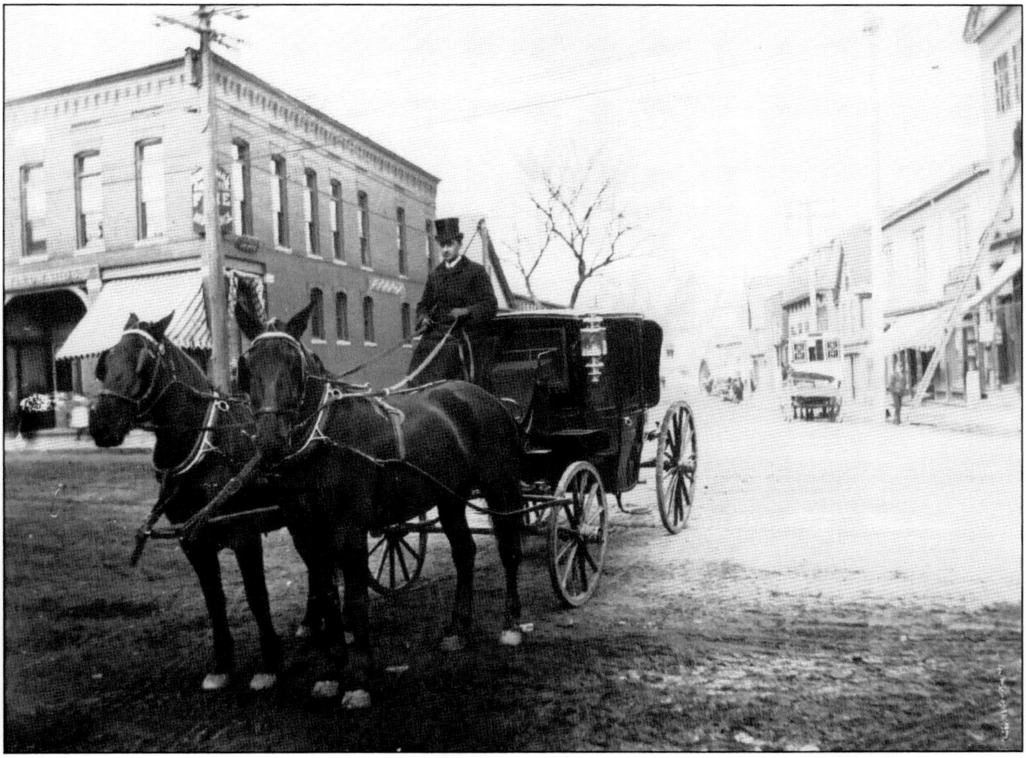

Arthur L. Roberts' Stable was located at 866 Main Street in the early 1900s. This photograph of a hack from the stable was taken at Main and Bridge Streets.

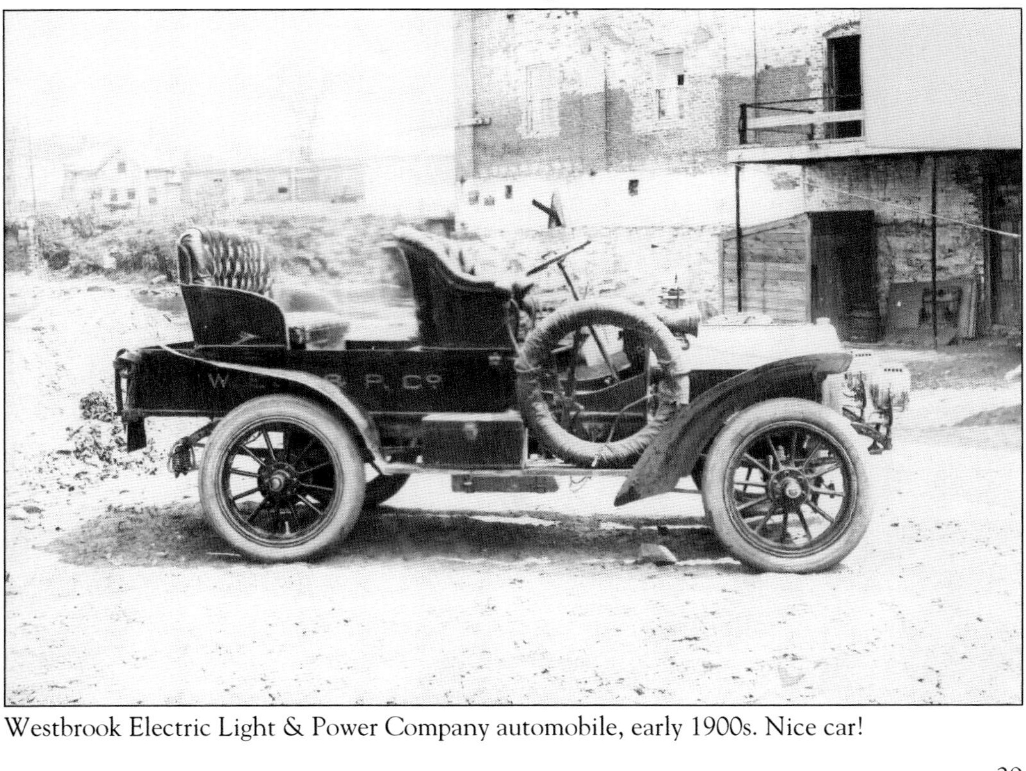

Westbrook Electric Light & Power Company automobile, early 1900s. Nice car!

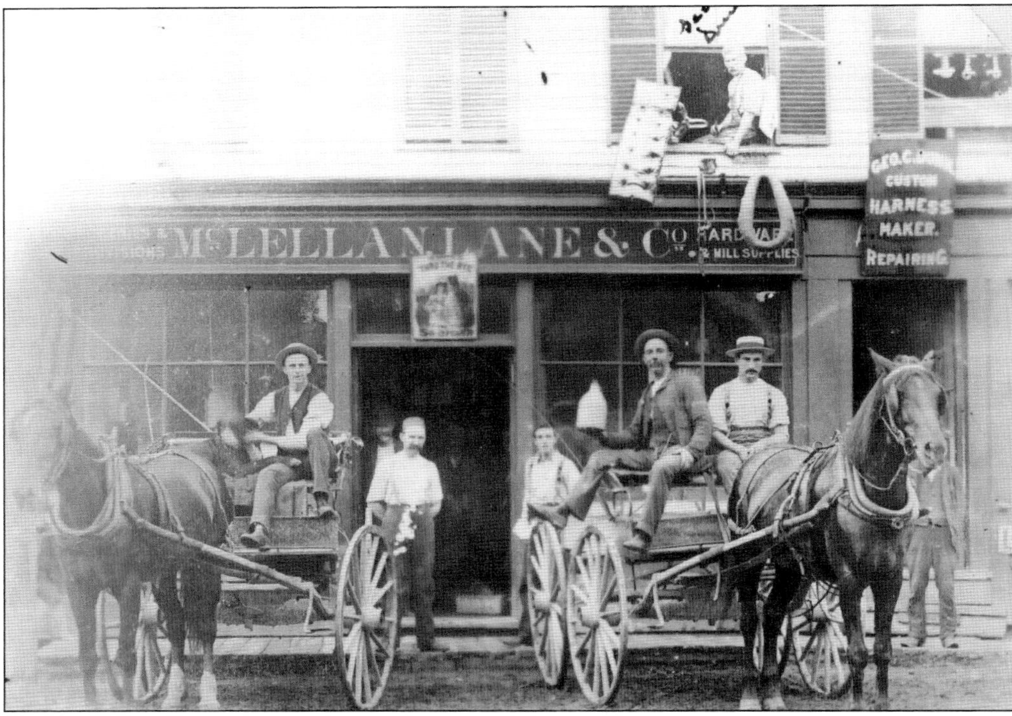

McClellan, Lane & Co. Hardware Store, on the corner of Main and Fitch Streets. George Dunn Custom Harness Makers is on the right. "And they're off!"

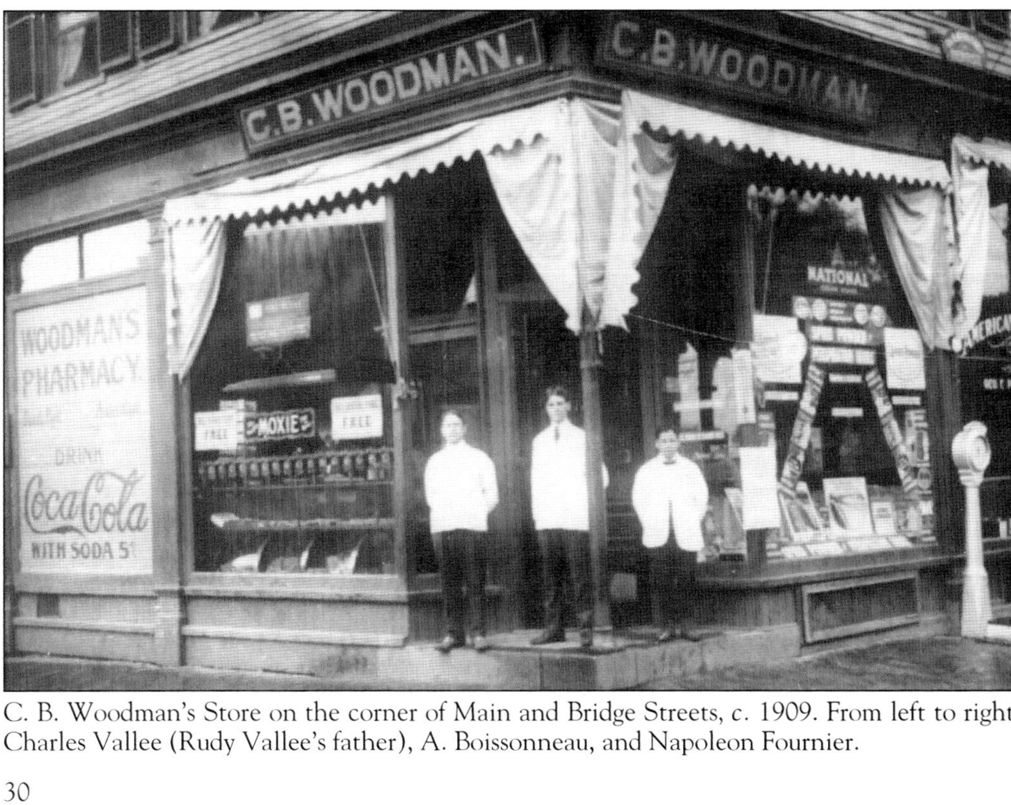

C. B. Woodman's Store on the corner of Main and Bridge Streets, c. 1909. From left to right: Charles Vallee (Rudy Vallee's father), A. Boissonneau, and Napoleon Fournier.

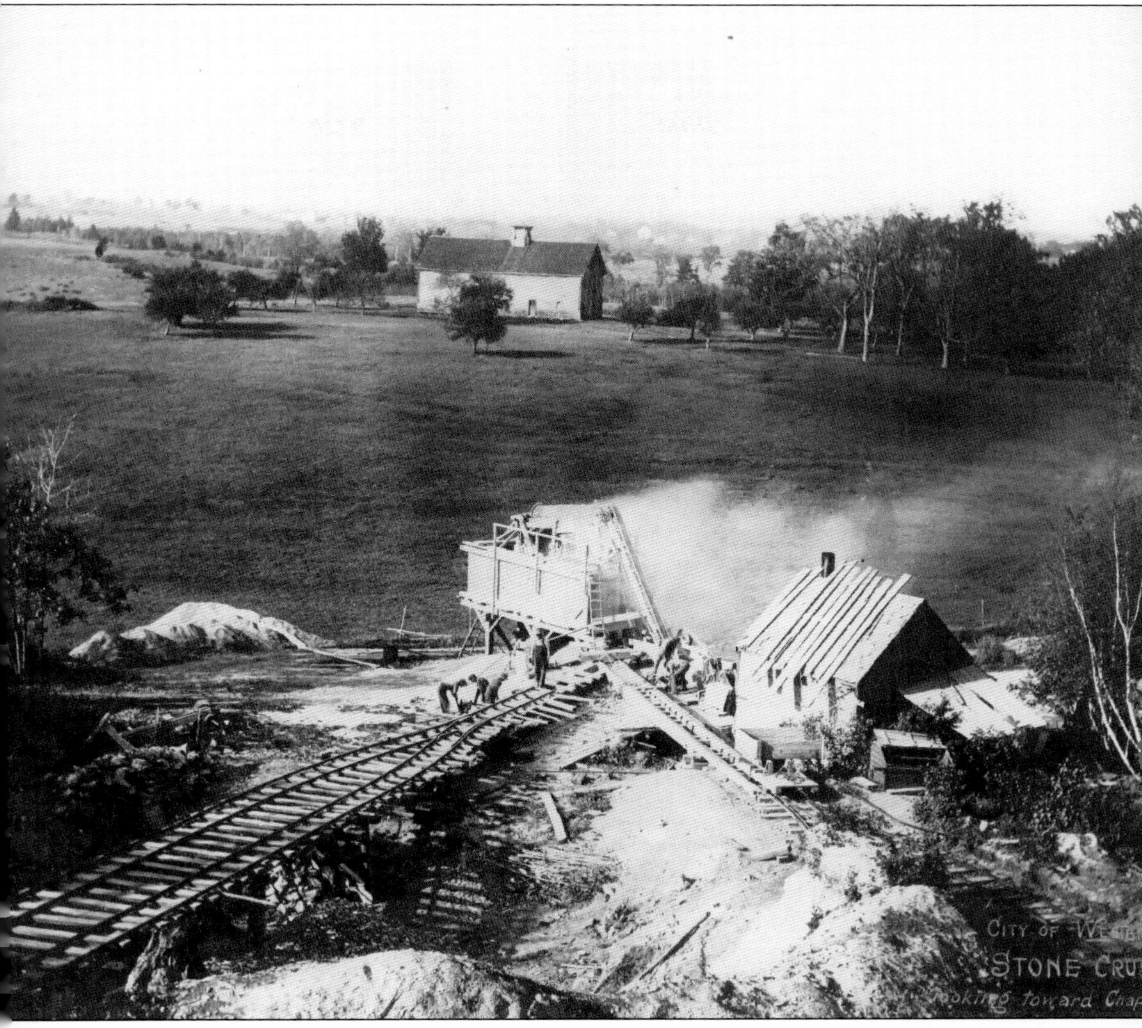

Edward Chapman Farm on Spring Street. The farm was acquired by the City of Westbrook, and the stone crusher was put into use c. 1912.

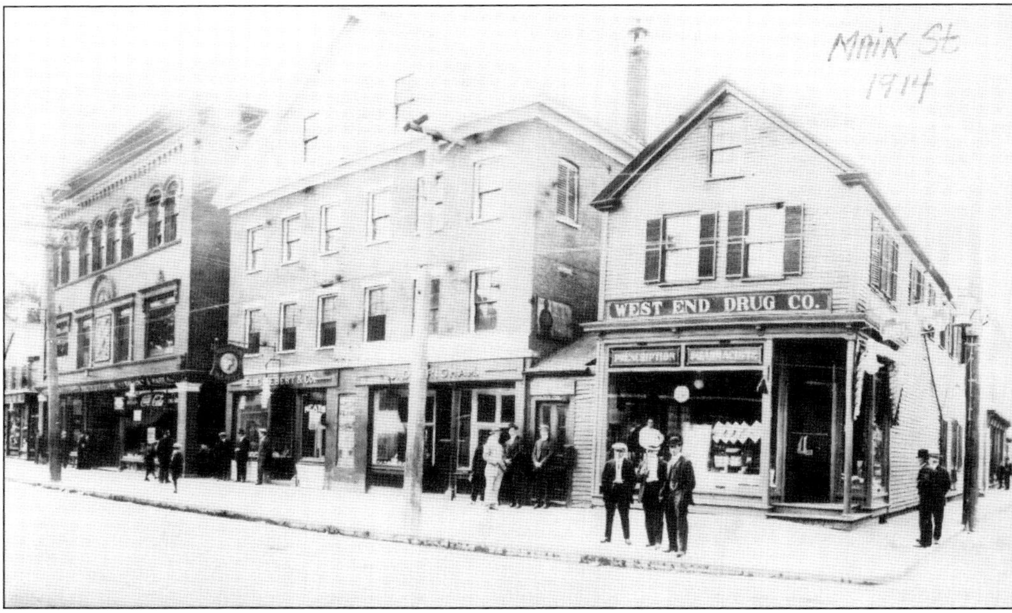

Main Street in 1914. Scates Block is to the far left and Fitch Street is on the far right.

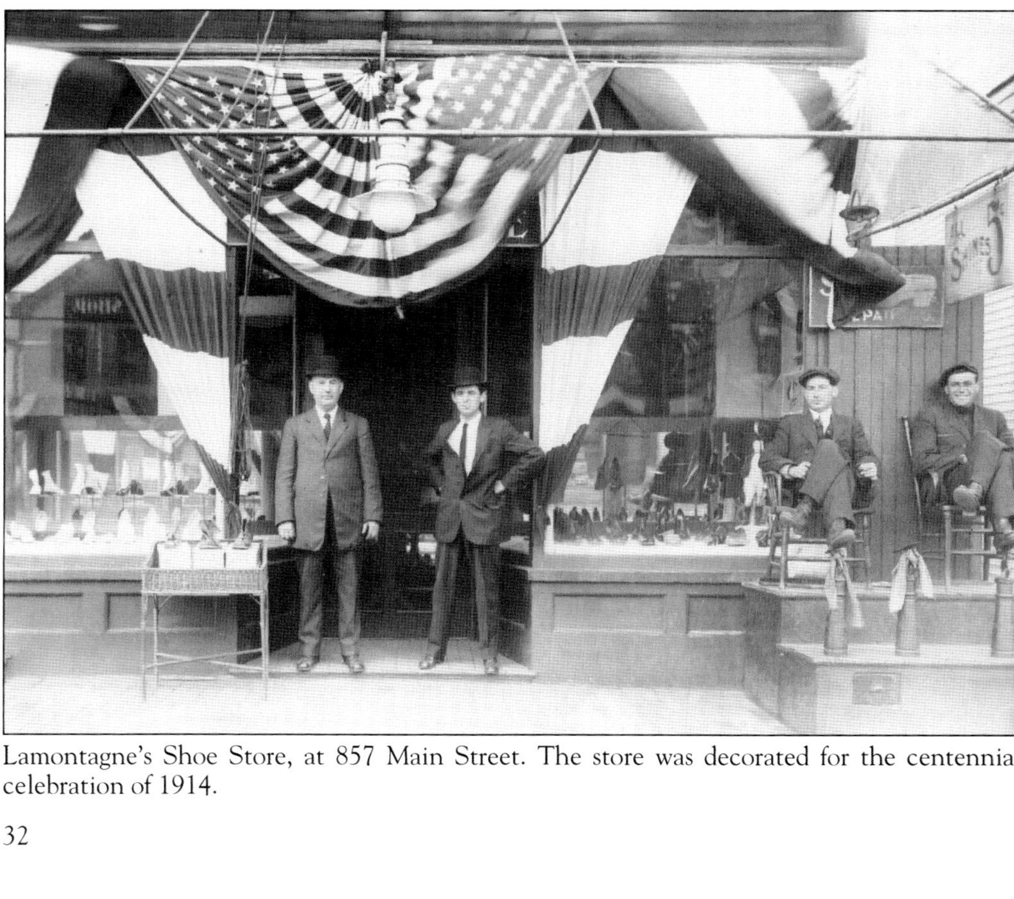
Lamontagne's Shoe Store, at 857 Main Street. The store was decorated for the centennial celebration of 1914.

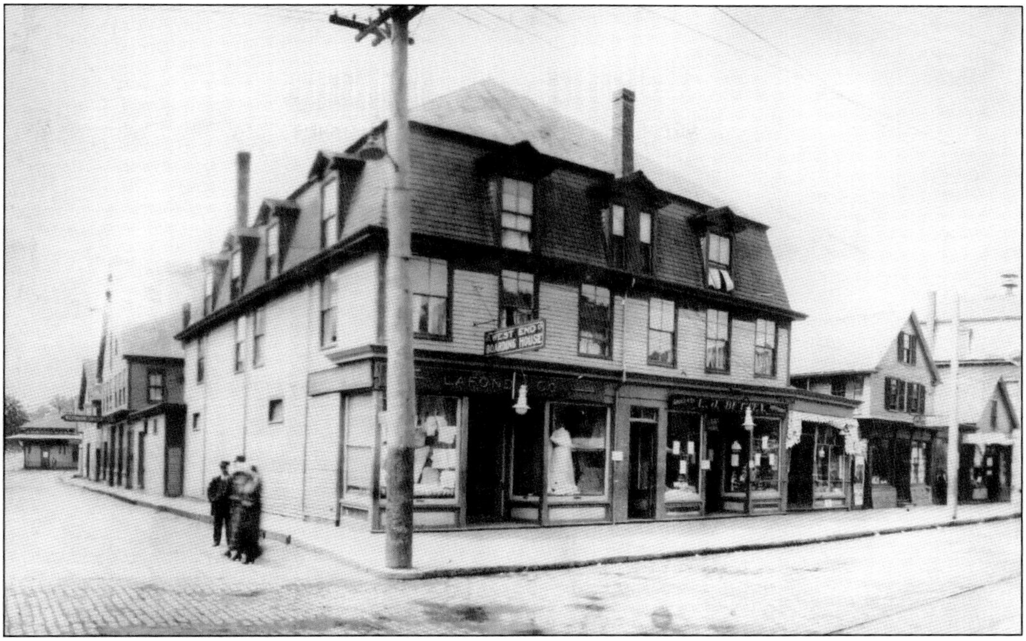

Corner of Fitch and Main Streets, 1914. Lafond & Company and L. J. Betty Company are featured. The railroad station can be seen to the rear of the street.

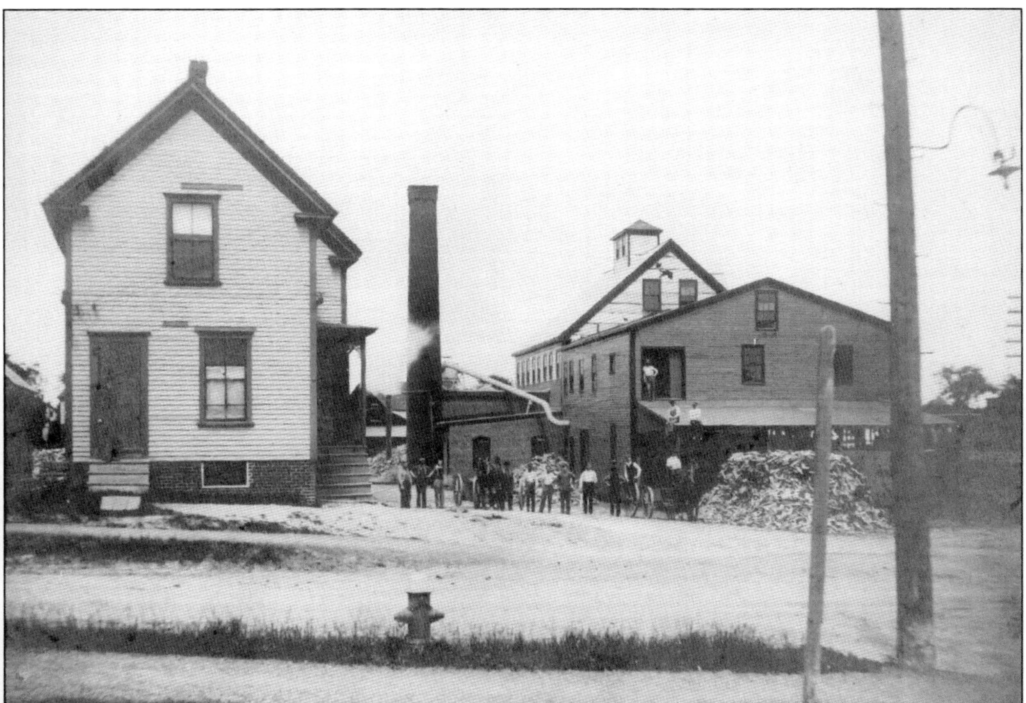

Ames Shovel & Tool Company at 55 Seavey Street, Cumberland Mills, *c.* 1915. Members of the crew stood outside to pose for this picture .

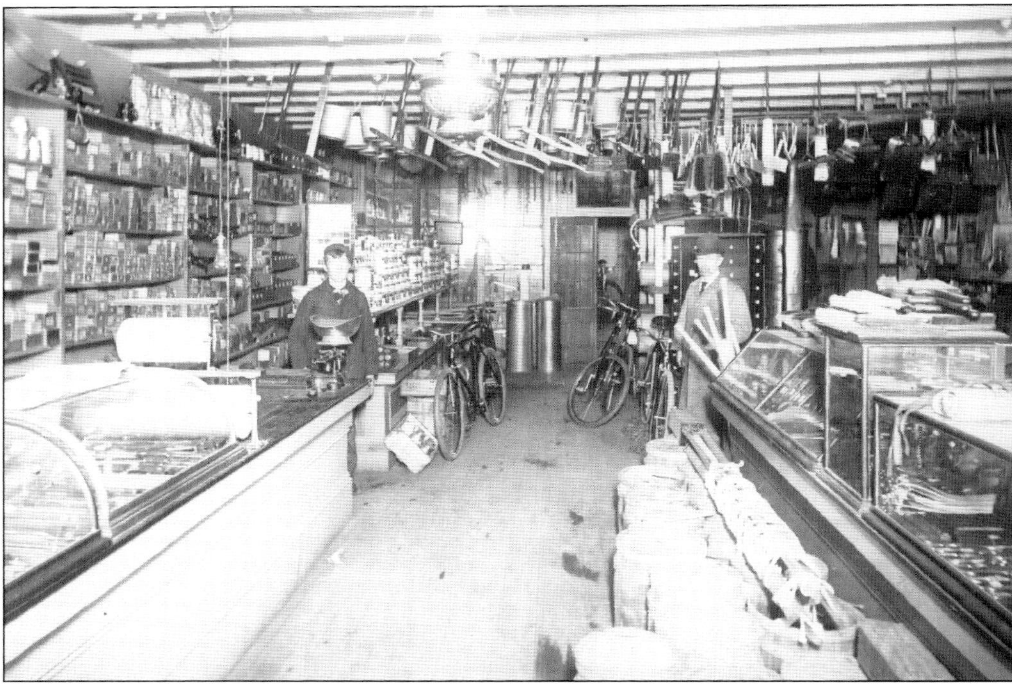

Knight's Hardware Store at 883 Main Street, in the early 1900s. Leland Knight is on the left and Walter Knight is on the right.

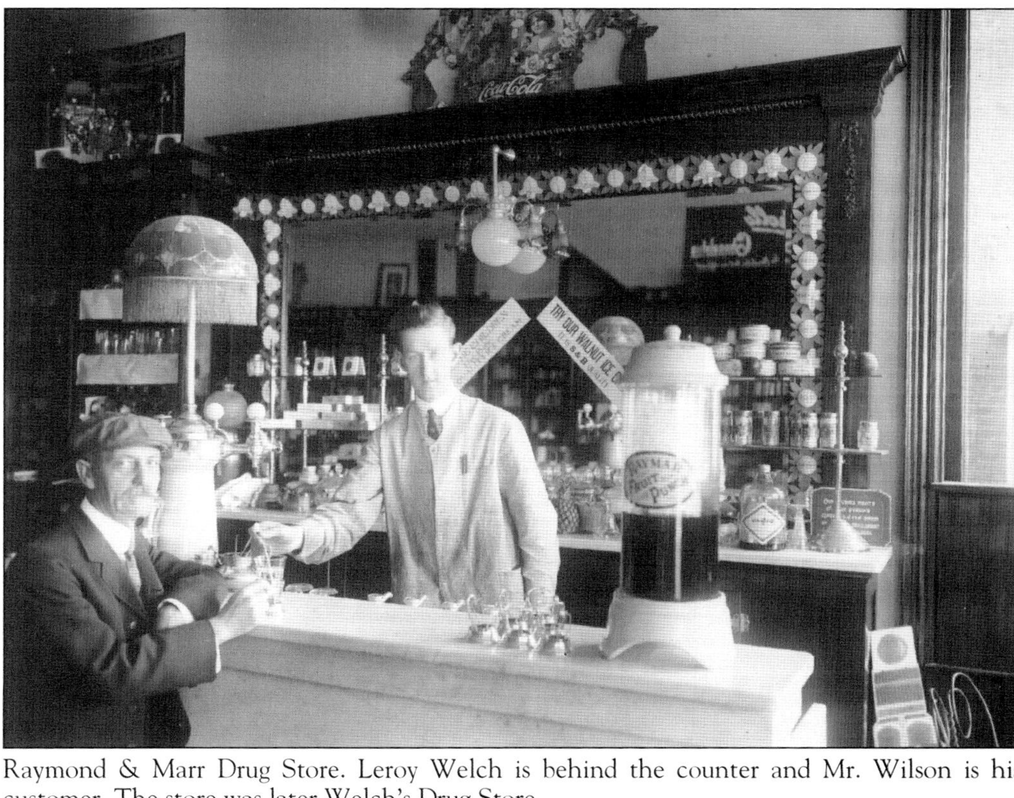

Raymond & Marr Drug Store. Leroy Welch is behind the counter and Mr. Wilson is his customer. The store was later Welch's Drug Store.

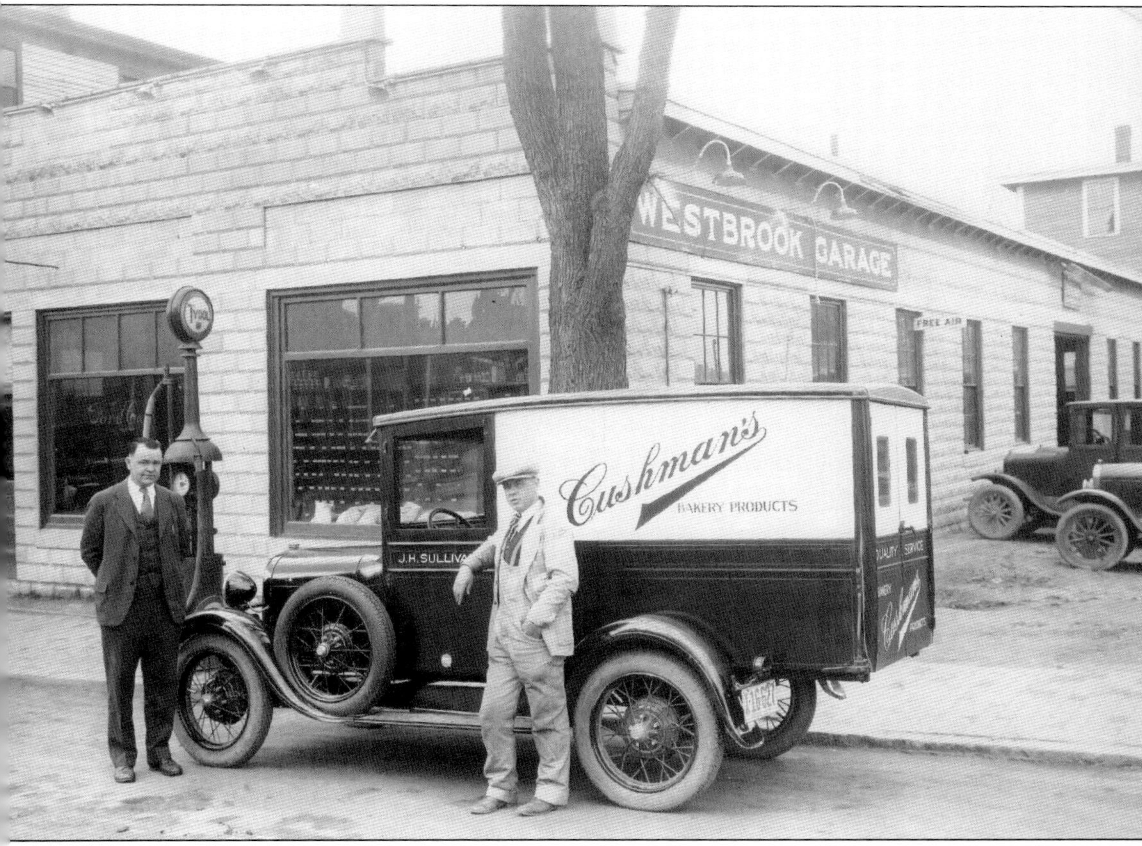

In front of Rowe's Garage (Later Rowe Motors) at the corner of Main Street and Stevens Avenue, 1930. Raymond Rowe (left), and James H. Sullivan (right) exchange pleasantries. Mr. Sullivan was a longtime Cushman Bakery truck driver. (Westbrook Historical Society Collection.)

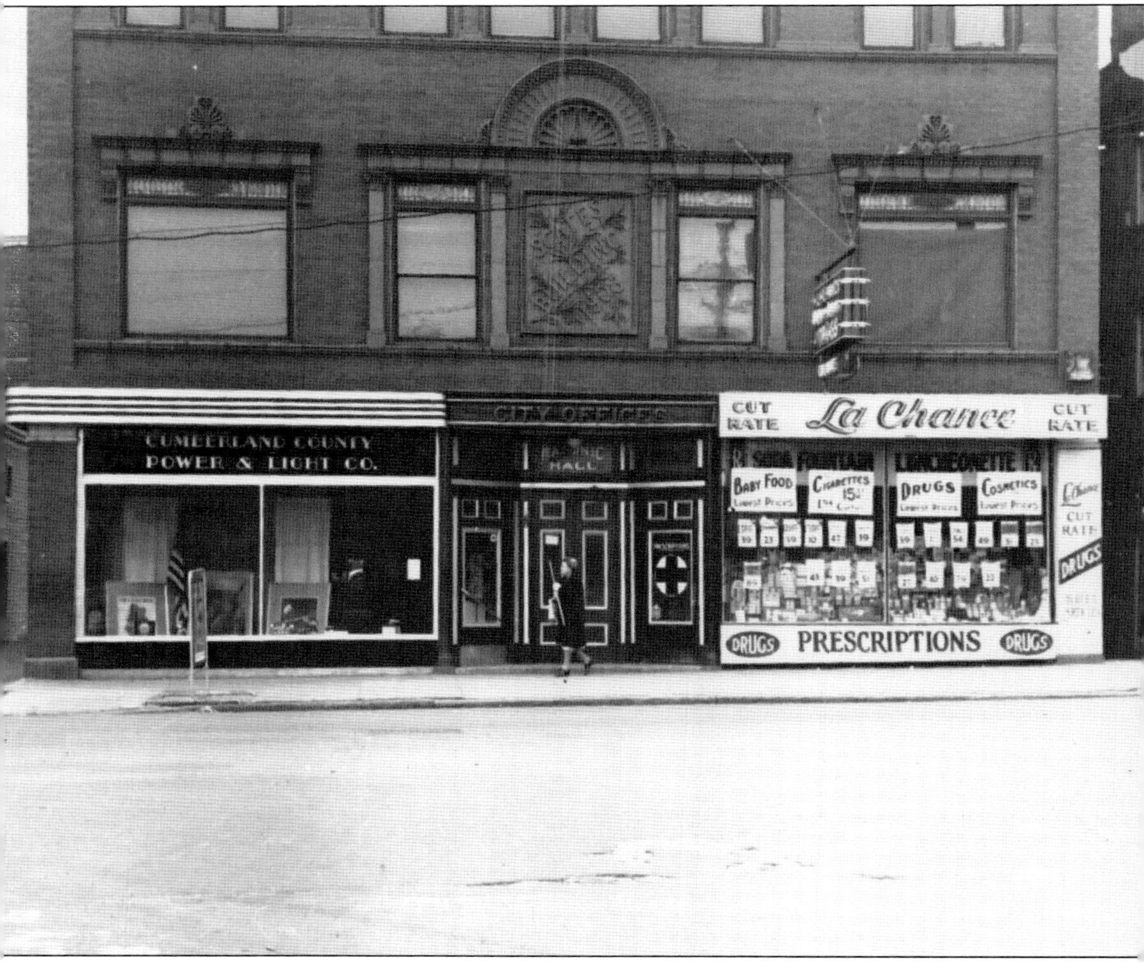

The Scates Building (1903–1981), located on Main Street opposite Bridge Street. The second floor housed the Westbrook city offices for many years. This building was demolished in 1981 as part of the Urban Renewal Project. The stained glass over the windows can be seen at the Walker Memorial Library at the entrance to the Local History Room.

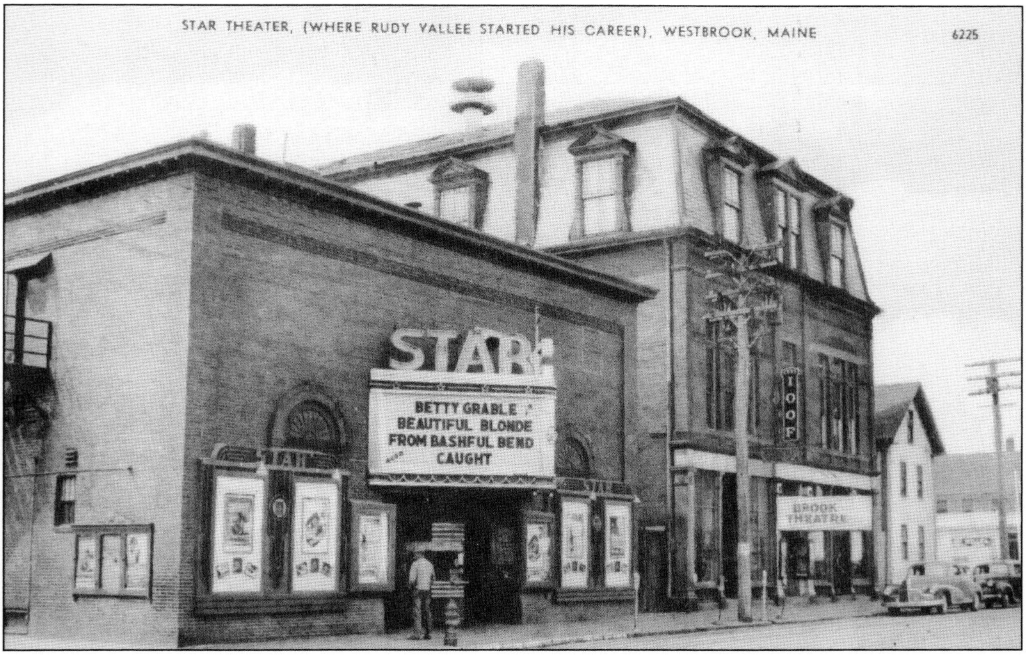

Star Theatre, 1949. Rudy Vallee, the "Vagabond Lover" of the '20s and '30s, got his entertainment start as an usher here. Many a romance began in the Star's balcony!

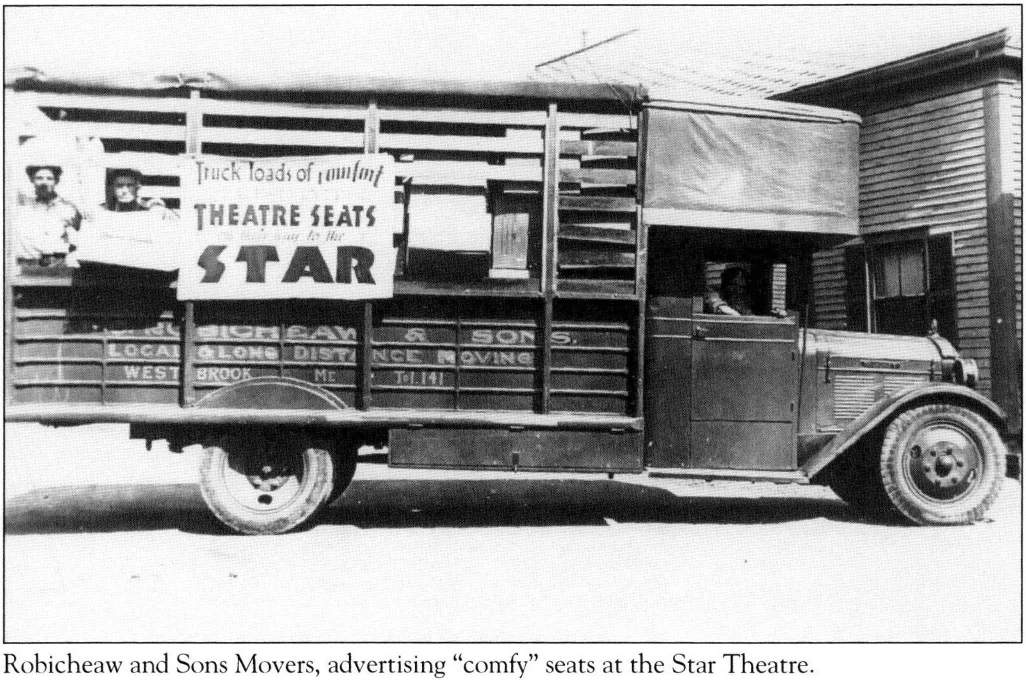

Robicheaw and Sons Movers, advertising "comfy" seats at the Star Theatre.

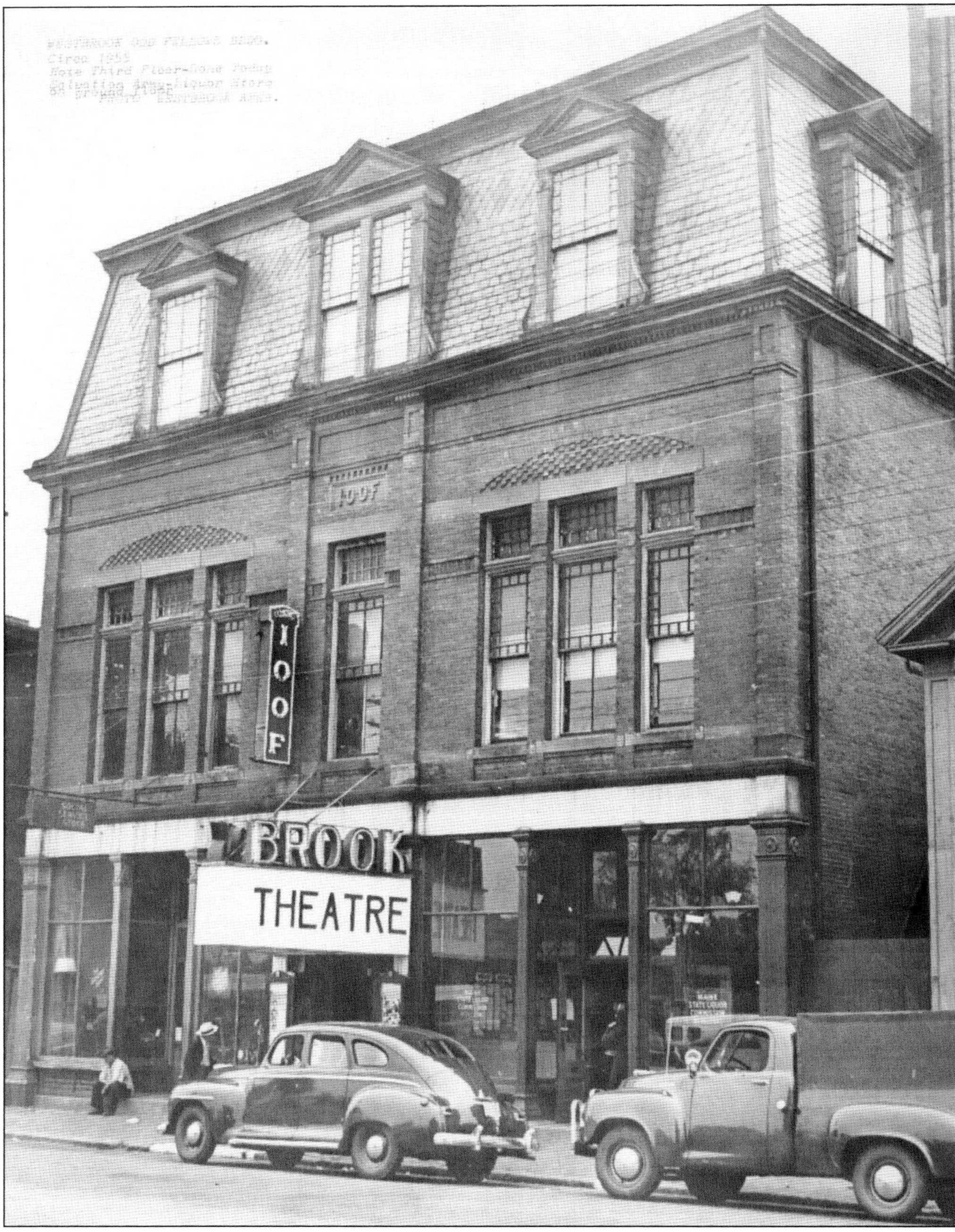

The Odd Fellows Hall Building, on the south side of upper Main Street. This was also the home of the Brook Theatre around 1950.

Three

Home and Family

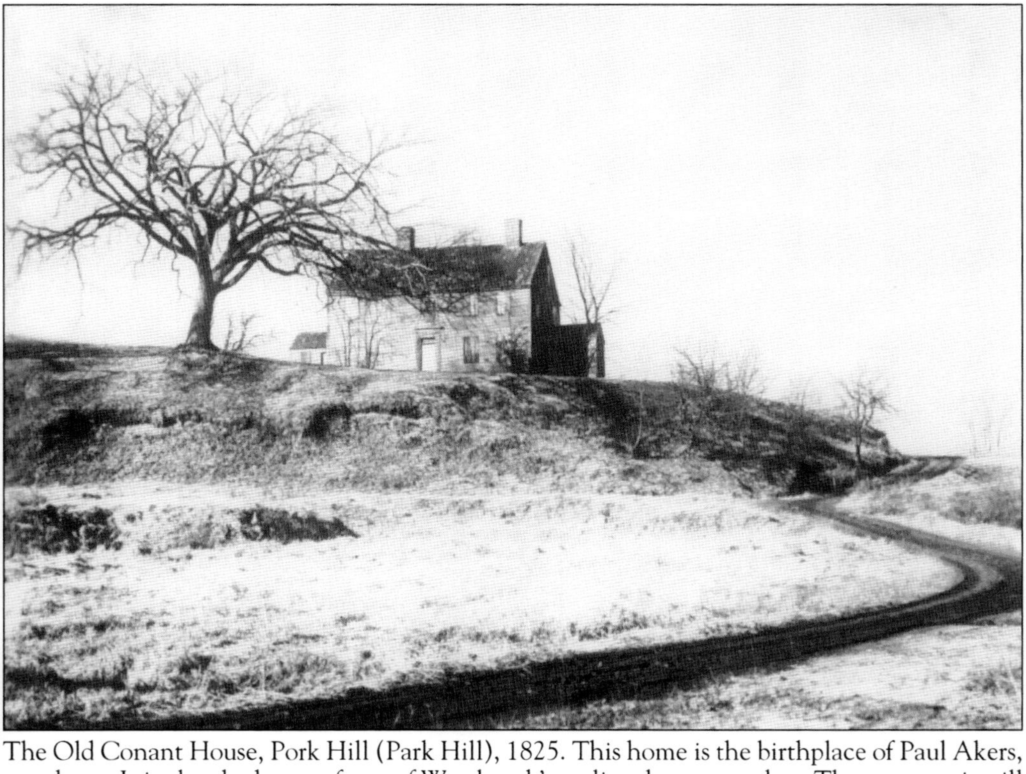

The Old Conant House, Pork Hill (Park Hill), 1825. This home is the birthplace of Paul Akers, a sculptor. It is also the home of one of Westbrook's earliest-known settlers. The property is still in the Conant family.

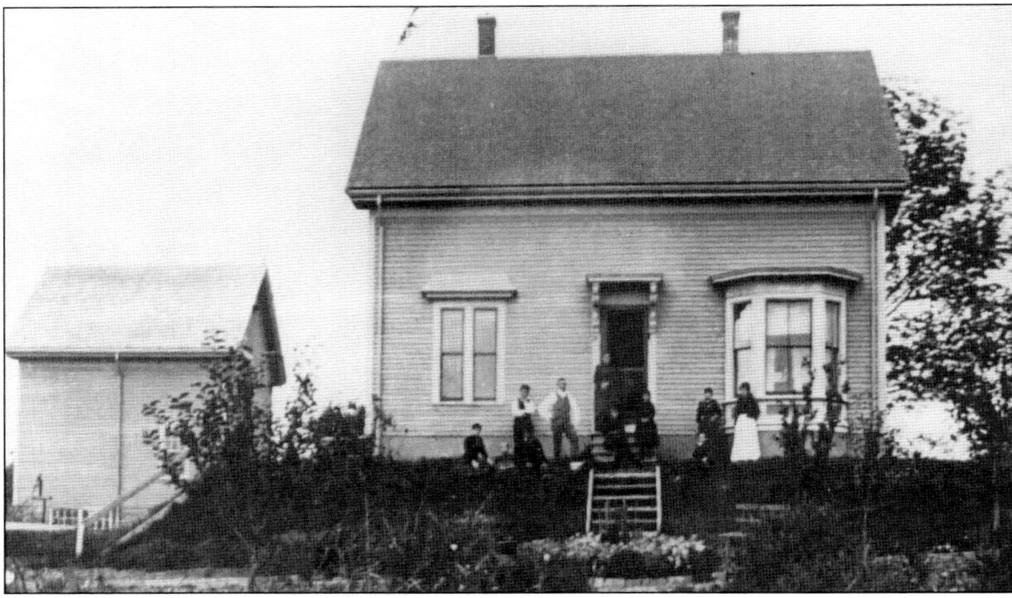

The Kinmond Home at 170 Pierce Street, with the family posing outside. The structure was built c. 1889 by Ernest F. Kinmond Sr., a house painter from Scotland. (Dorothy Lachance Collection.)

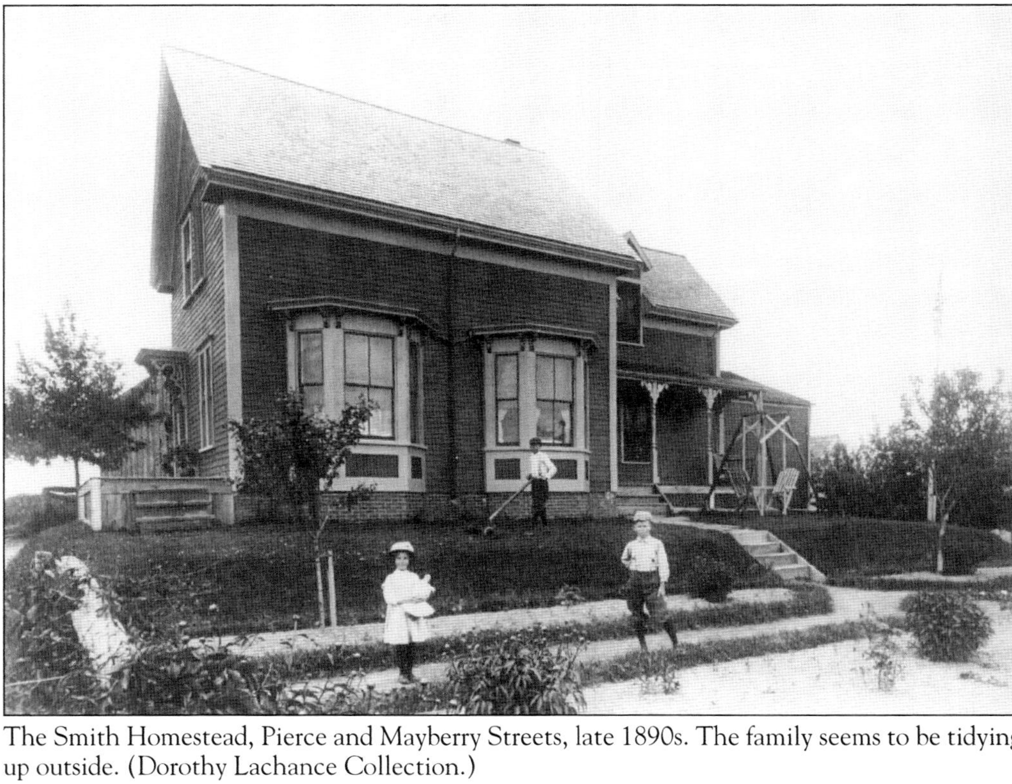

The Smith Homestead, Pierce and Mayberry Streets, late 1890s. The family seems to be tidying up outside. (Dorothy Lachance Collection.)

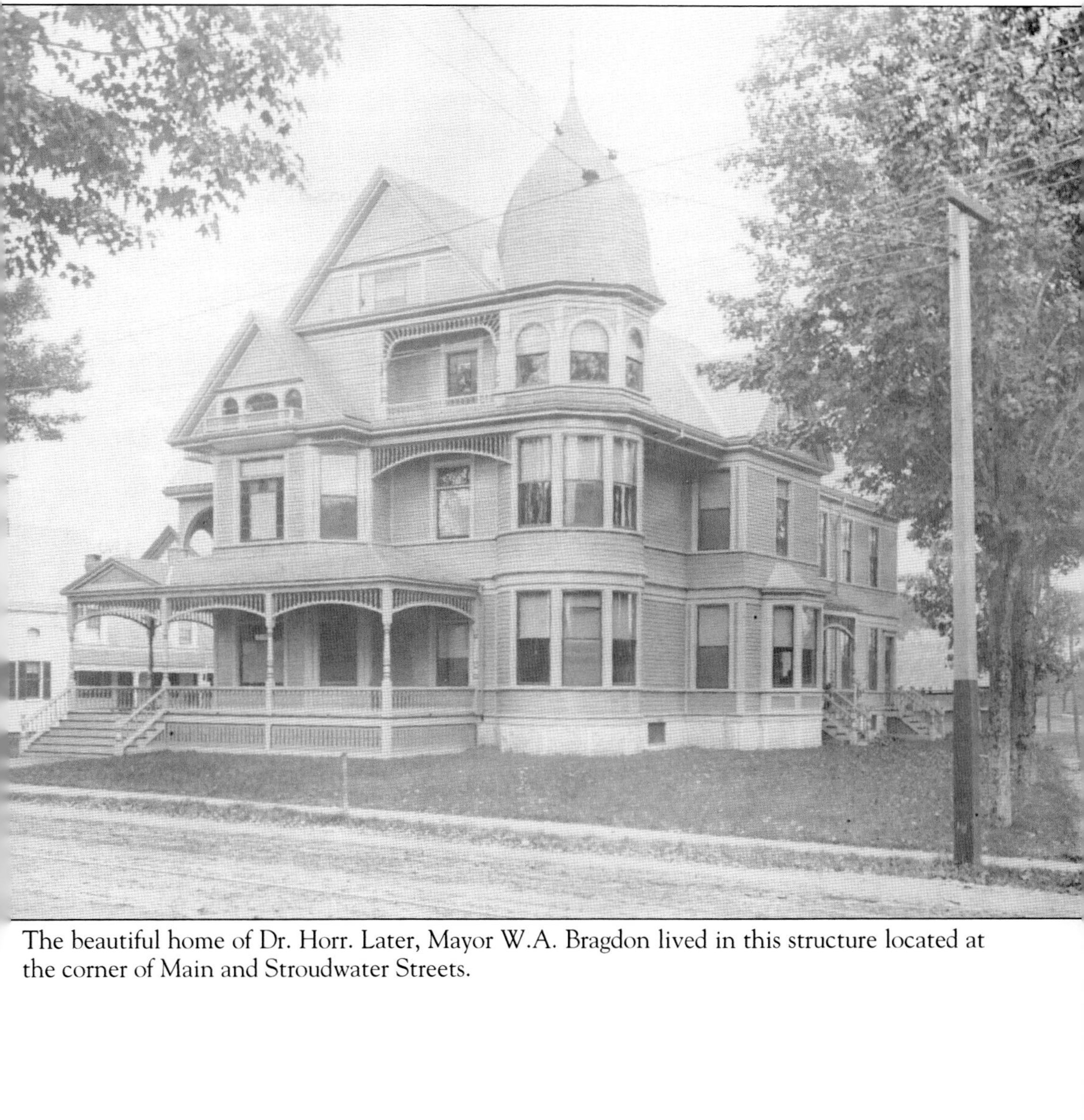

The beautiful home of Dr. Horr. Later, Mayor W.A. Bragdon lived in this structure located at the corner of Main and Stroudwater Streets.

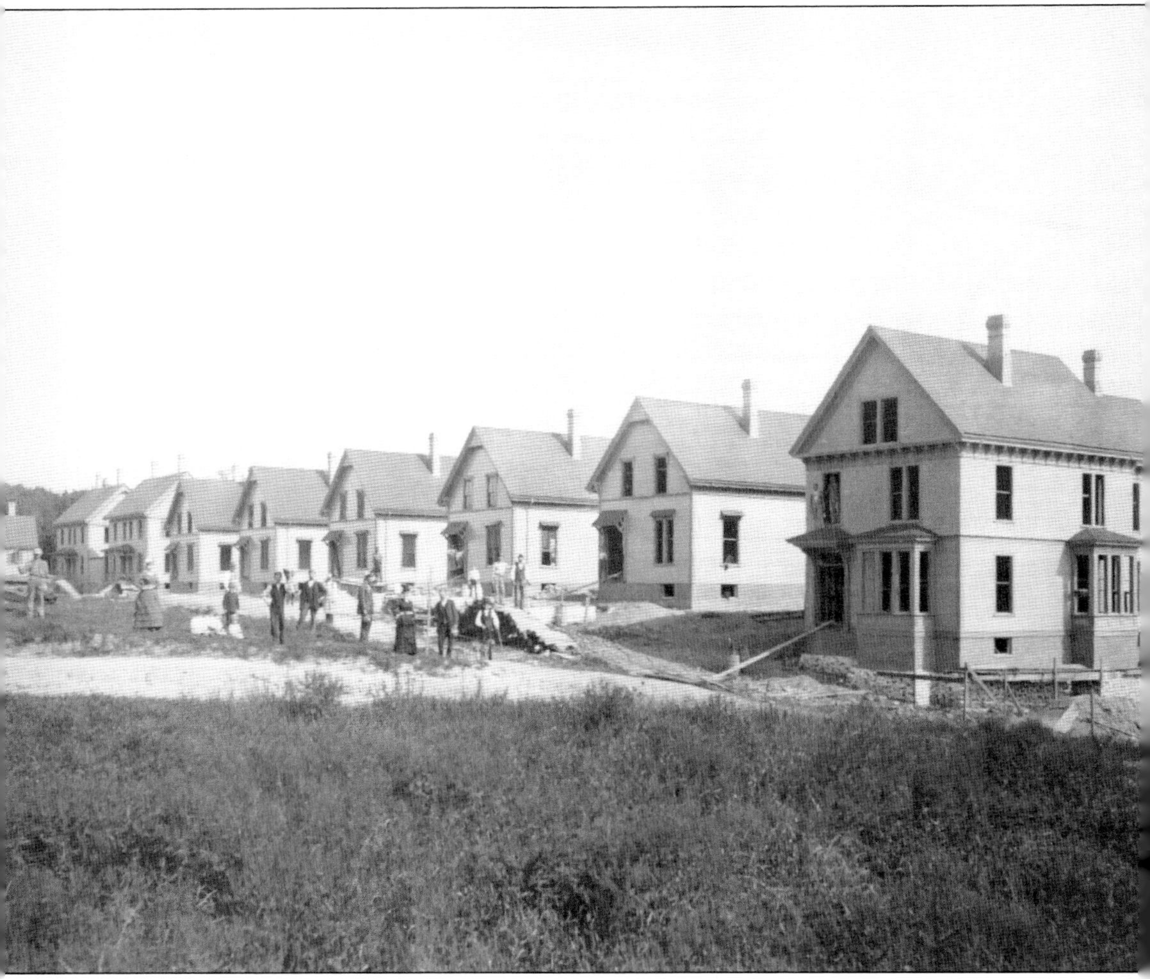

"Scotch Hill," *c.* 1890. In this rare image, readers can see tenement houses being built on "Scotch Hill," so named because of the many Scottish people who came to work in the Haskell Silk Mill. The "hill" was located on Walker Street. (Conant Collection.)

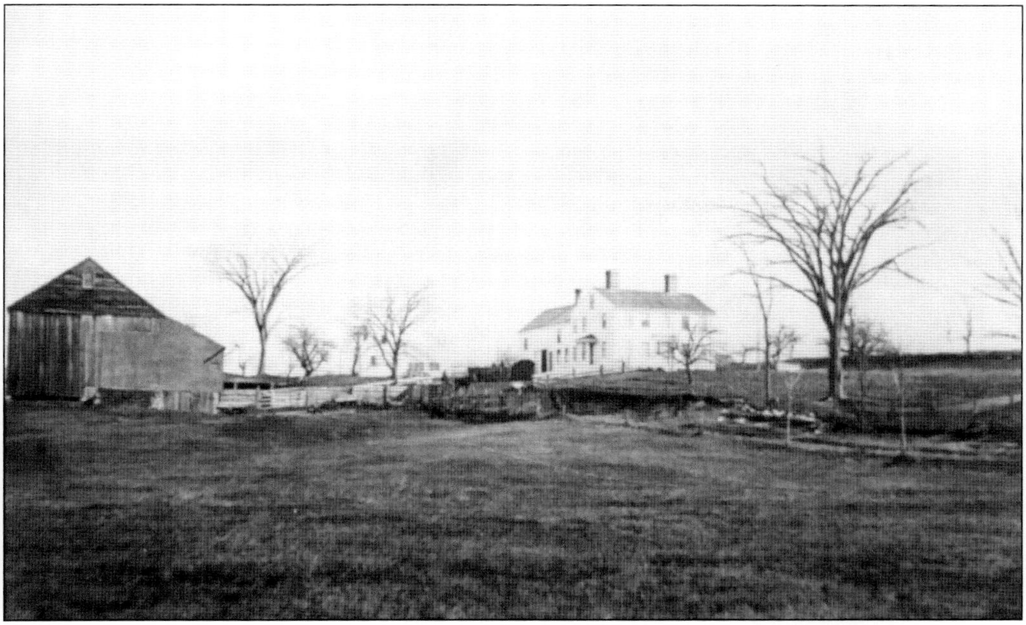

The Lamb House, located on what is now known as Deer Hill, Cumberland Mills.

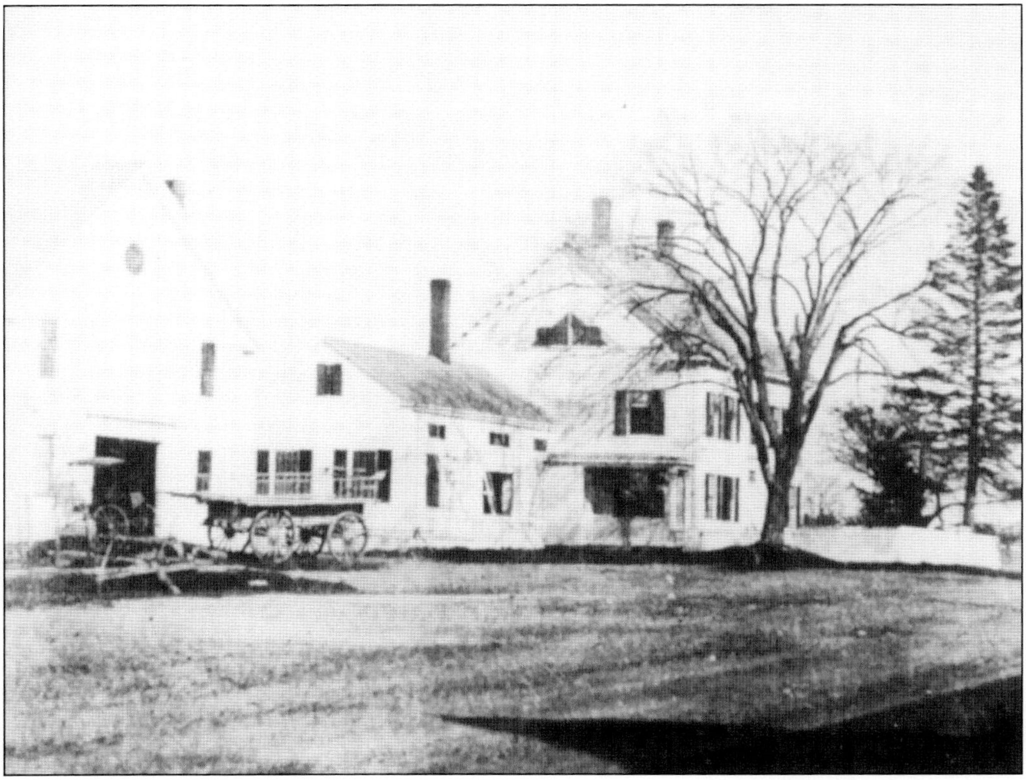

The Raymond House, built in 1805 by Captain Amos Winslow. The house, along with ninety acres, was deeded to Samuel Raymond in 1842.

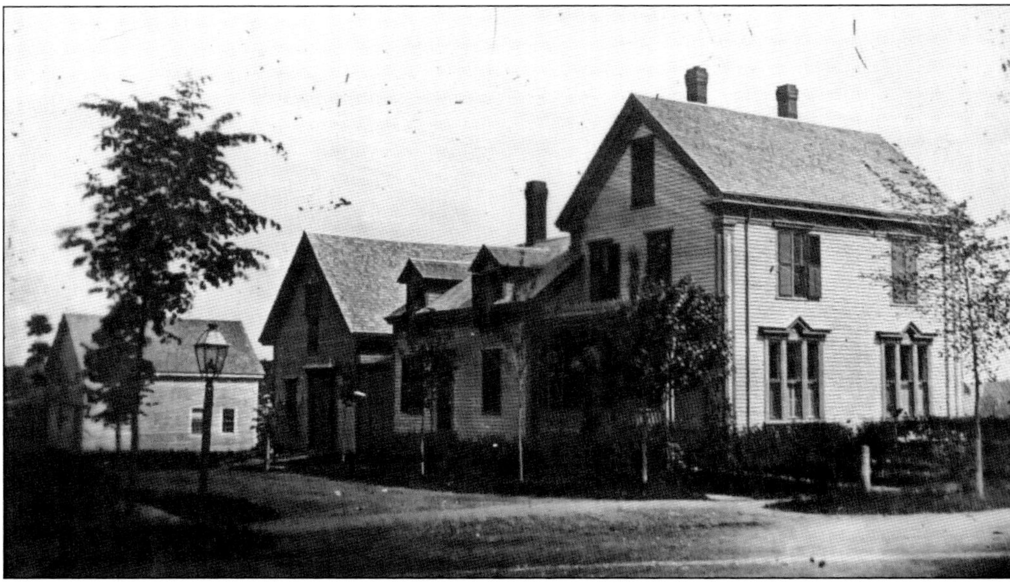

The B. G. Pride Home on Main Street.

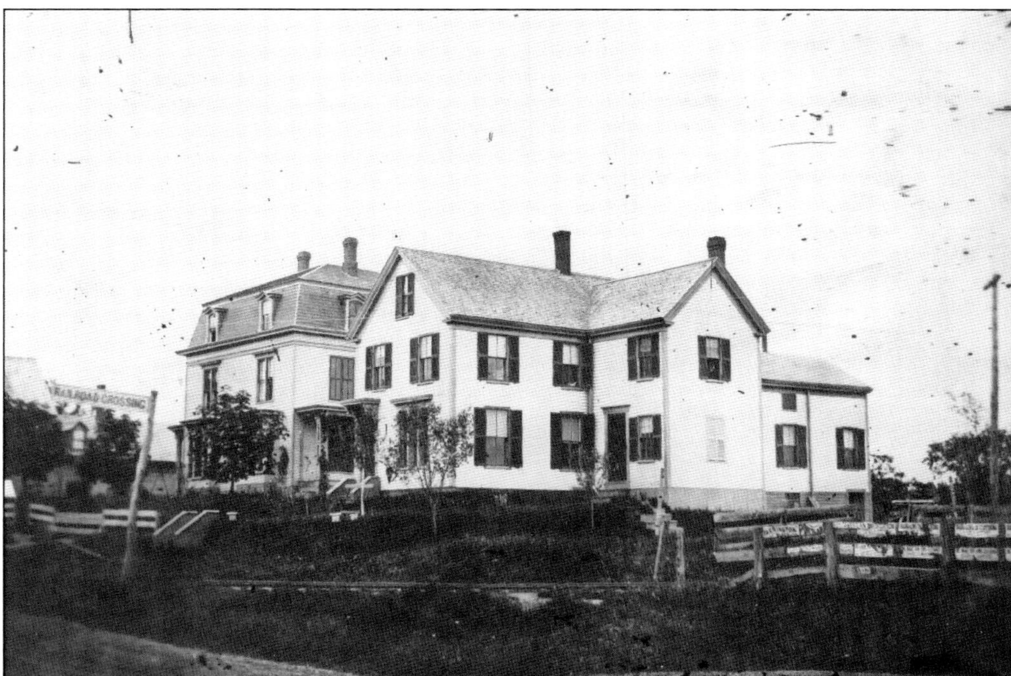

The Larrabe Home, Main Street, Cumberland Mills.

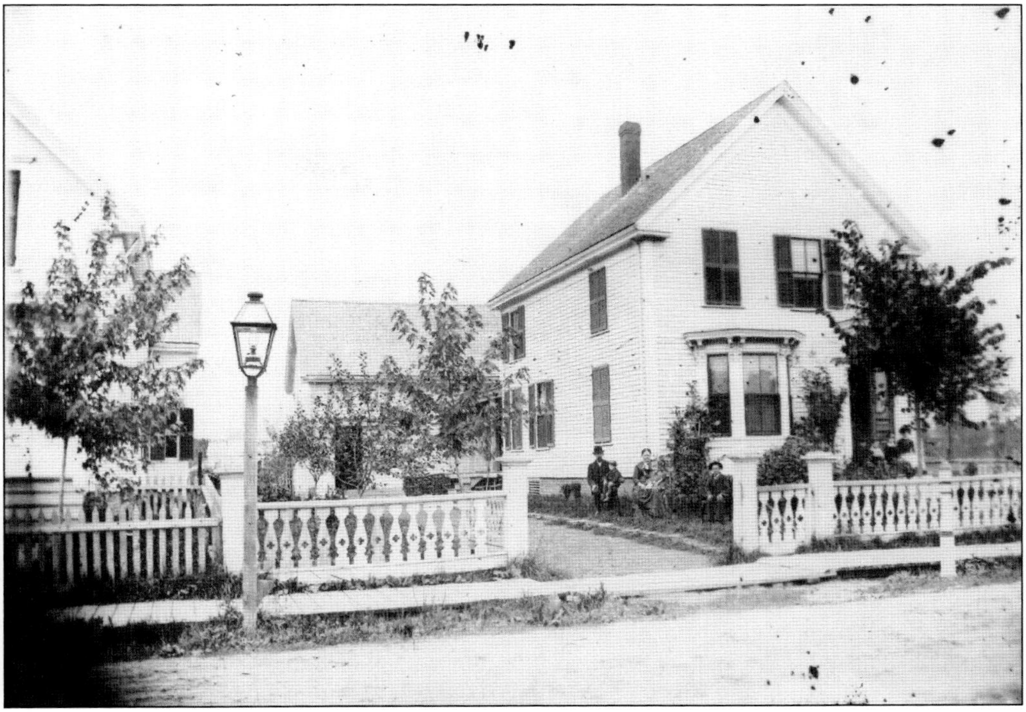

The Watson House on Main Street. The family posed outside for this picture.

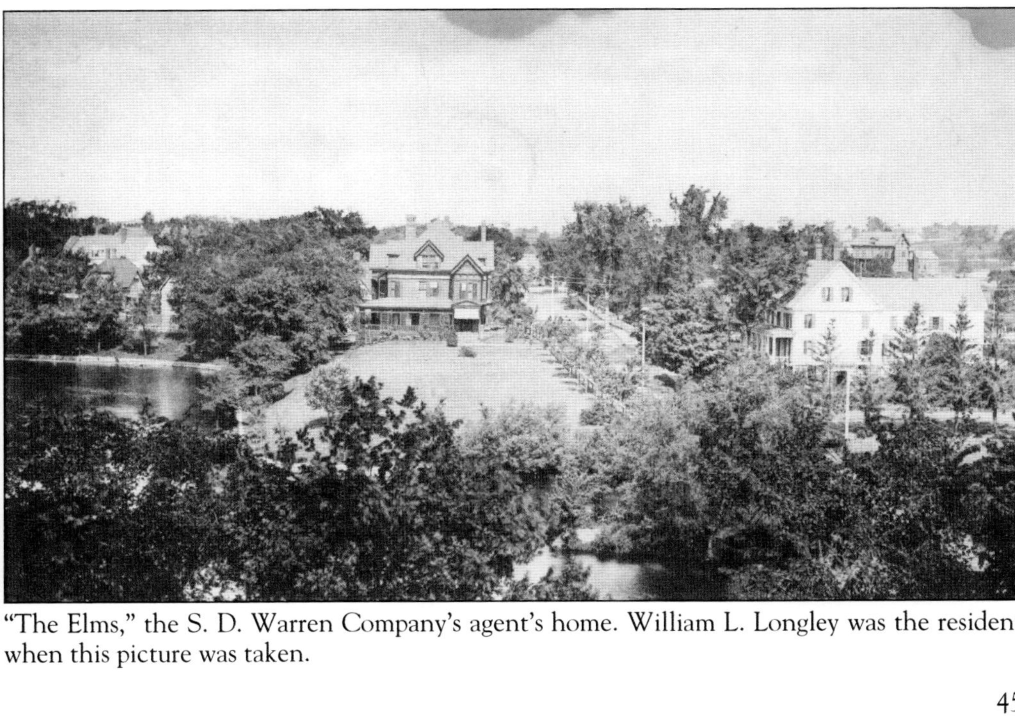

"The Elms," the S. D. Warren Company's agent's home. William L. Longley was the resident when this picture was taken.

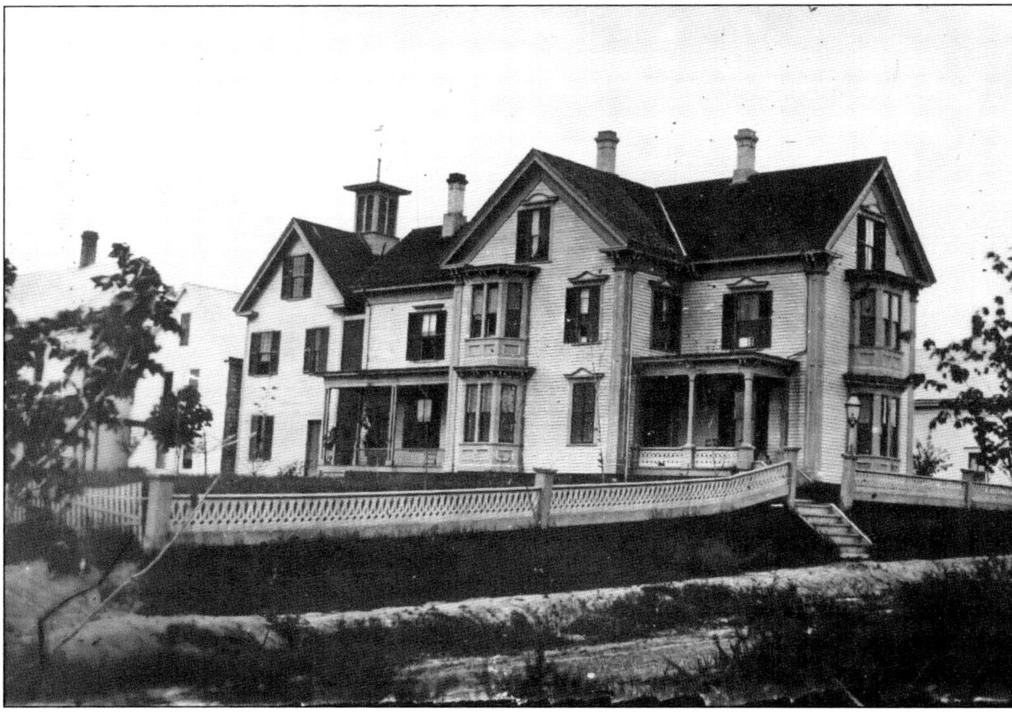

The Pride House, at 70 Mechanic Street.

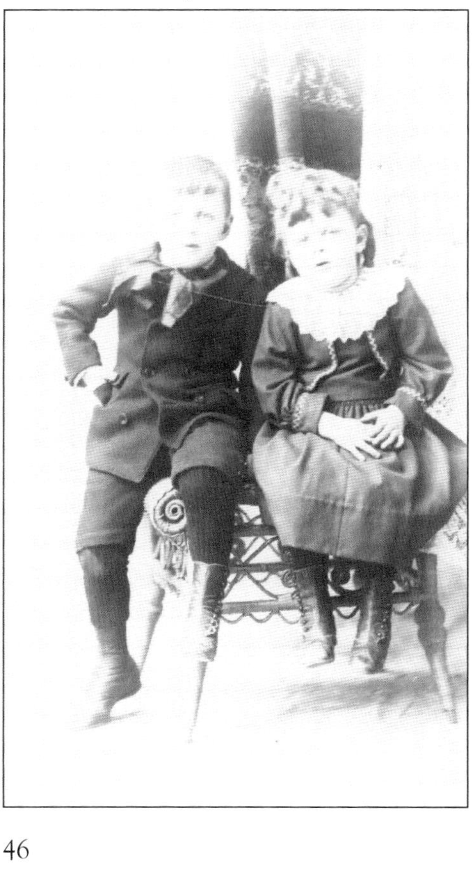

Percy and Philip Conant. The Conants were the descendants of one of Westbrook's earliest settlers. (Conant Collection.)

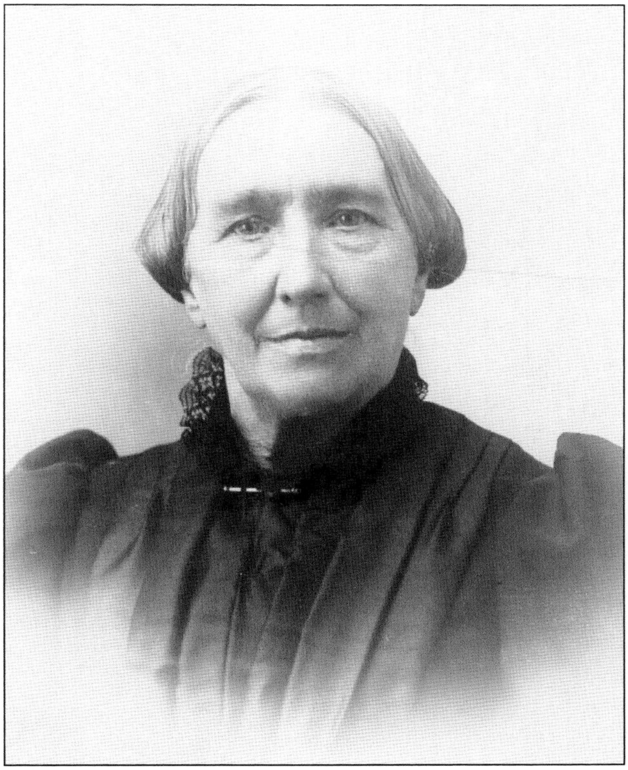

Captain and Mrs. Quinby. Quimby Avenue was named for this family (when the "n" became an "m" is unknown). Mrs. Quinby was the grandmother of Ellie Hawes.

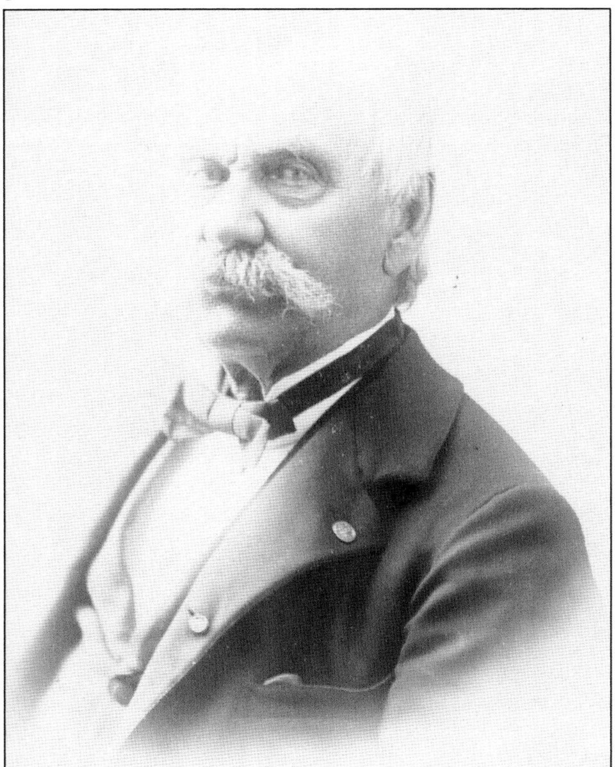

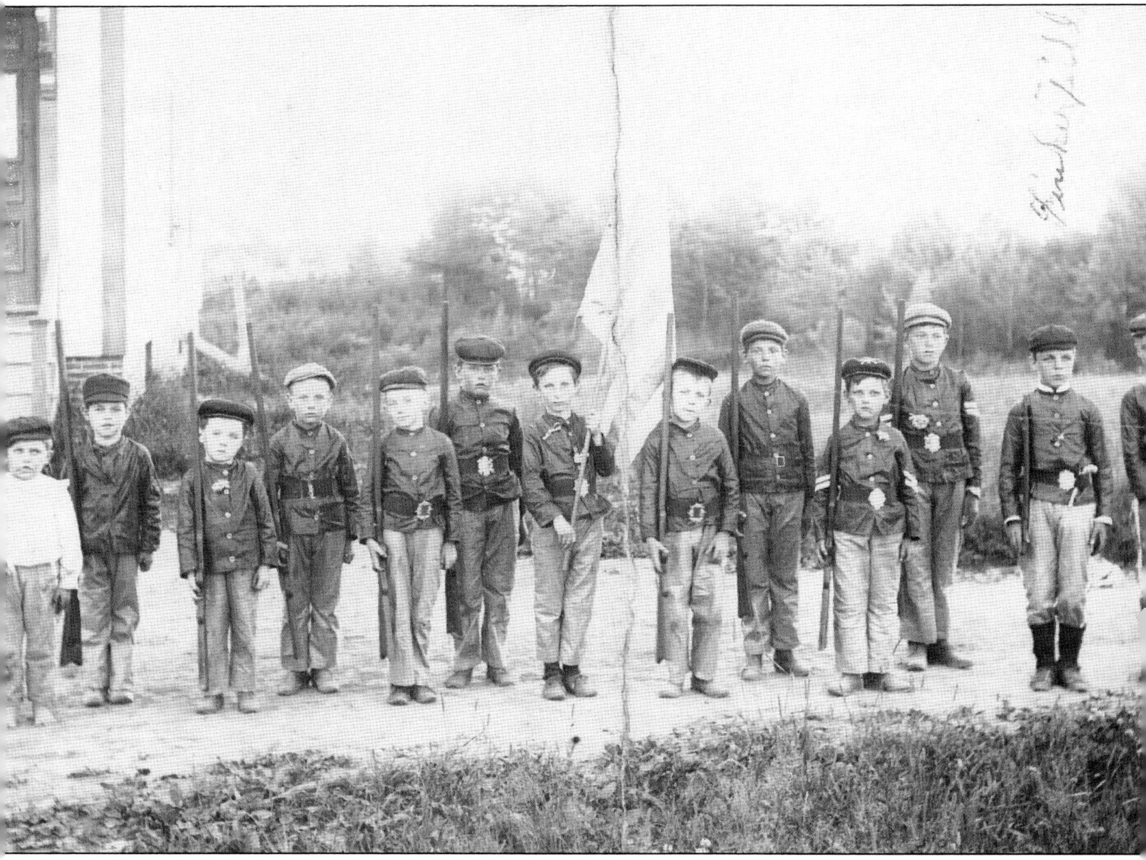

The Irish Hill Gang, 1898. This tough-looking gang came from the upper Saco Street area that was known as "Irish Hill." Members of this gang included: Ray Mayberry, William Bell, Thomas Killian, John Burroughs, Stephen Burke, Earle Mayberry, Perley Lornin, Alex Jones Gardiner, Tinker Fields, and Robert Parsons. Three of the group were not identified.

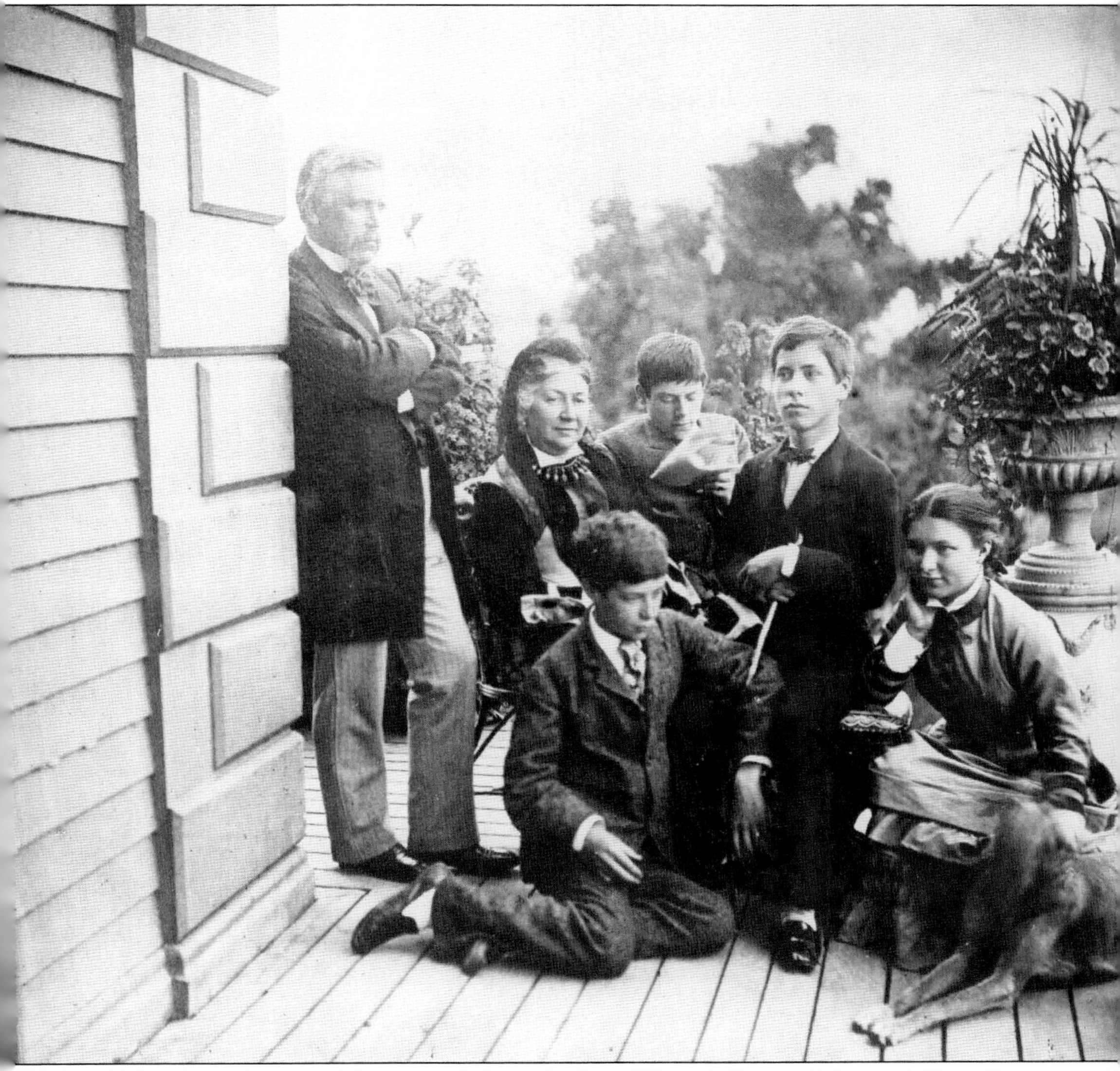

Mr. and Mrs. Samuel Dennis Warren and their children, Edward, Henry, Fiske, and Cornelia. The Warrens posed for this portrait on their porch about 1872.

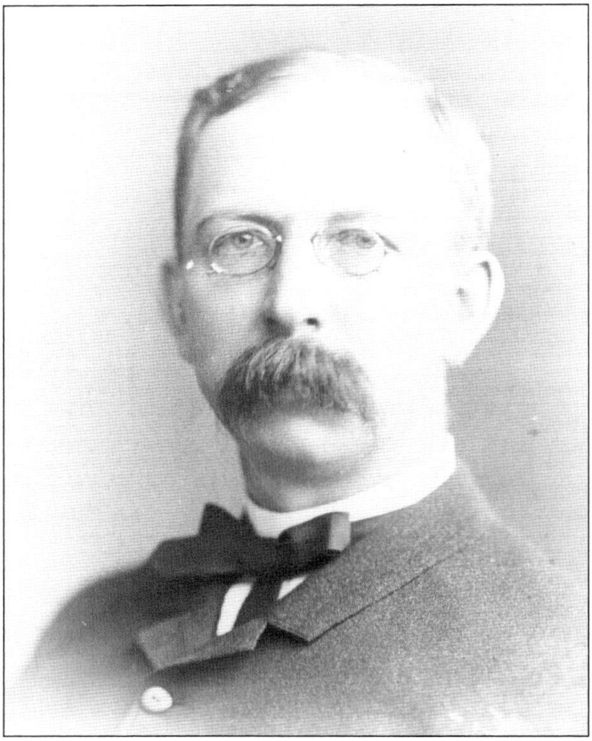

Thurston Burns, the second principal of Westbrook High School.

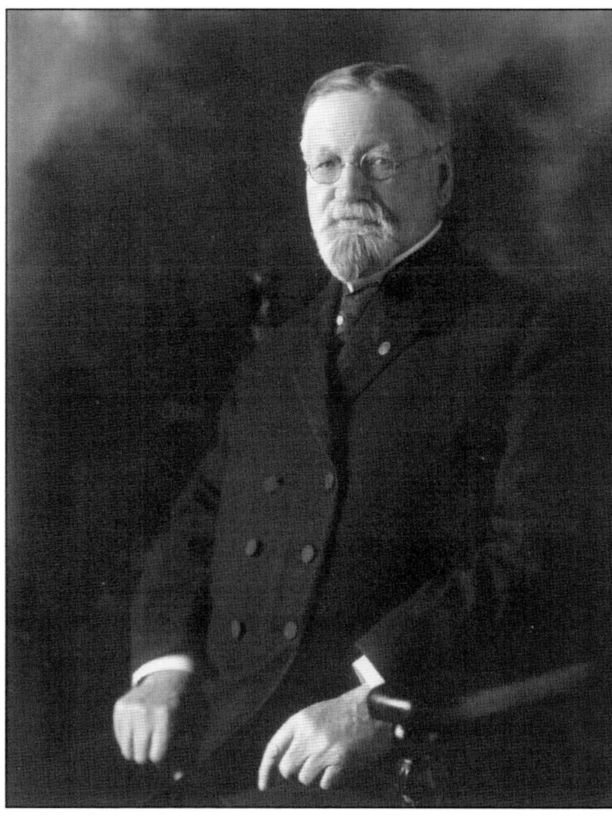

Woodbury Kidder Dana (June 7, 1840–May 24, 1942). Among his many civic contributions, this mill-owner was also a trustee of the Walker Memorial Library.

Wedding picture of Arthur David LaPointe and Anne Marie Lemieux, 1903. Posing in this manner, with the groom seated and the bride standing, was a practical way for the bride to show off her beautiful dress. (LaPointe Family Collection.)

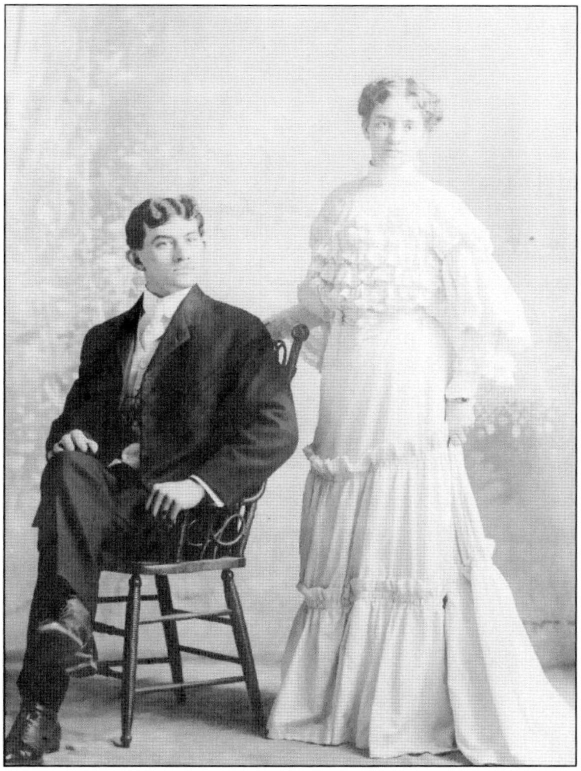

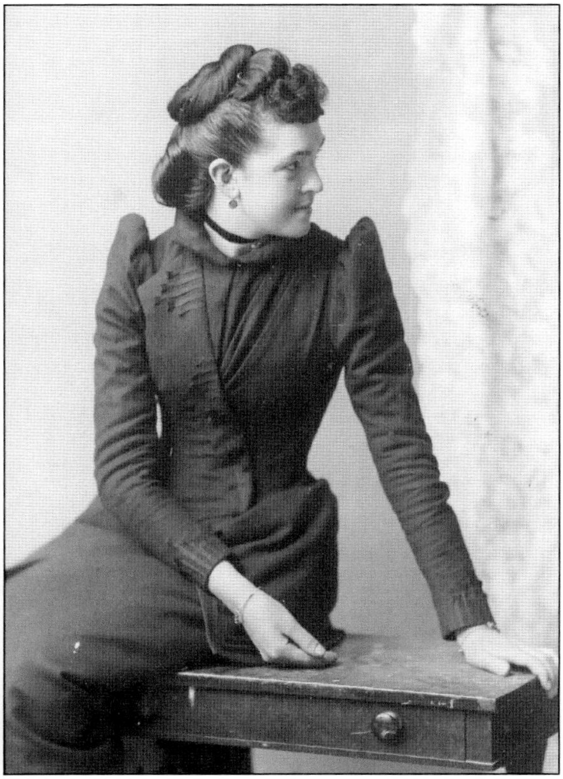

Marie LaPointe Lemieux, *c.* 1880. Mrs. Lemieux was the mother of Dr. Leo C. Lemieux, an osteopathic physician and one-time mayor of Westbrook. (LaPointe Family Collection.)

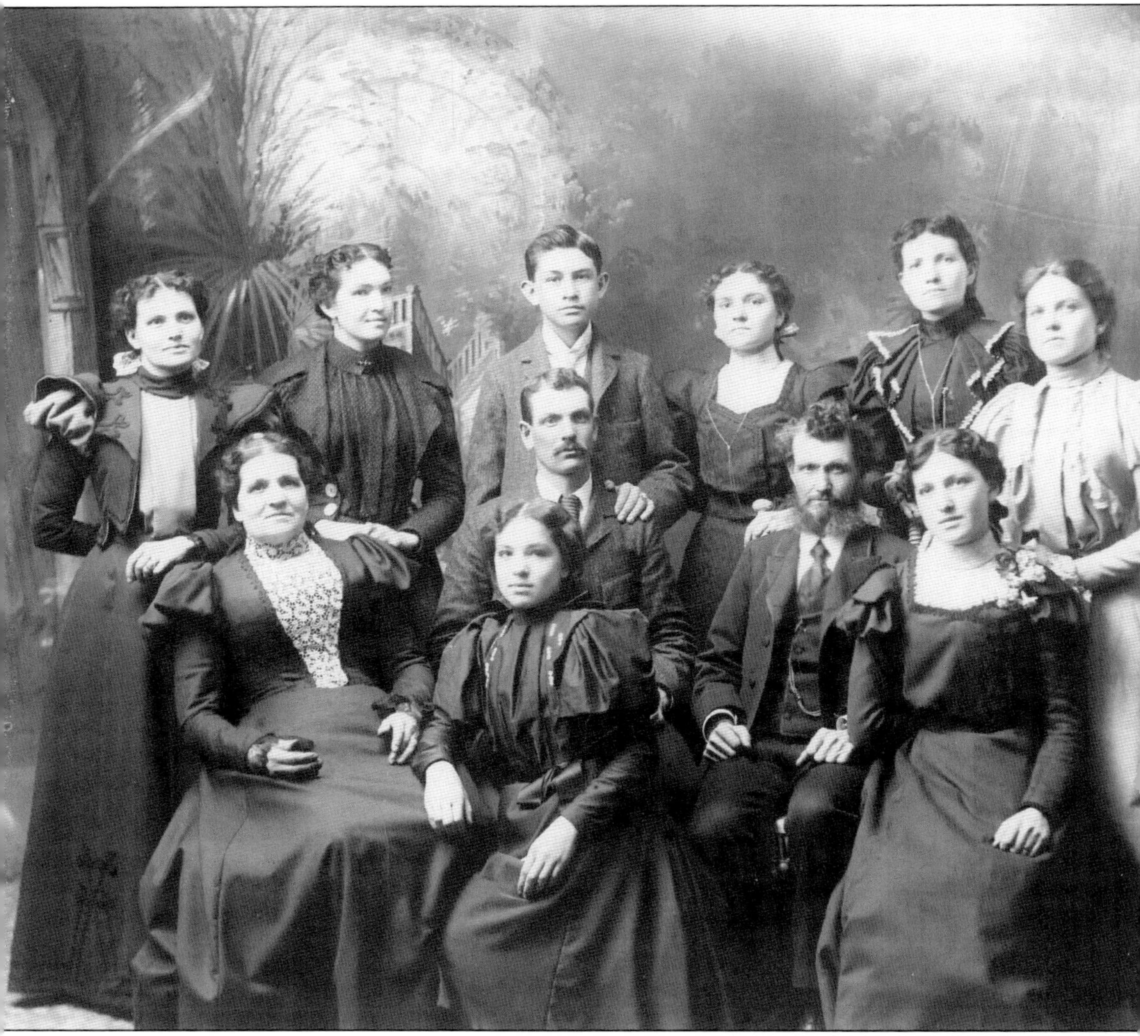

LaPointe Family, 1880. From left to right: (bottom row) Grandmother LaPointe, Laura LaPointe Guimond, Grandfather LaPointe, Christina LaPointe Robitaille; (center) Ernest LaPointe; (top row) Mathilde LaPointe Desjardins, Marie LaPointe Lemieux, Arthur LaPointe, Dina LaPointe Vaillancourt, Ernestine LaPointe Thuotte, and Alice LaPointe Desilets. (LaPointe Family Collection.)

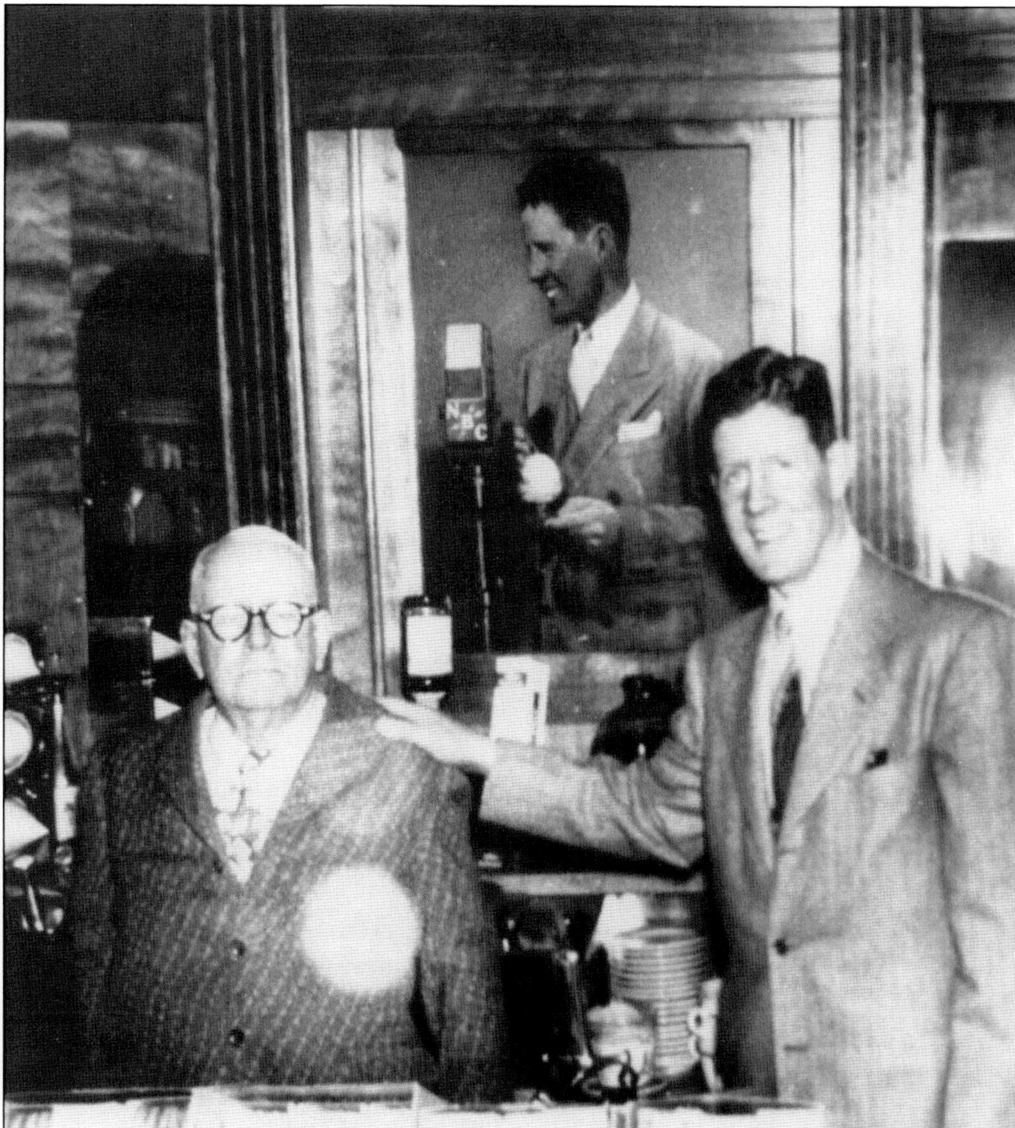

Rudy Vallee poses with his father, Charles, in the latter's drug store on the corner of Main and Bridge Streets (hence the name "Vallee's Square"). The picture of Rudy in the background may be seen at the Walker Memorial Library, where it hangs as a gift of Roland Albert.

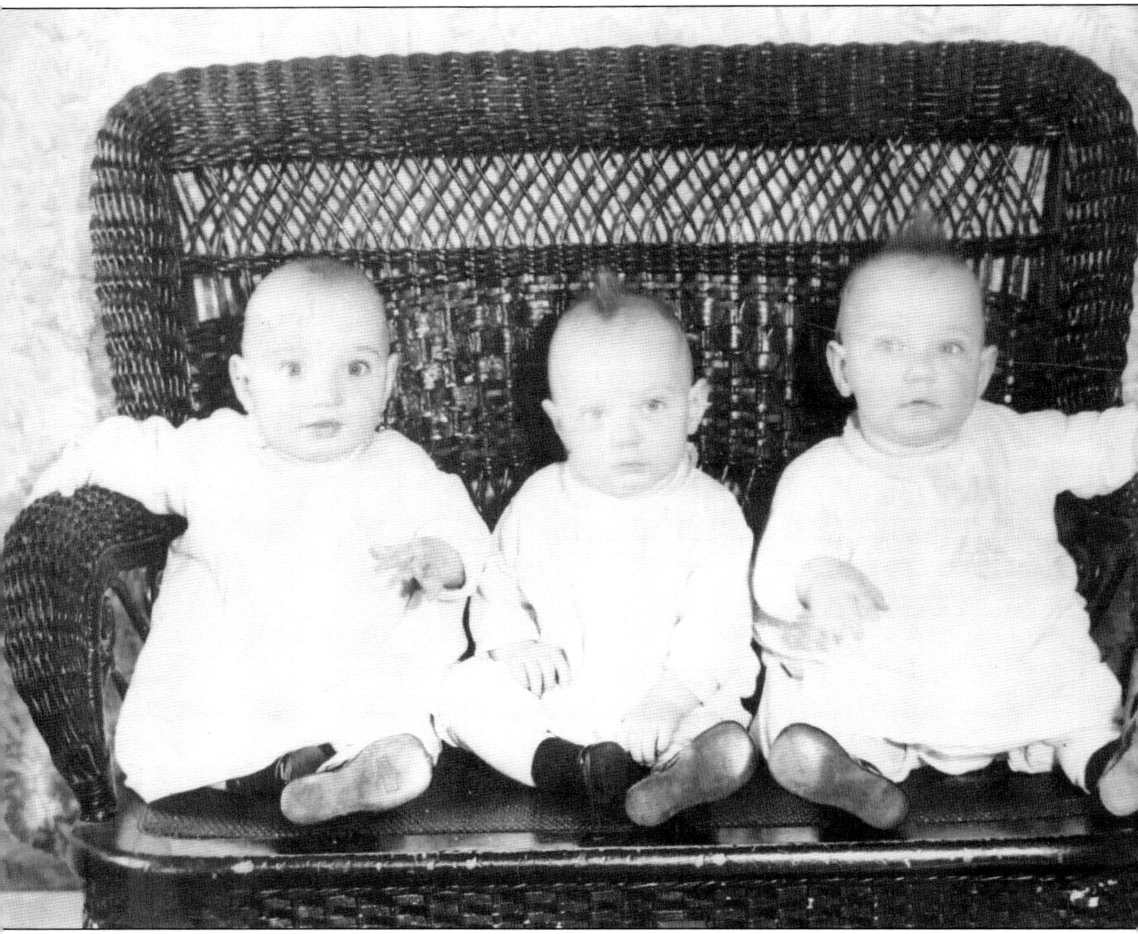

Westbrook's first triplets, born to Hazel and Eugene LeConte in February 1931. These were the sixth, seventh, and eighth of their ten children. They were named Norwood, Norris, and Norman. Mr. LeConte was a longtime mechanic for the City of Westbrook and also served on the Westbrook City Council.

Four

Churches and Schools

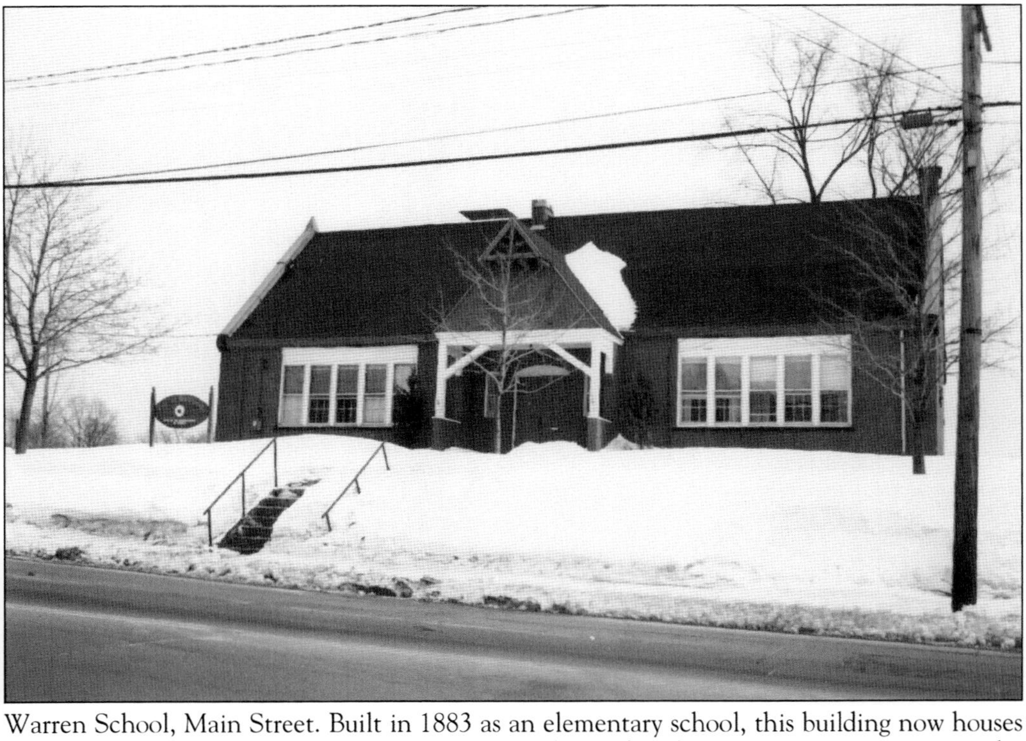

Warren School, Main Street. Built in 1883 as an elementary school, this building now houses the offices of the superintendent of schools. Nothing played a more important part in the development of any town than its churches and schools. Westbrook was no exception. This section presents examples of this development, illustrated through photographs.

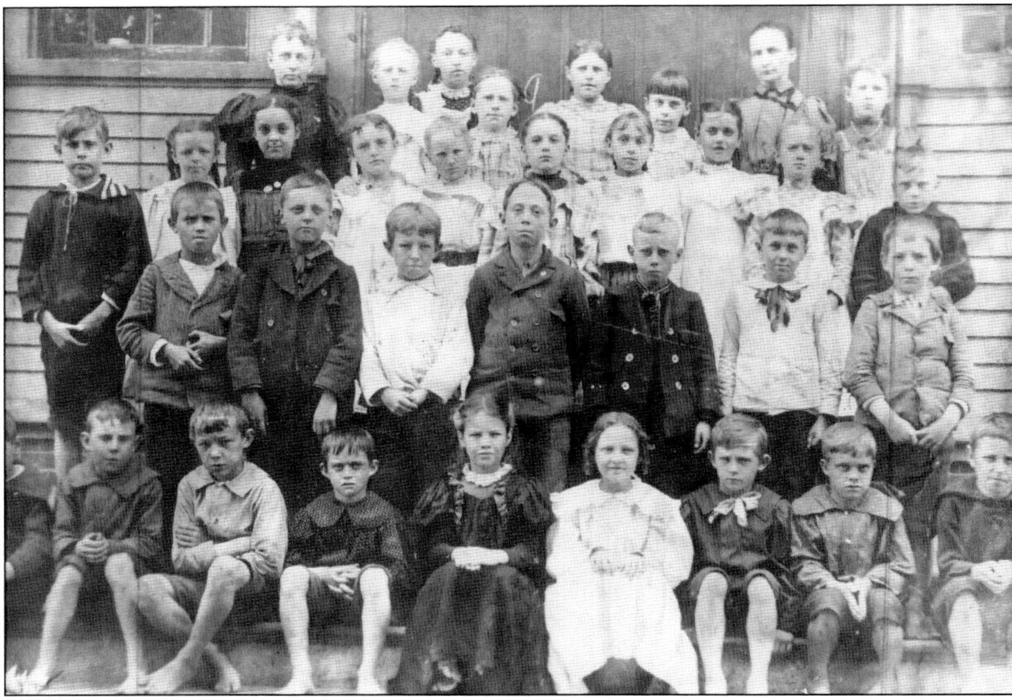

Brown Street School, built in 1891. Julia M. Doyle, a longtime teacher at the Brown Street School, is pictured here with one of her classes. The school burned in 1958 and is now the site of Barton's Florist.

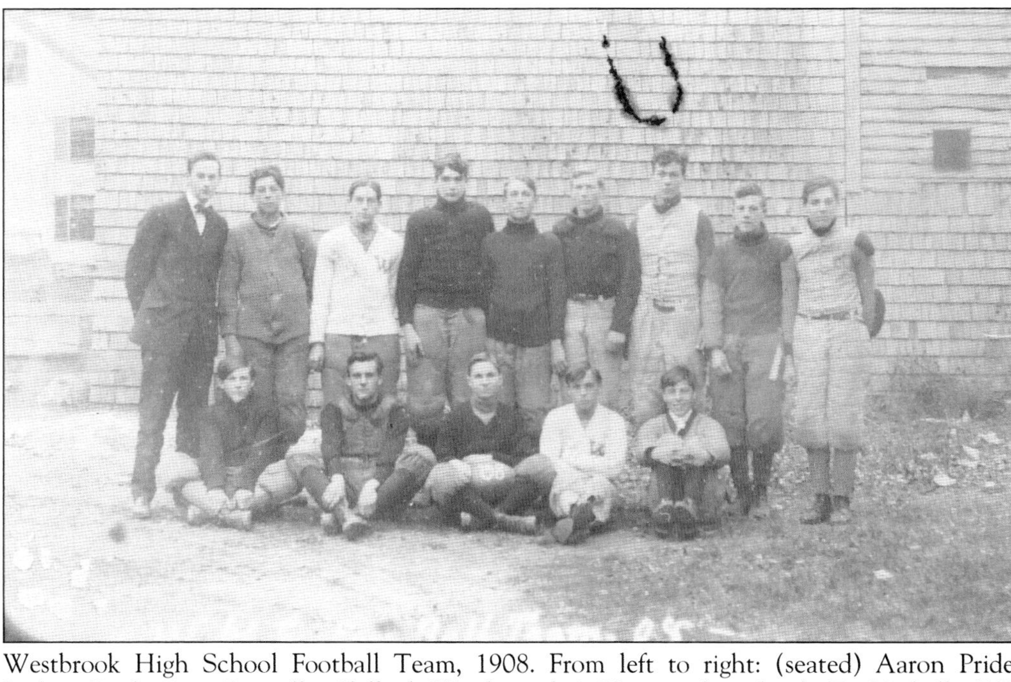

Westbrook High School Football Team, 1908. From left to right: (seated) Aaron Pride, Parker Pool, Ray Burwell, Clifford Ward, and ? Hogan; (standing) T. Haskell, E.K. McFarland, Charlie Boyce, Ralph Wentworth, Gus Staples, ? Walls, Cy Philpot, Warren Stuart, and R. Decormier.

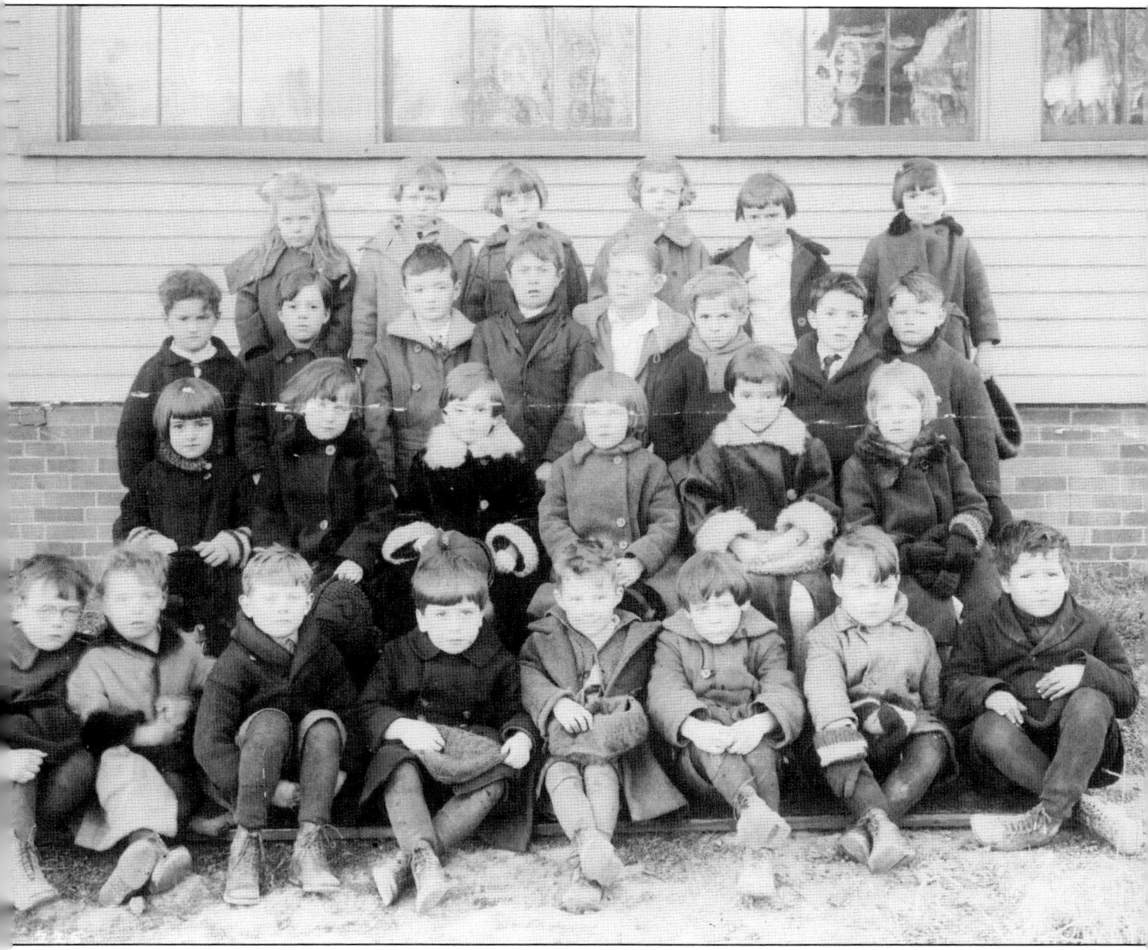

First Grade at Valentine School, 1926. From left to right: (front row) Kenneth Barbour, James Chilcot, Harold Pride, Gerald Fluett, Eugene Berg, Roger Caron, Philip Kirkpatrick, Stanley Mayberry; (second row) Dorothy St. Pierre, Irene Moreau, Pauline Graper, Shirley Lowell, Alberta Dugas, Mary Allen; (third row) Edward Smith, Arnold Higgins, William Clarke, Peter Phillips, Ridgewell Allen, Edward Spencer, Charles Fortin, Roland Philmore; (back row) Gladys Gordon, Ruth Smith, Esther McFarland, Dorothy Anderson, Irene St. Pierre, and Margaret Laffin. (Berg Family Collection.)

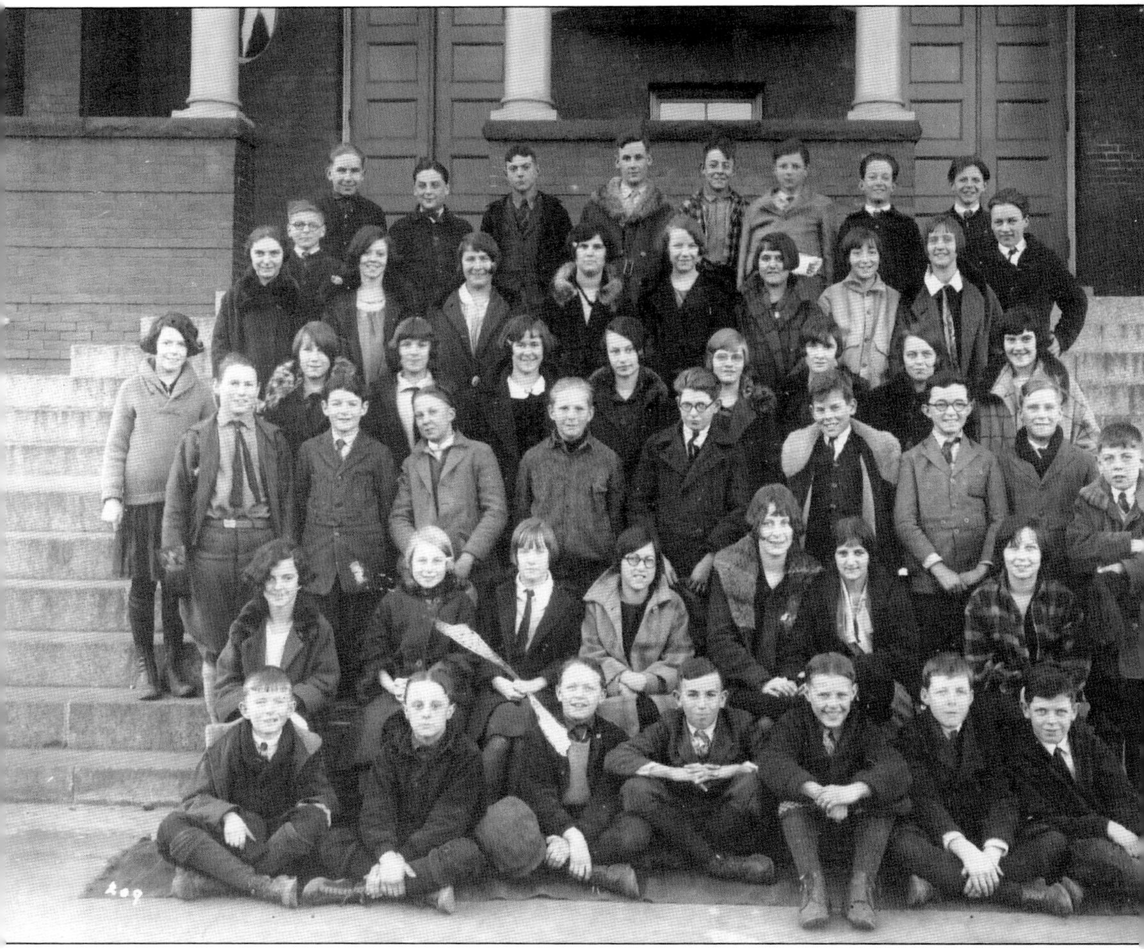

Forest Street School Class of 1927. From left to right: (front row) Warren Pratt, George Merrill, George Smith, Charles Teague, Kermit Kelly, Leslie Graham, William Bryan; (second row) Flora Berry, Helen Lewis, Sylvia Gordon, Ruth McKenney, Elizabeth Roby, Beaulah Greenleaf, Ruth Varney; (third row) Owen Pride, Lester Berry, Milton Nelson, Irving Nielson, Philip Stultz, Alvin Polley, Wilson Herring, Millard Keller, Leonard Richardson; (fourth row) Alice Saunders, Hazel Davis, Mildred Doucette, Barbara Quimby, Christine Prince, Rena Crague, Bernice Bassett, Esther Wilson, Margaret Roberts; (fifth row) Mary Jameson, Arlene Anderson, Yvonne Blake, Rena Palmer, Doris Harmon, Sarah LaBrie, Abbie Burnell, Dorothy Esty; (sixth row) Elmer Randall, Frederick Raymond, Harold Lord, Franklin Hannaford, Richard Billings, Gus Randall, Richard Lopez, Walter Randall, and Roland Fraser.

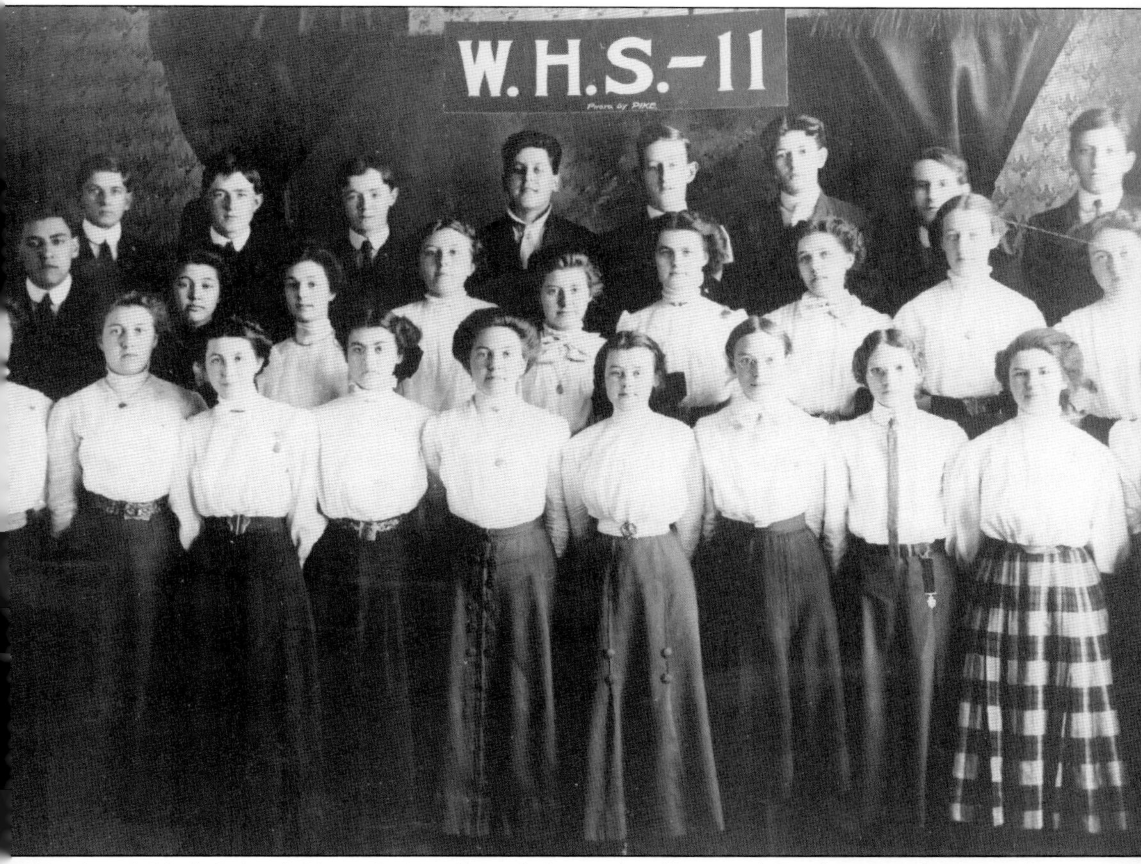

Westbrook High School Class of 1911. From left to right: (first row) Bertha Guptil, Mae Fisk, Lillian Bragdon, Lena Sherman, Emma Gerhardts, Elizabeth Redlon, Helen Mann, Ruth Norton, Ruth Scates, Clata Sisson; (second row) Romeo Decormier, Carrie Jordan, Polly Burnell, Lillian Strout, Ruth Carll, Stella Smith, Laura Hawkes, Julia Burke, Hazel Gleason; (third row) Philip Verril, Clifford Waltham, Tommy Lillian, Milburn McAloney, Roy Welch, Roy Wheldon, Robert Parkhurst, and Russell Moses. (Berg Family Collection.)

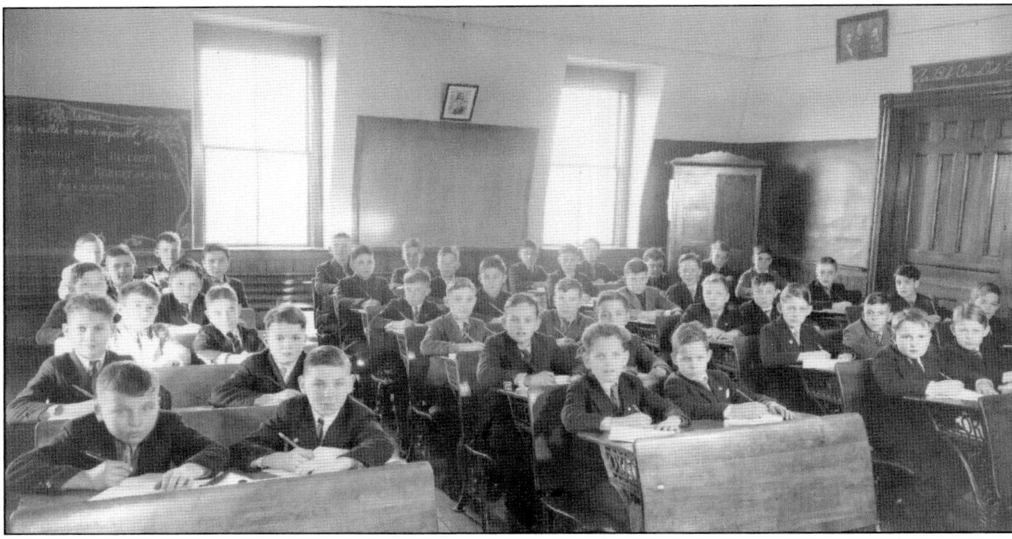

St. Hyacinth's School Class of 1937. Front to back: (first row) Louis Fournier, Edgar Savoie, Andy Metivier, John Lestage, ? Delcourt, unknown; (second row) Roger Guimond, Richard Moreau, Amie Labrecque, Donald Begin, unknown, Bill Theriault. (third row) Eddie Savoie, Rudy Michaud, Eugene J. Thibeault (Jack), Roger LeBorgne, Roma Drouin, Bill Duclos; (fourth row) Paul Dufour, Vin Label, George LaFrance, Robert Godin, unknown, Robert Arsenault; (fifth row) Leo Pedneau, Emile Labrecque, Paul Benard, Leandre Roy, Andre Jolette, ? Bernier; (sixth row) Robert Breton, Arthur Arsenault, unknown, Kit Nadeau, Elmer Martin, ? Lemieux; (seventh row) Conrad Tardif, ? Roberge, Gerald Delcourt, Edgar Barriault, and Yoland Landry. (Joseph E. Thibeault Collection.)

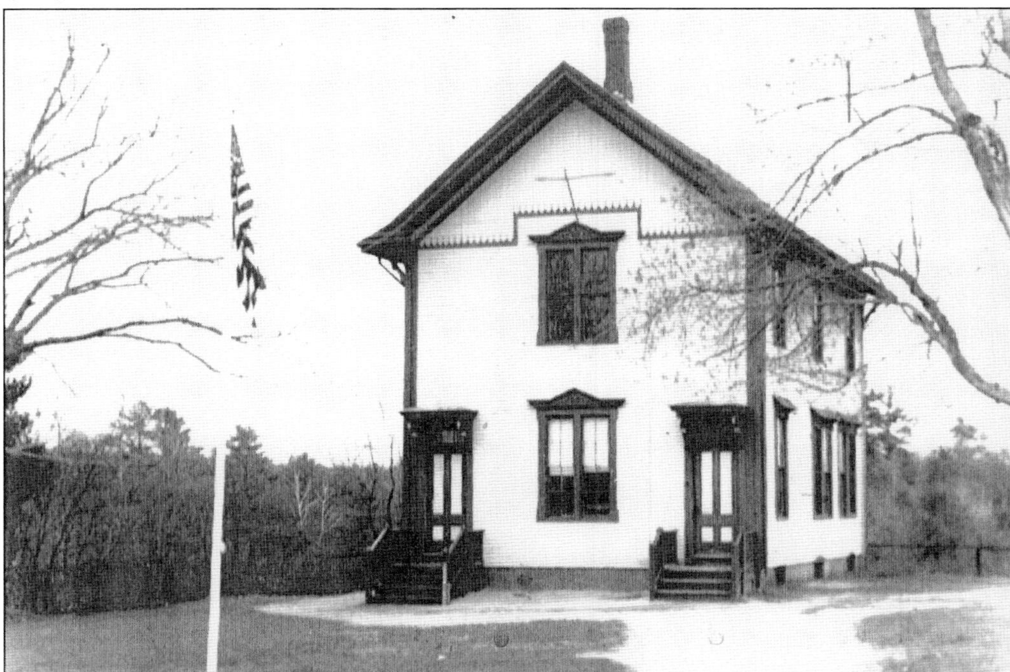

Highland Lake School. Located on Duck Pond Road near Bridgton Road, this school was razed in the 1970s.

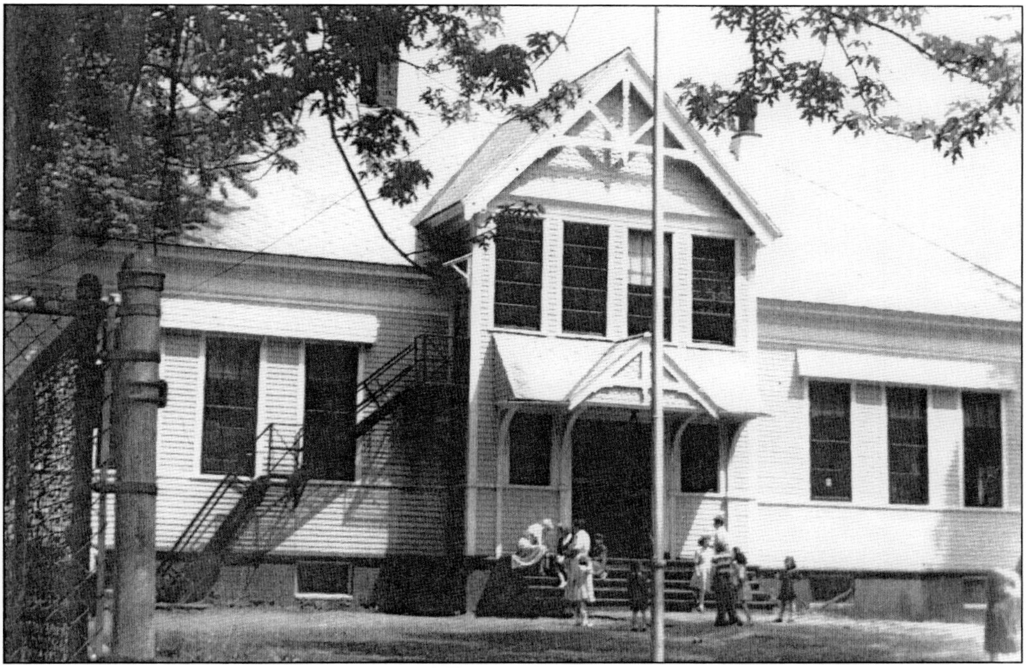

Brown Street School, *c.* 1886. This school was destroyed by fire in 1958.

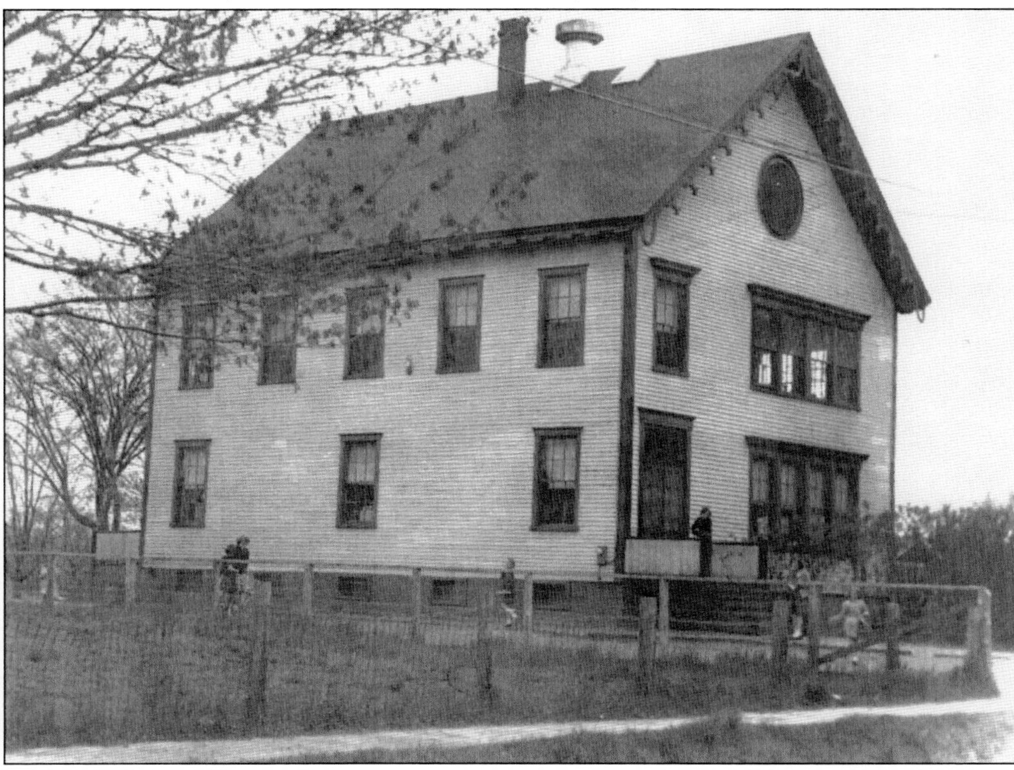

Valentine School. Originally located on Main Street near the Old Westbrook High School, this building was used as both a grammar school and a high school. It was moved to its present site on East Valentine Street in 1887 and was converted to apartments in the 1970s.

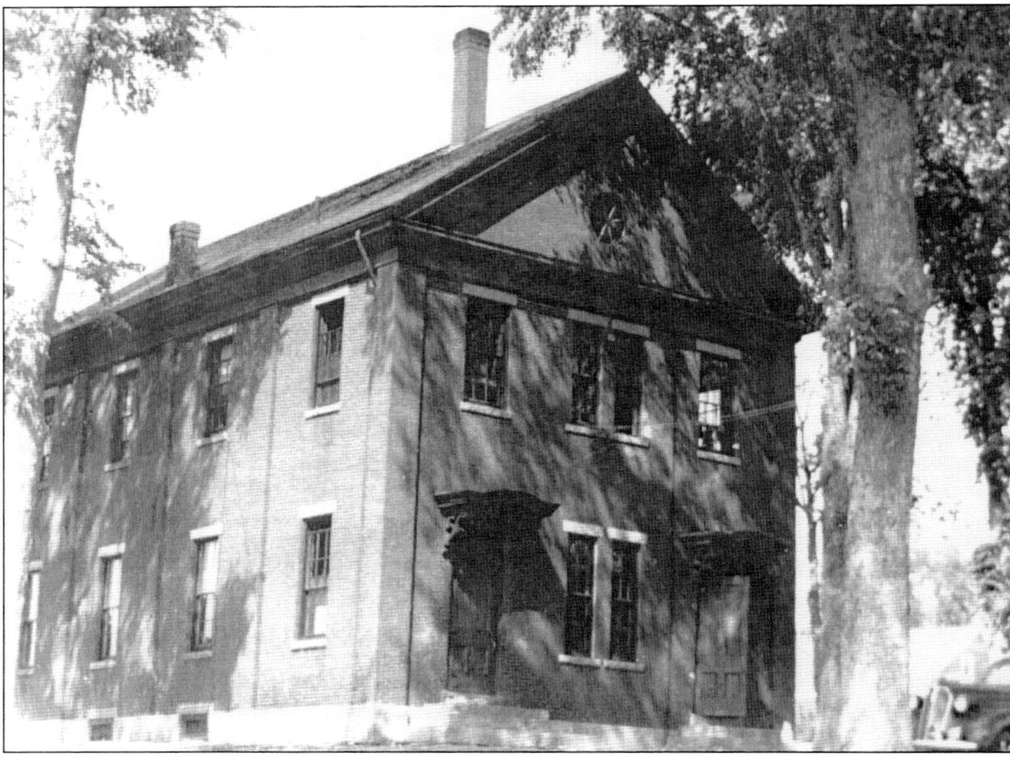

Pride's Corner School. Located on Bridgton Road near Pride Street, this building was razed in the 1960s.

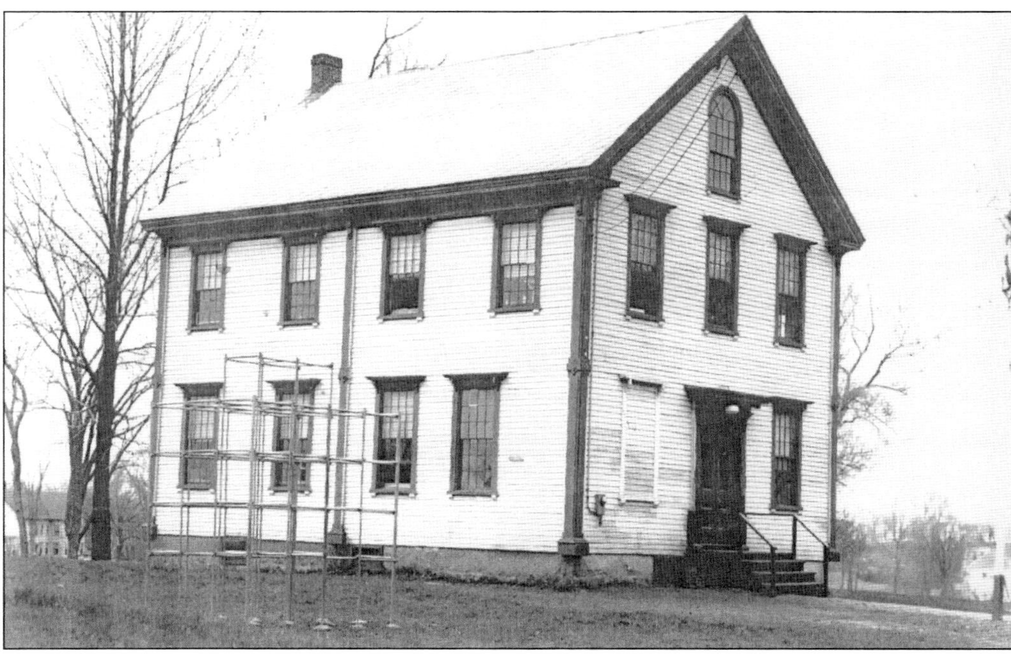

Saco Street School, built in 1868 and used as an elementary school until 1953. Many renovations were made, and the building is presently the home of the Westbrook Knights of Columbus.

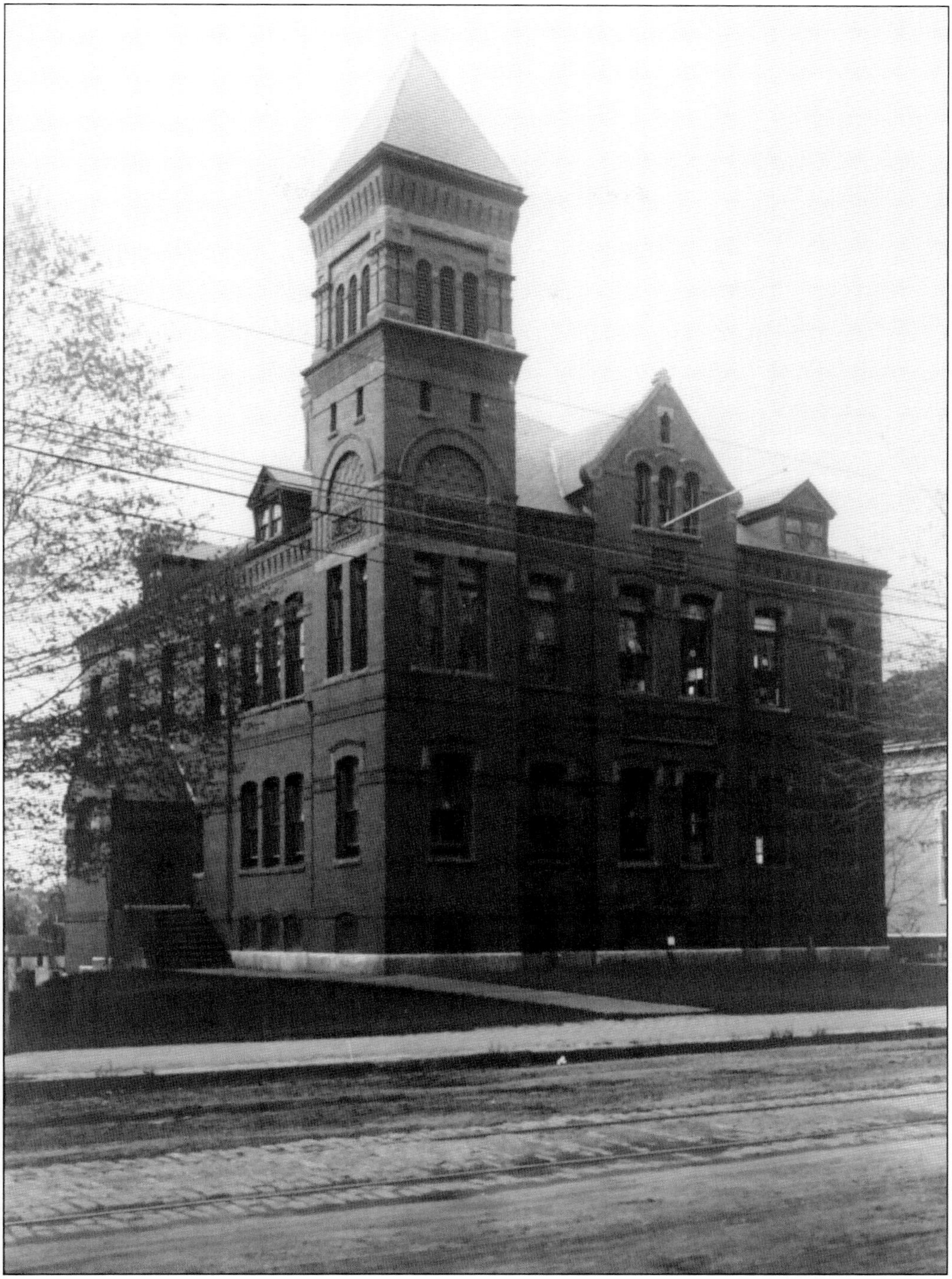

Westbrook High School, 1911. Built in 1886, this building has also been used as a junior high school. It now stands relatively empty. A 1936 addition of a gymnasium and classrooms at the rear houses the City of Westbrook Recreation Department and other rooms used by the Westbrook Historical Society. Advisory referendums have urged the preservation of the school, but lack of funding has prevented any immediate plans for renovation. (Berg Family Collection.)

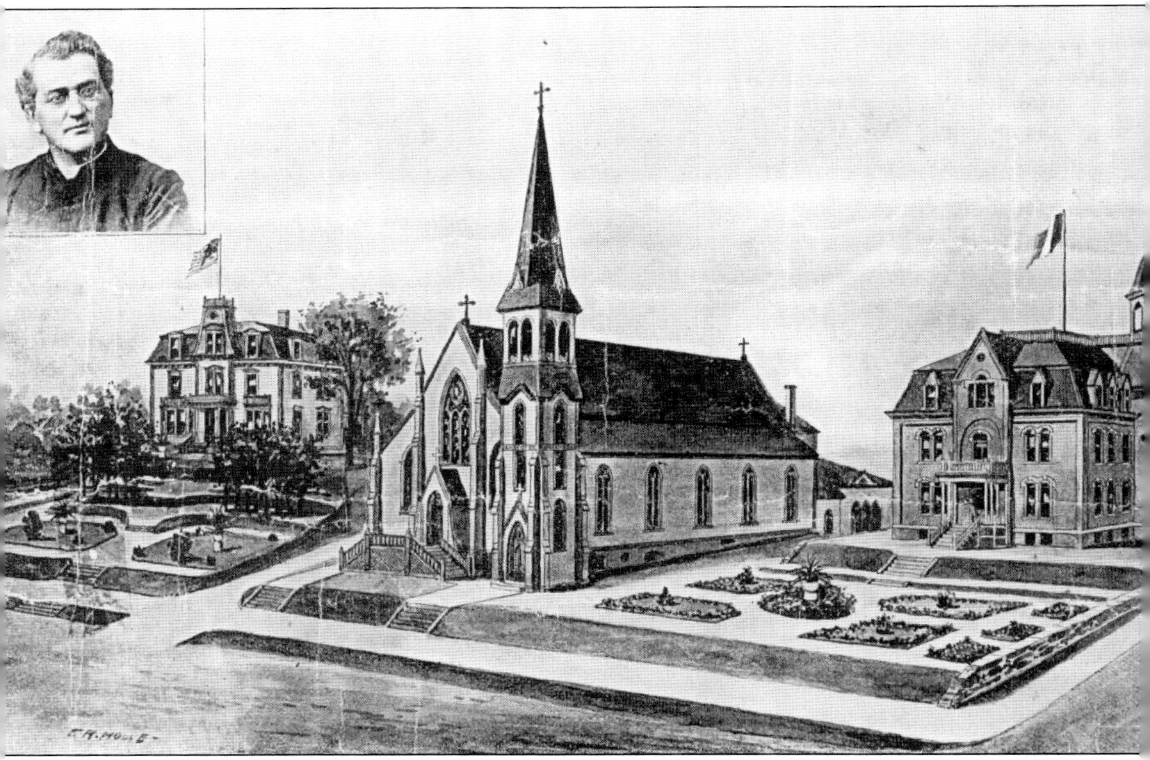

St. Hyacinthe Parish Complex on the northerly side of Brown Street, 1894. Some buildings that can be seen here: The Rectory (left), First Church (center), and the Parish School and Convent (right). Pastor A.D. DeCelles is present at the upper left. (St. Hyacinthe's Historical Society.)

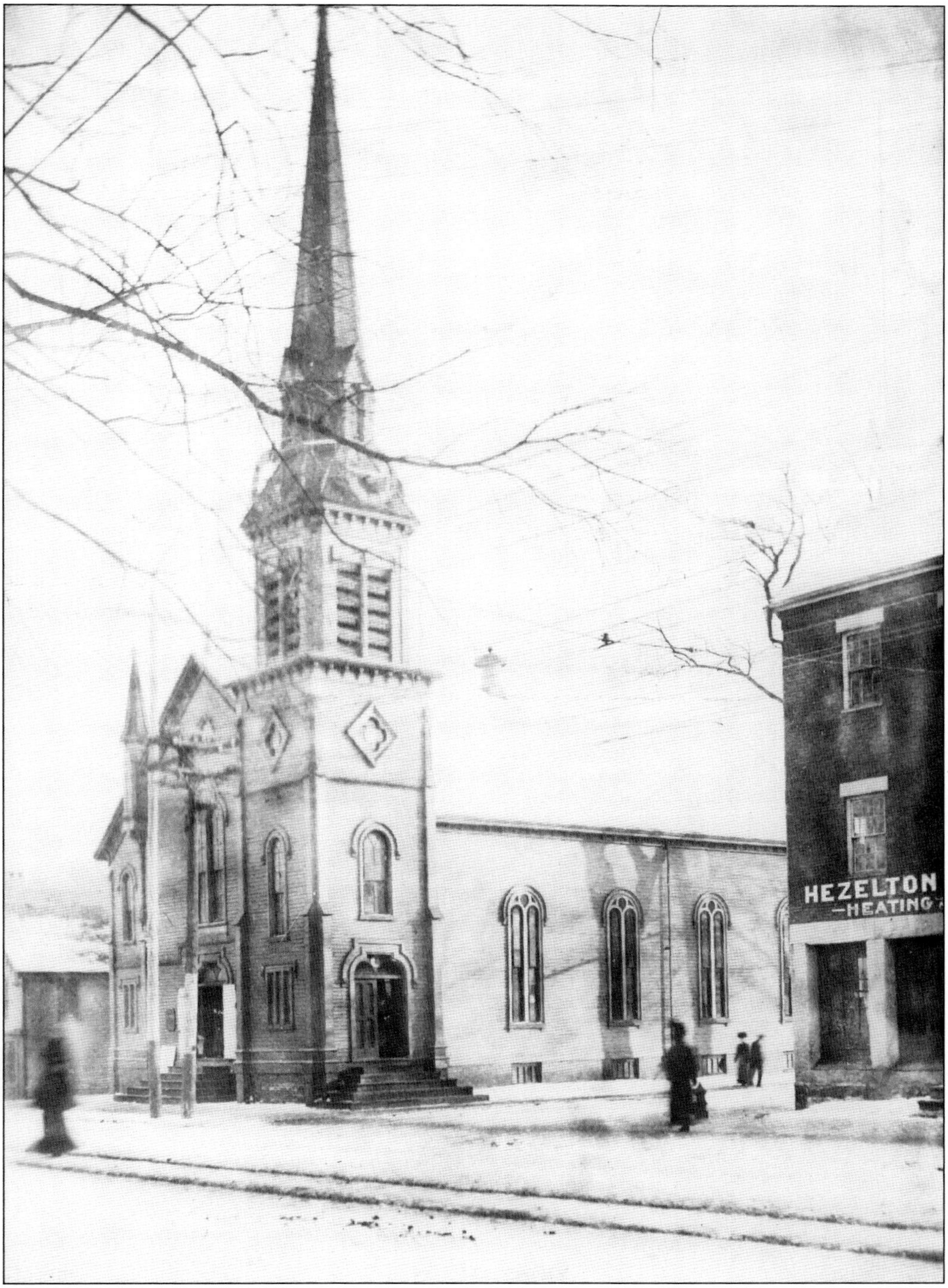

Westbrook Congregational Church, on the corner of Main and Brackett Streets. A landmark symbol in many of the existing pictures of Westbrook's Main Street, the church was demolished in the 1970s both as part of the Urban Renewal Project and as a result of a merger with the Warren Congregational Church. A new church was erected at that time at 810 Main Street.

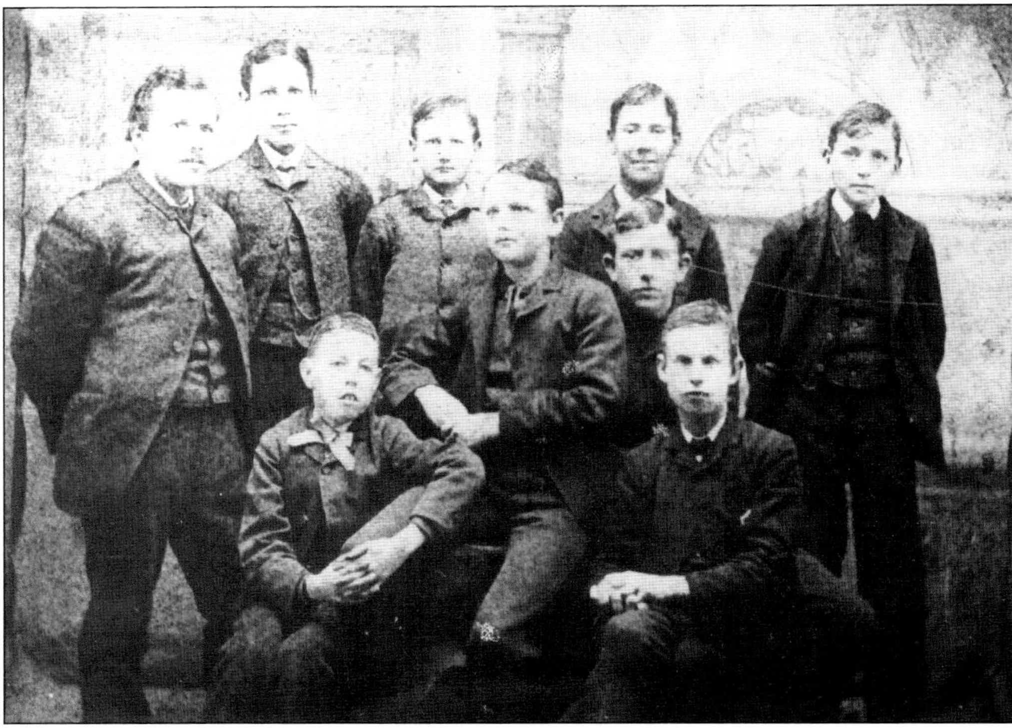

A Sunday school class at the Methodist Episcopal Church. From left to right: (front row) Guy Woodman, Fred Spear; (second row) W.R. Bragdon (teacher), ? Hazelton, John Knight; (back row) Alfred Libby, Walter Wayson, George Knowlton, and Win McClellan.

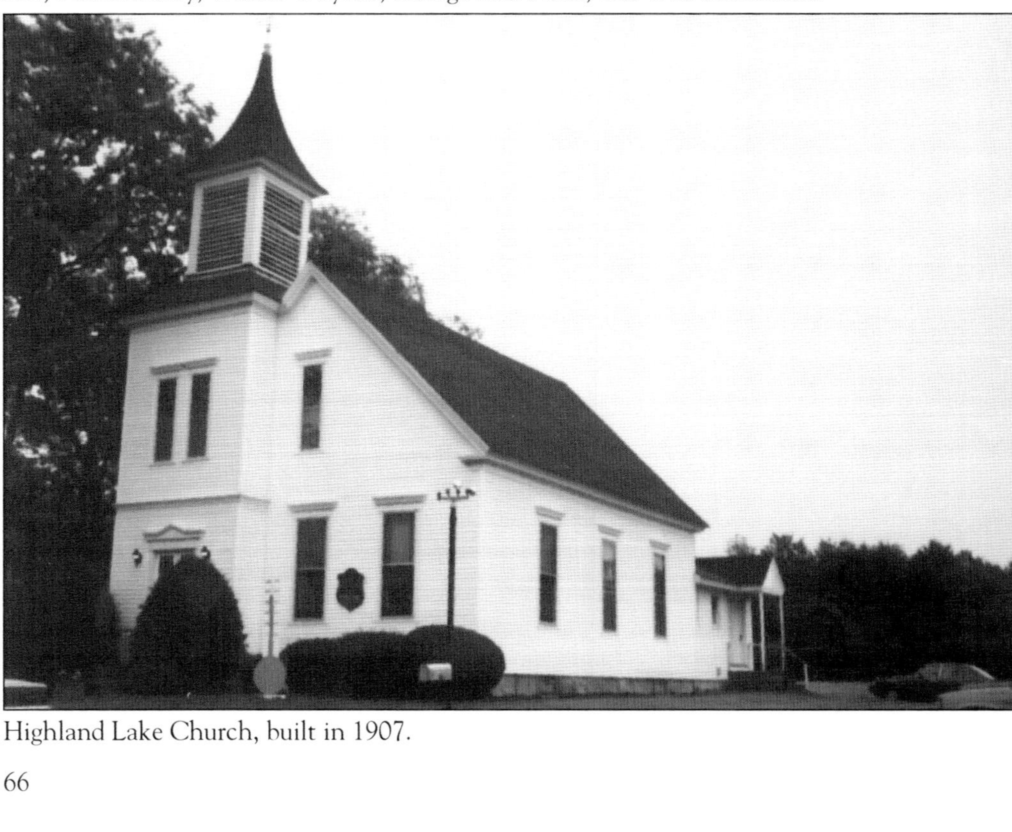

Highland Lake Church, built in 1907.

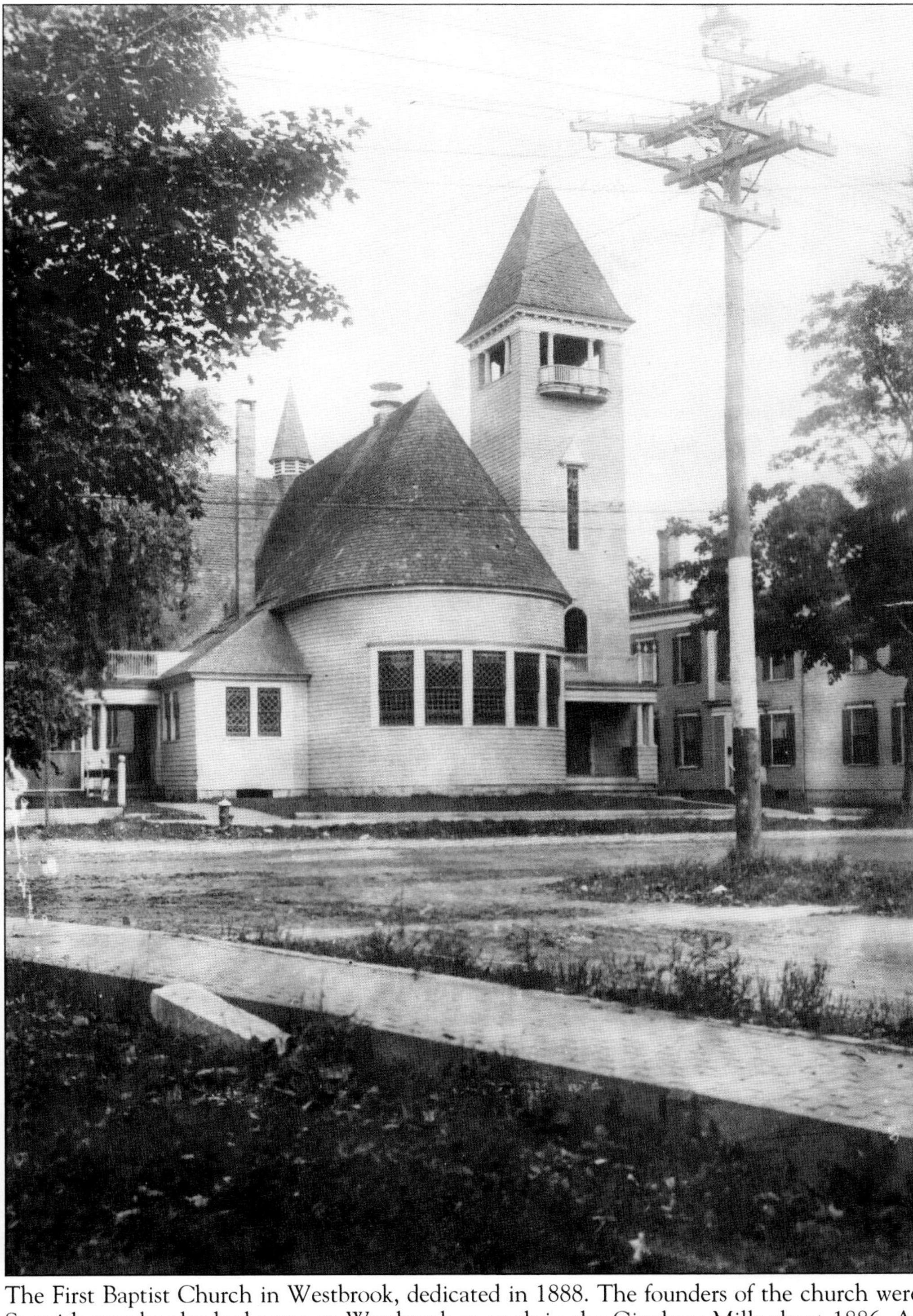

The First Baptist Church in Westbrook, dedicated in 1888. The founders of the church were Scottish people who had come to Westbrook to work in the Gingham Mills about 1886. At first, they organized Sunday school meetings in a private homes. Due to the group's increasing numbers, the site and building on Main Street were acquired and the church edifice was built.

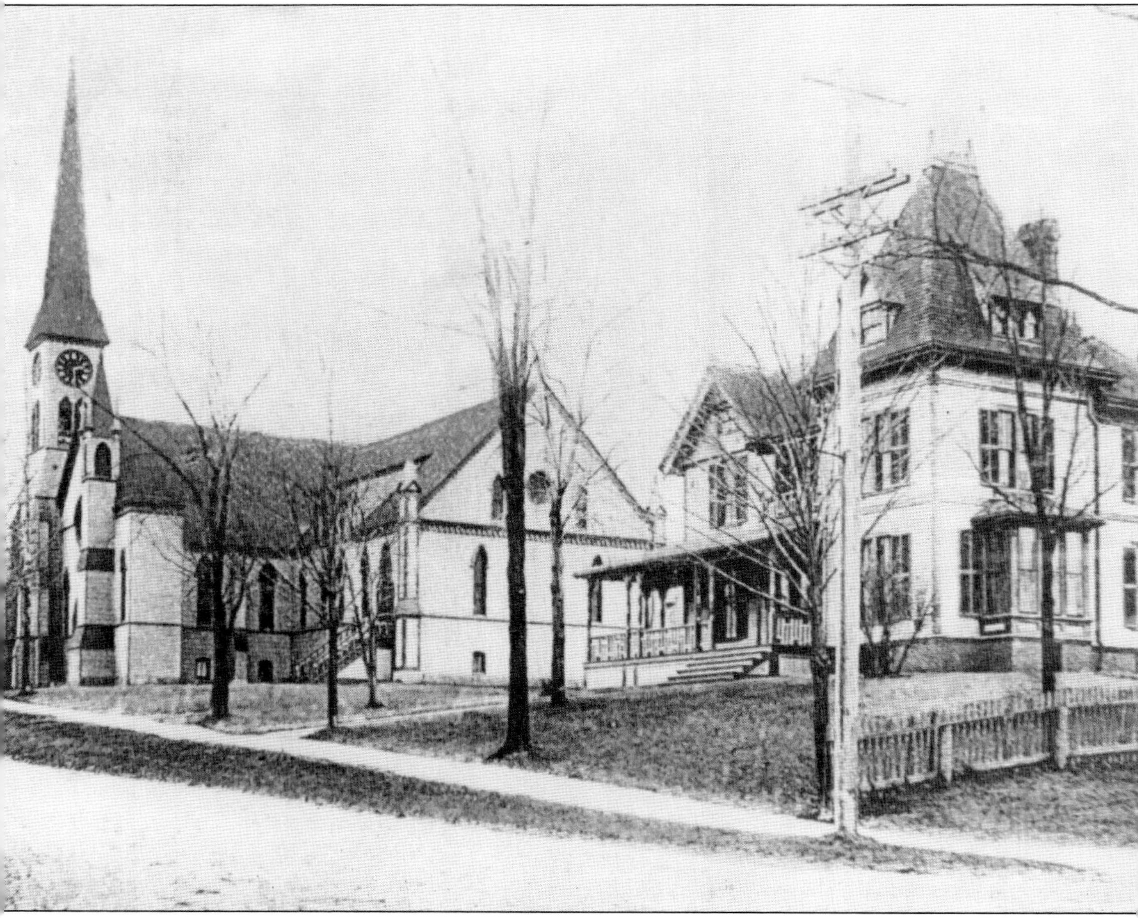

Warren Congregational Church, organized in 1869. Samuel D. Warren donated land and considerable financing for the church and later built the parsonage shown on the right. This parsonage has been moved and is now located on upper Cumberland Street near the Windham line. The church was demolished in the 1970s and the congregation merged with the Westbrook Congregational Church, moving to a new location at 810 Main Street. The City of Westbrook has since purchased the site shown for use by the Westbrook Police Department. The Whitney Rose Garden is being cultivated on the spot where the church one stood. (Roland D. Tetrault Collection.)

Five

Community Life and Entertainment

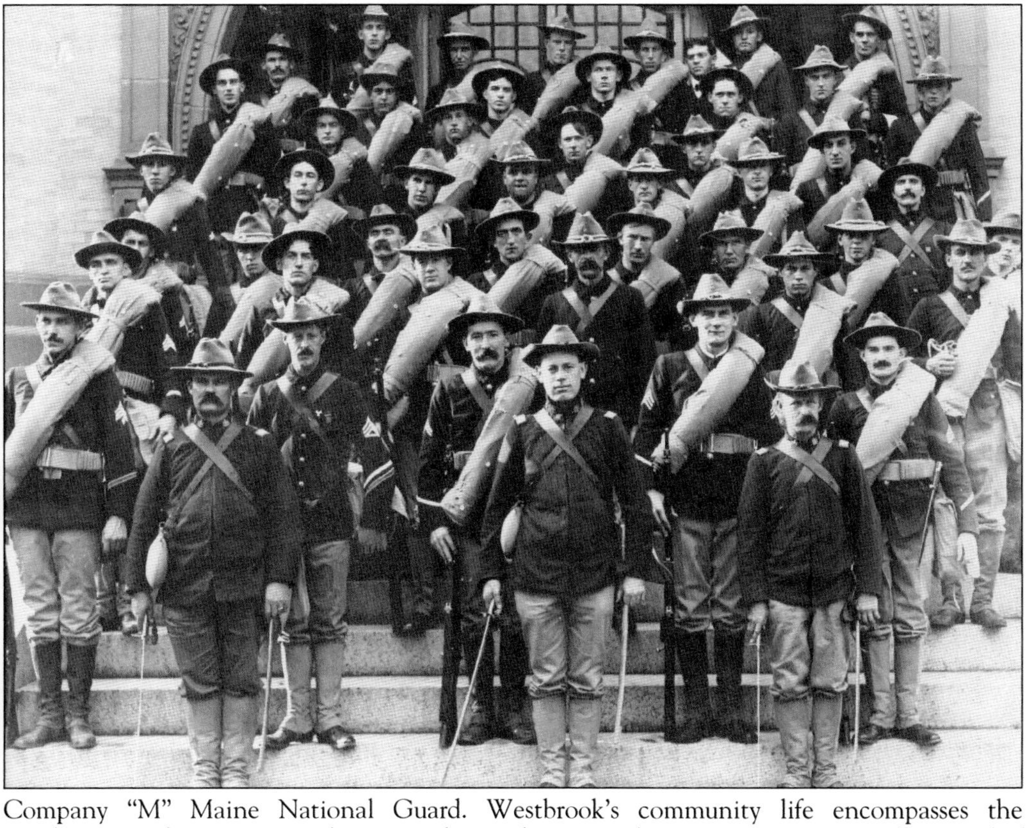

Company "M" Maine National Guard. Westbrook's community life encompasses the involvement of its citizens in their civic duties, their contributions in community affairs, and of course their ability to entertain and be entertained. The next chapter highlights some of these important activities.

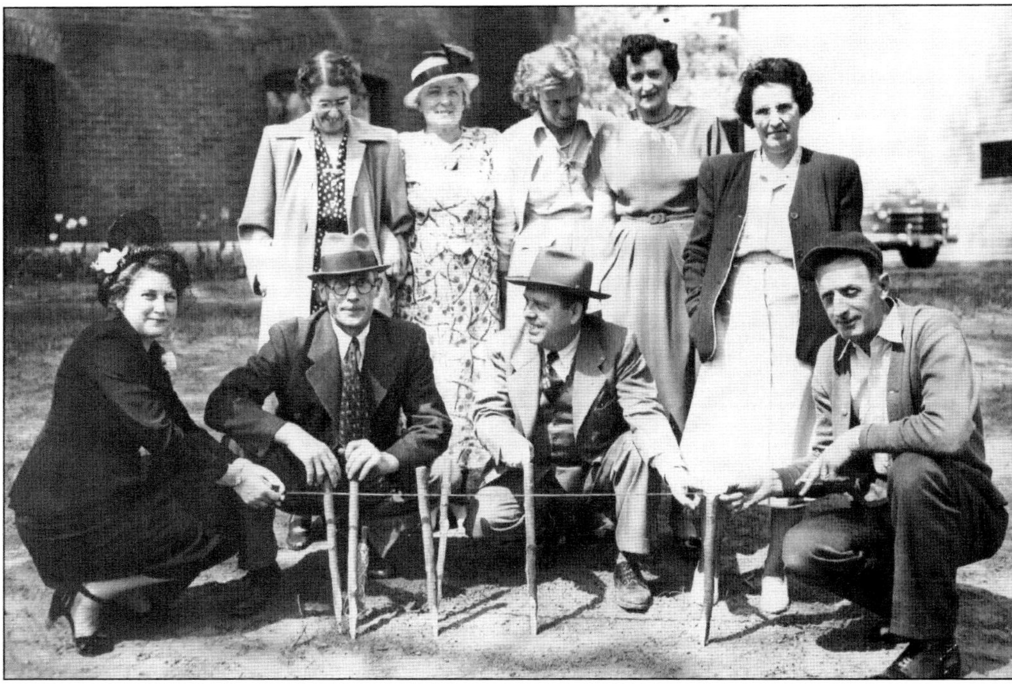

Walker Memorial Library garden, 1950. Marking out the plans for the library garden are, left to right: (front) Oswald McFarland, August Arndt, Mayor Ernest Porell, Leroy Lombard; (back) Myrtle Fuller (librarian), Mrs. Carl Bertelsen, Mrs. Franz Hansen, Mrs. Carl Hansen, and Mrs. Roy St. Clair.

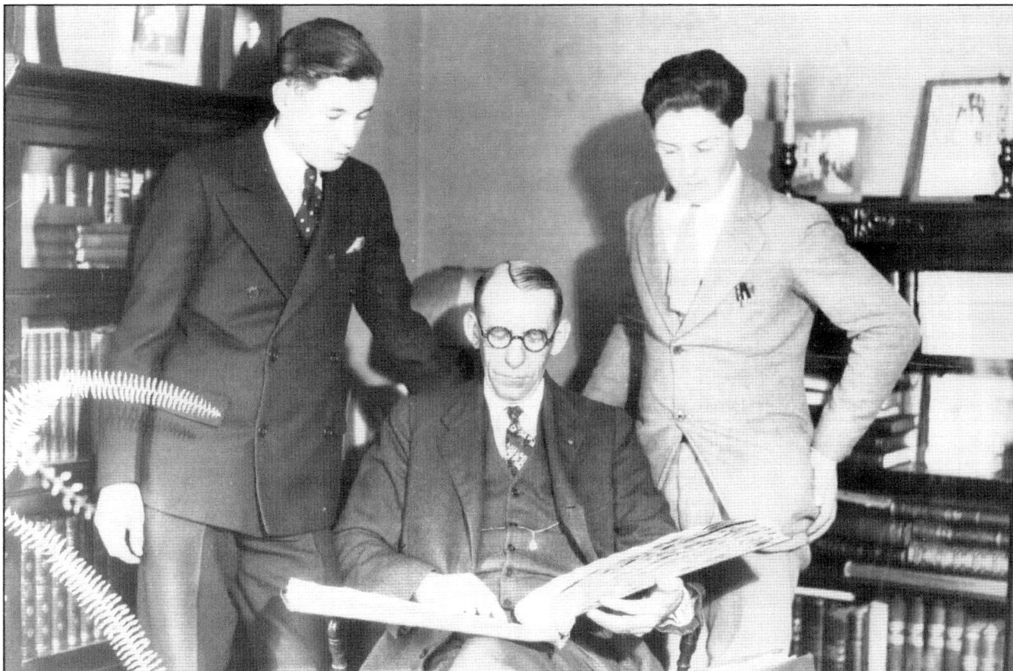

Harry Pride and his Boy Scout troop, 1928. Mr. Pride donated many hours to the development of Boy Scouts in Westbrook.

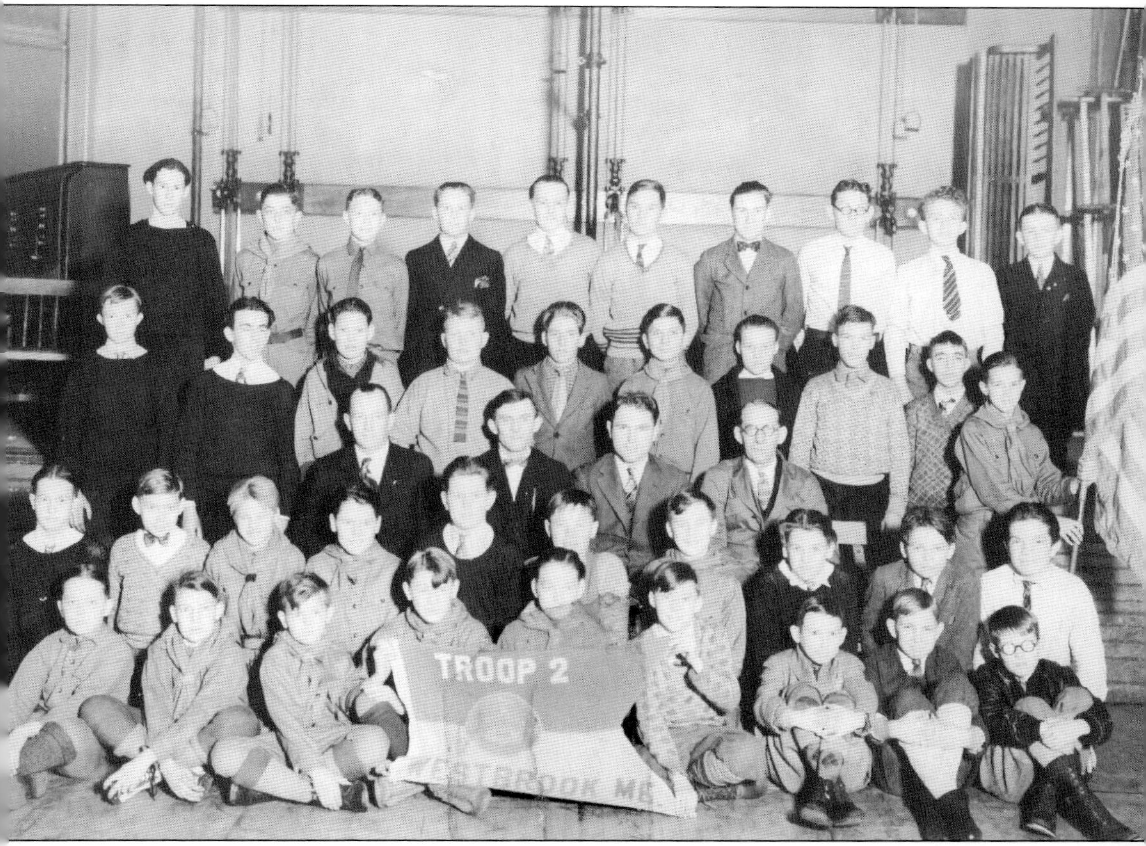

Westbrook Boy Scout Troop 2, 1928/29. From left to right: (front row) Wyvern Richardson, Elmer Riggs, Robert Polley, Fred Martin, Wade Harmon, Everett Ladd, Philip (Chicken) Leighton, Axel Hansen, Earl Christensen; (second row) Robert Babb, Linwood Doughty, Vernon Chaplin, William Cape Jr., Albert Hunter Jr., Perley Kenny, Ernest Speirs, Robert Doucette, Charles Dyer, Harold Harmon; (third row) Earle Babb, Dana Ladd, Charles Weir, Harry Pride; (fourth row) Philip (Honey) Nelson, Charles Teague, Carl Peterson, Lawrence Nielson, Harold Warming, Pedro Peters, Walter Christensen, Minot Pitts, Philip Larabee, Dana Babb (color bearer); (back row) Earle Pride, Leonard Richardson, George Smith, Irving Nielson, Clayton Curitt, Lawrence Plummer, Dwight Leighton, Owen Wood, Frank Willcome Jr., and Warren Pratt. Mrs. Marshall of Portland is behind the piano.

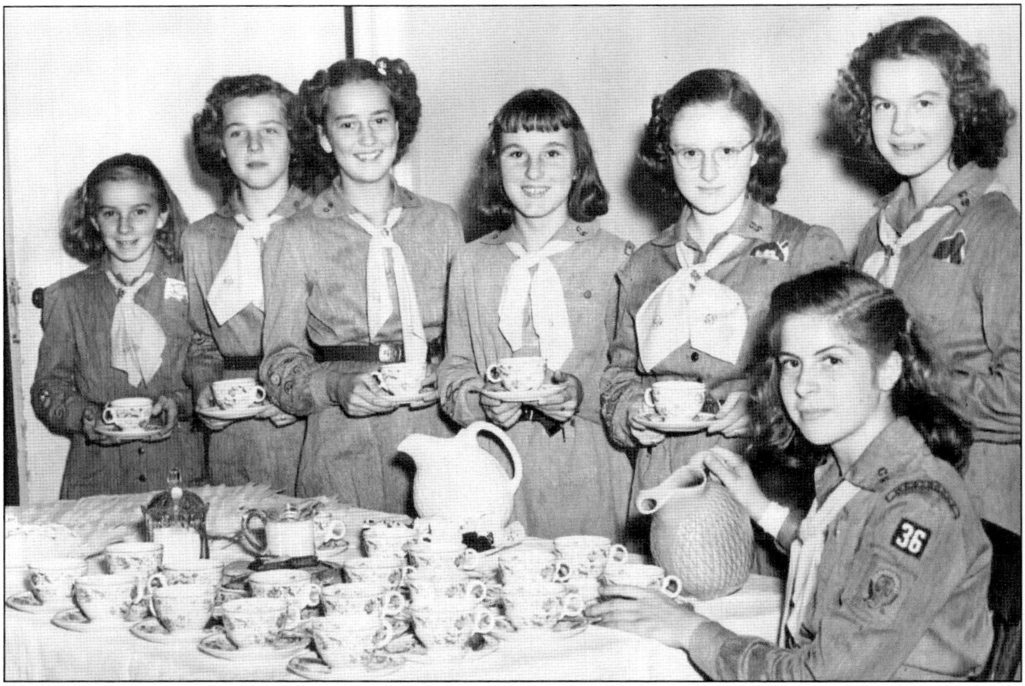

Westbrook Girl Scout Troop 36, 1948. From left to right: (seated) Patricia Clarke; (standing) Joan Tetreault, Wanda Christensen, Sally Ann Percival, Donna Spiller, Ellen DeWolfe, and Dianne King.

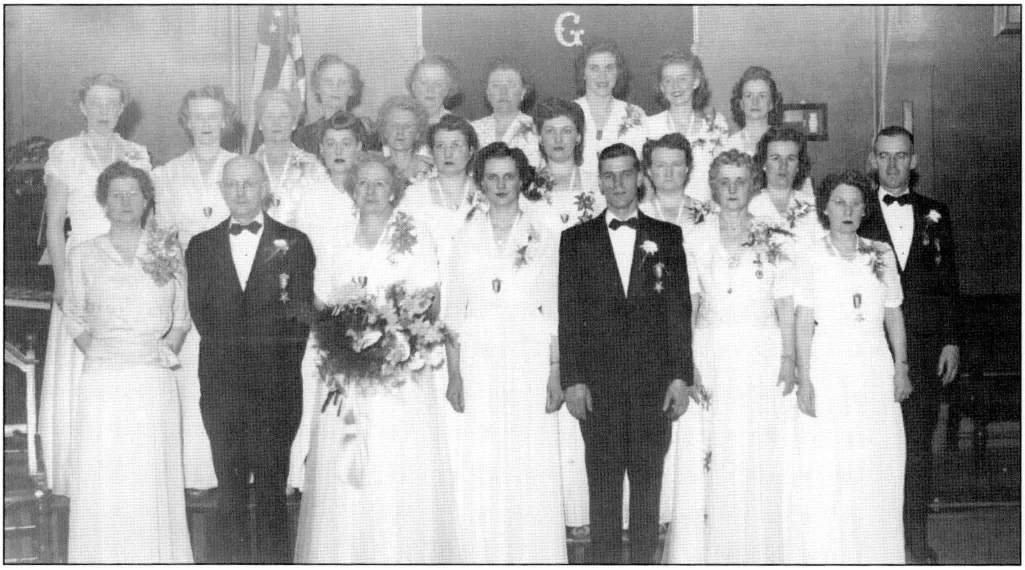

Beulah Chapter No. 5, Order of the Eastern Star, 1946. From left to right: (first row) Marcia Craft (Genesta Chapter–Bath, installing officer), Willis Holbrook, Louise Holbrook, Winnifred Marsters, Irvine Marsters, Sara Shaw (Genesta Chapter–Bath, past grand matron), Mildred Buzzell; (second row) Phyllis Stigman, Lillian Potter, Wilma Jordan, Dorothy Smith, Clyda Chick, Ivy Waterhouse, Marguerite Flint, Vernona Soper, Dorothy Collins, Leigh Flint; (third row) Frances Asker (Mizpah Chapter district deputy grand matron), Bertha Laffin, Kathy Nichols, Florence Goff, Muriel Swett, and Nancy Harper.

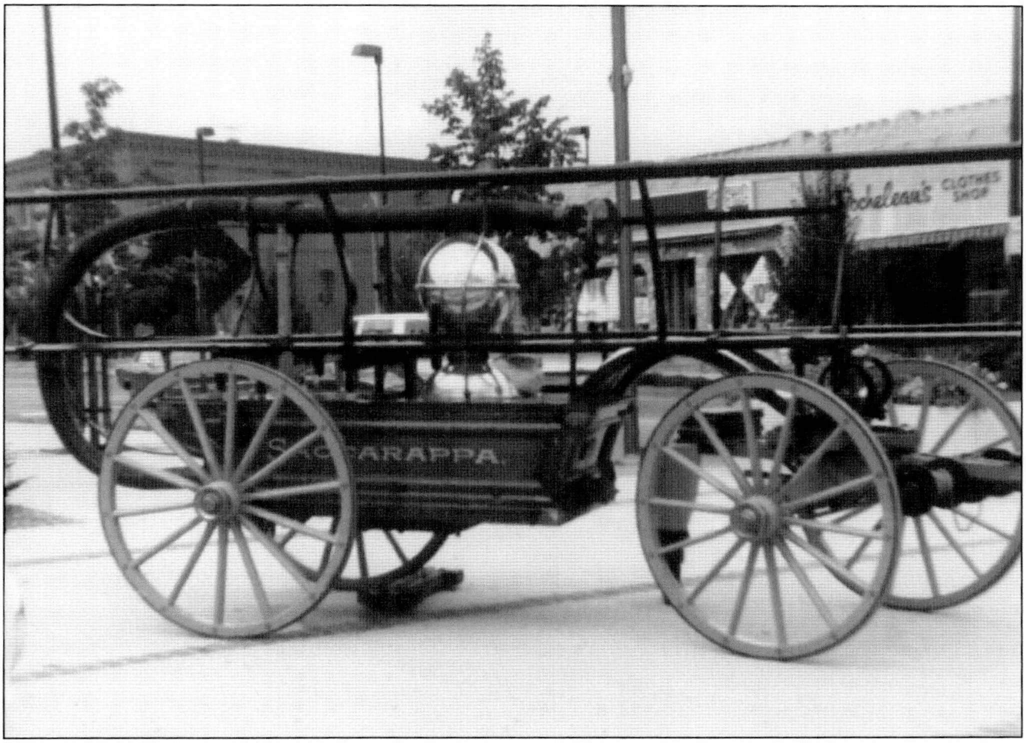

The "Saccarappa," 1867. This vehicle assisted the early fire fighters in Westbrook. This photograph by C. N. Hiel was donated to the Walker Memorial Library by "Bill" Clarke.

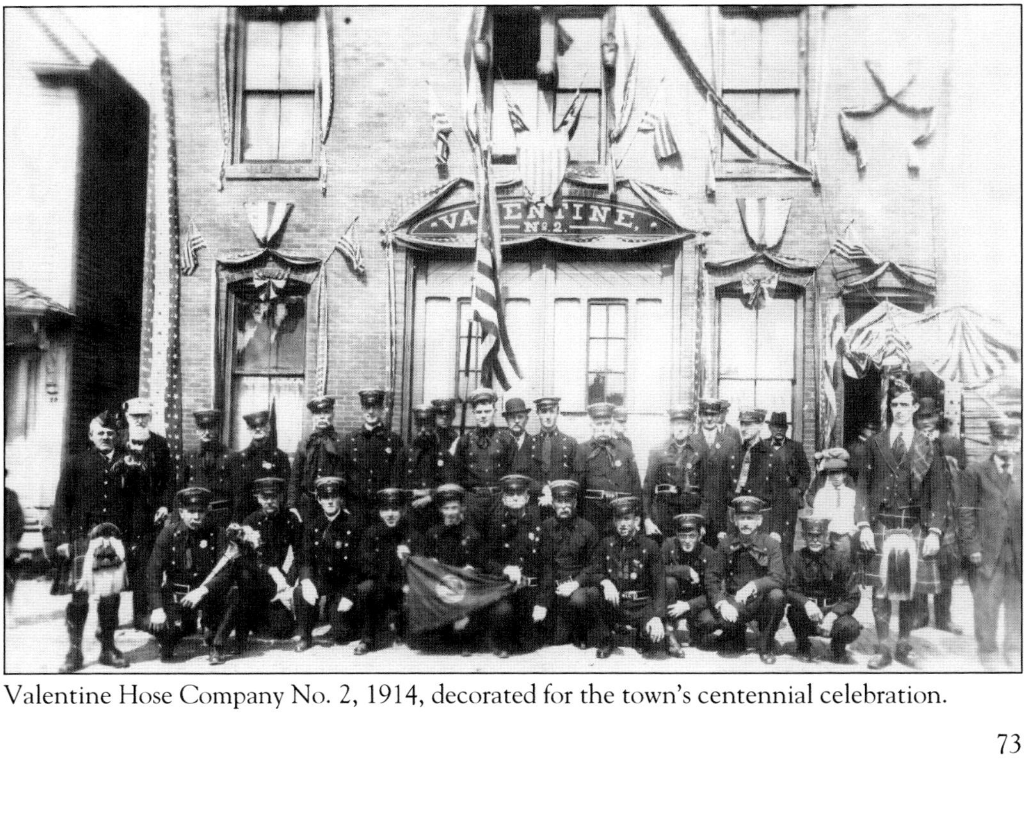

Valentine Hose Company No. 2, 1914, decorated for the town's centennial celebration.

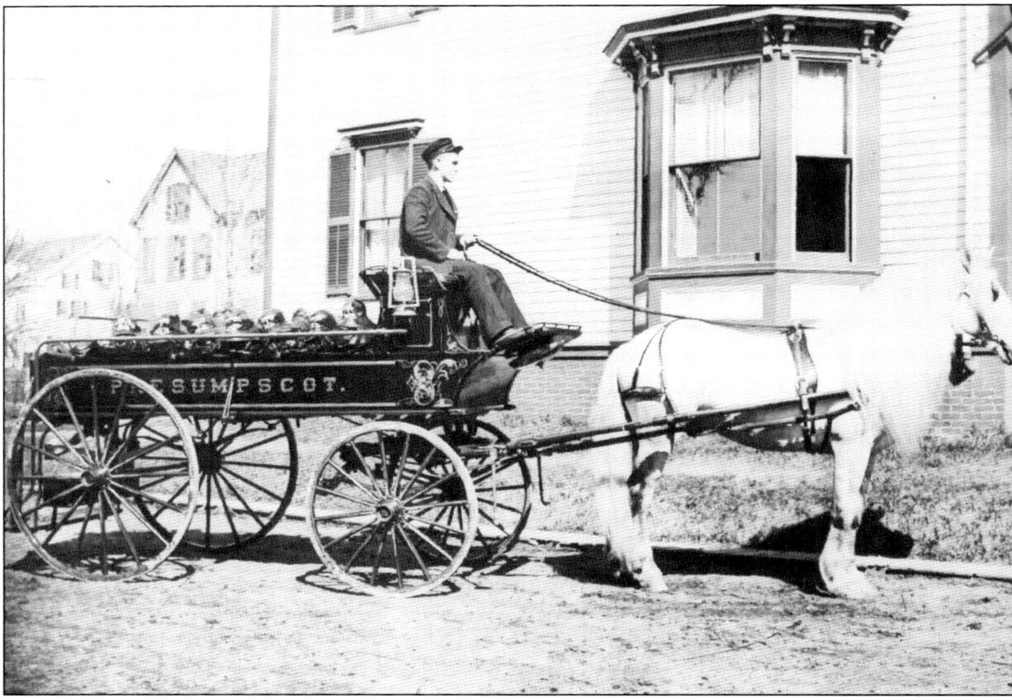

Presumpscot Hose Company No. 1., Charlie Trafton, driver.

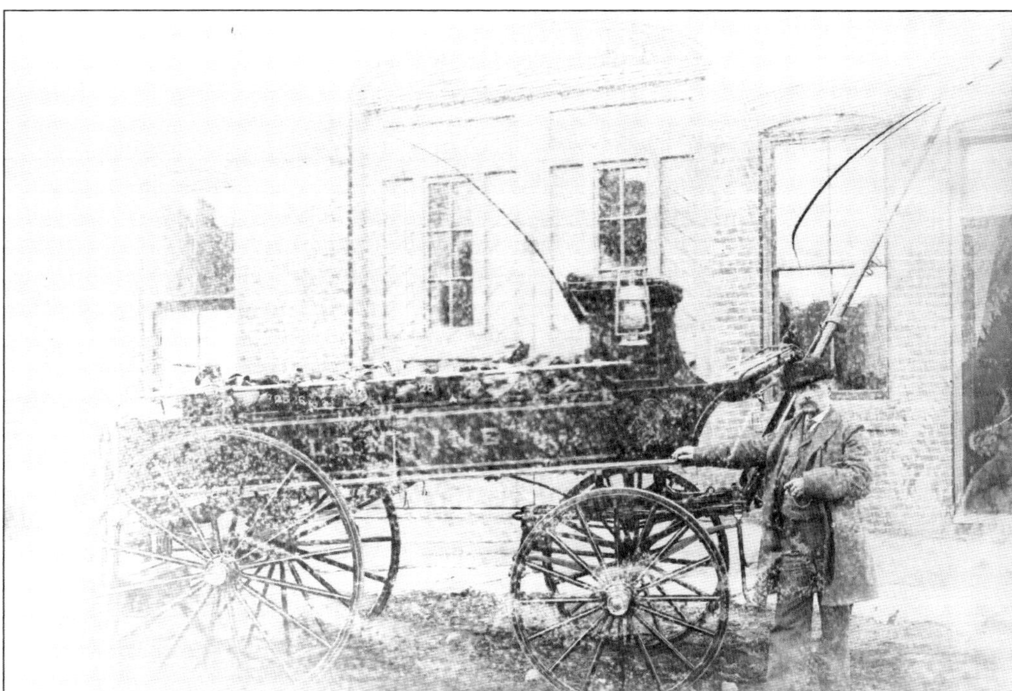

Valentine Hose Company No. 2., Chief Dick Leighton.

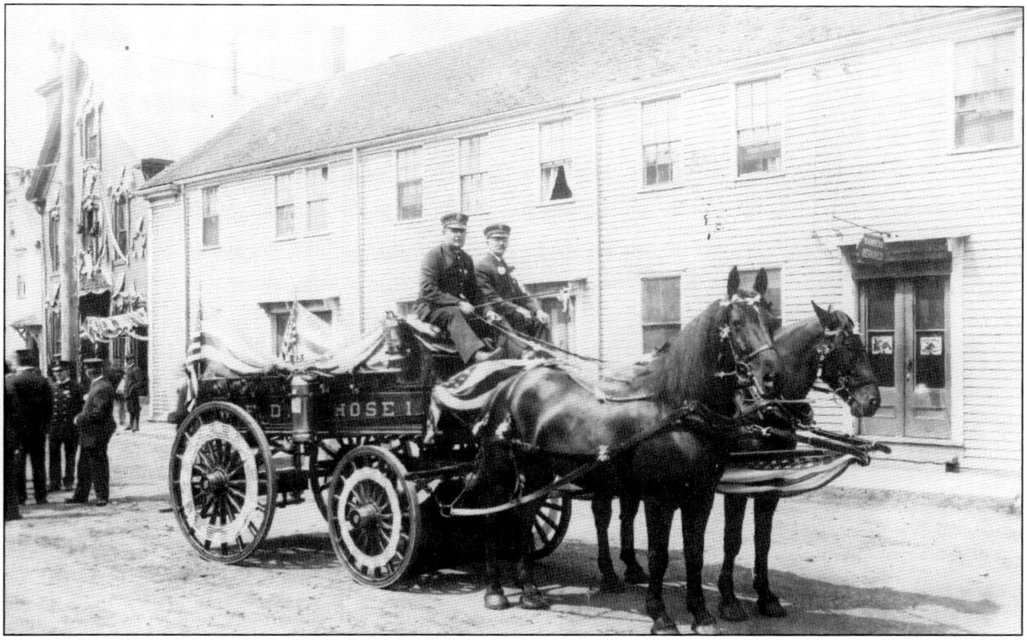

Westbrook Fire Department Hose No. 1, 1914.

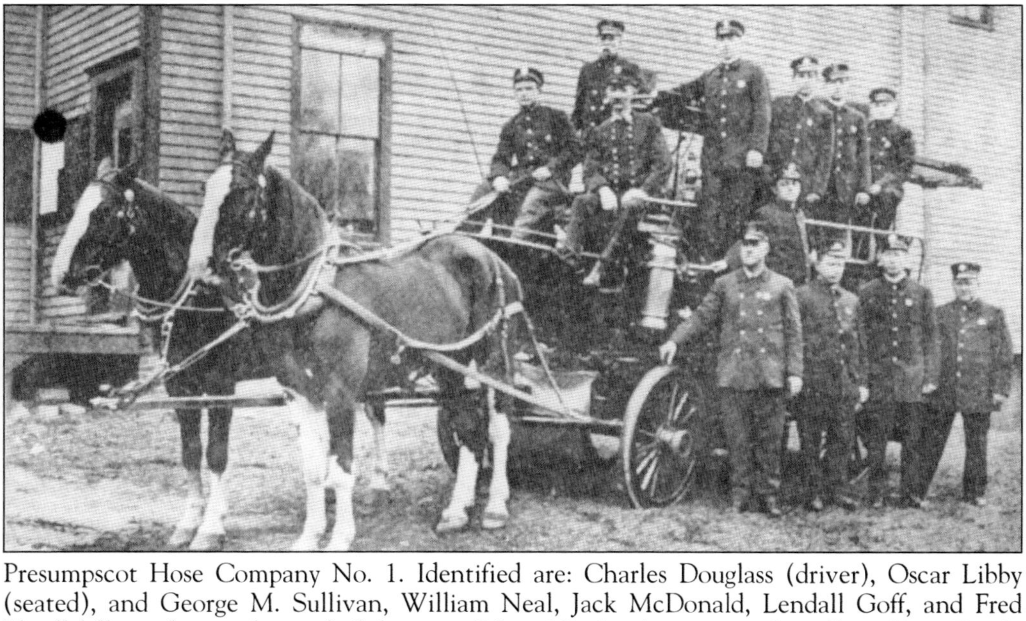

Presumpscot Hose Company No. 1. Identified are: Charles Douglass (driver), Oscar Libby (seated), and George M. Sullivan, William Neal, Jack McDonald, Lendall Goff, and Fred Elwell (all standing in the rear). Others are: Edward Barker (on running board), and Lew Frank, Thurman Green, James Kelley, and Edward Hawkes (all standing).

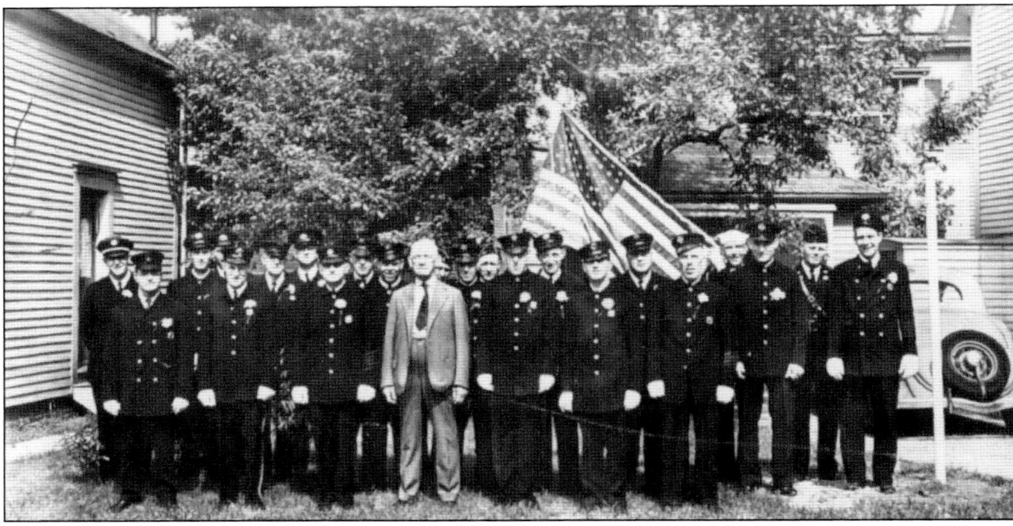

Presumpscot Hose No. 1, 1942. Identified are: Chief Burrows, H. B. Frank, Arthur Swett, Clarence Weeman, George Dineen, Frank Riggs, Earl McFarland, Grover Hooper, Henry Griffiths, Rudney Fields, James Trafton, Charles Hale, James Kinmond, Arol Hawkes, Edward Anderson, Everett Parker, Eugene York, Albert Griffiths, Edmund Cohon, Elmer Riggs, Clarence Pinkham, Norris Berry, and Kenneth Riggs.

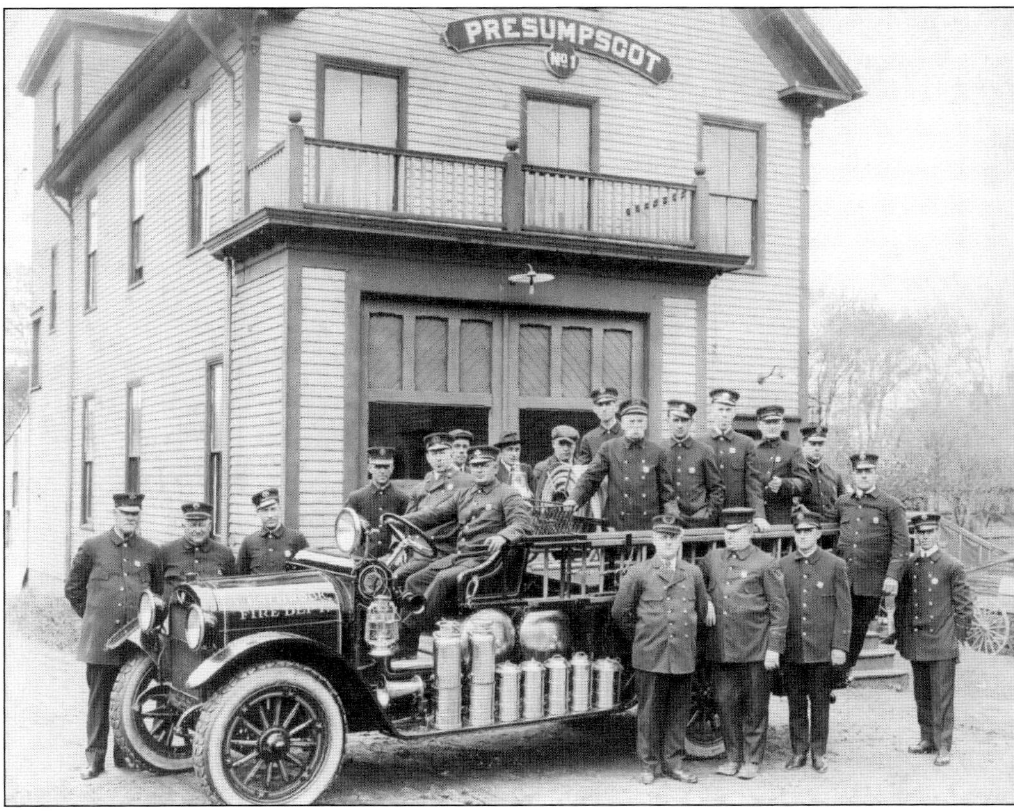

Presumpscot Station No.1.

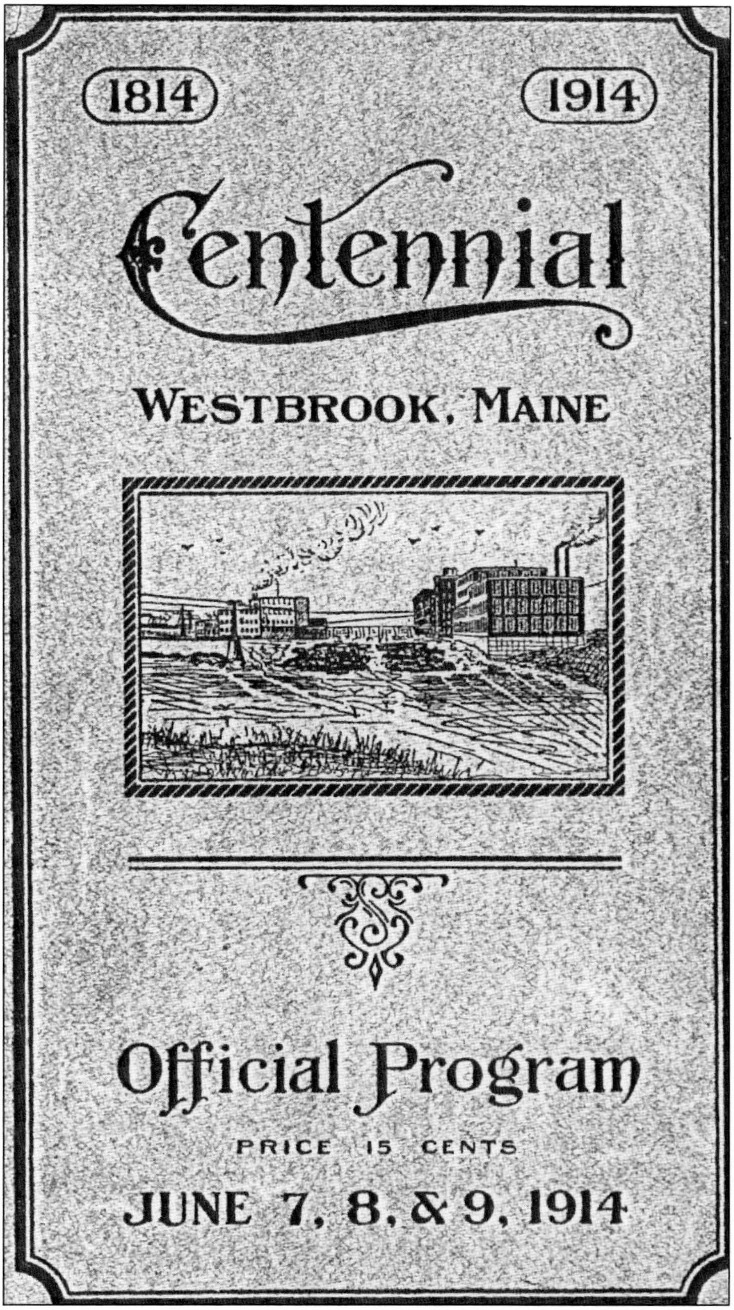

Westbrook was incorporated as a town in 1814 and the centennial celebration was a three-day event on June 7, 8, and 9, 1914. There were special services in all the churches on Sunday, June 7. Monday was Children's Day, featuring a parade, a baseball game at Warren League Grounds, canoe races, and a canoe pageant on the Presumpscot. Tuesday included another ball game; a Grand Military, Civic , and Trades Parade; the dedication of Riverbank Park; and an athletic meet for students. The celebration concluded with a fireworks display "consisting of the grandest display of fireworks ever produced east of Massachusetts." This was a gala celebration and many pictures were taken. The next few pages are but a sampling.

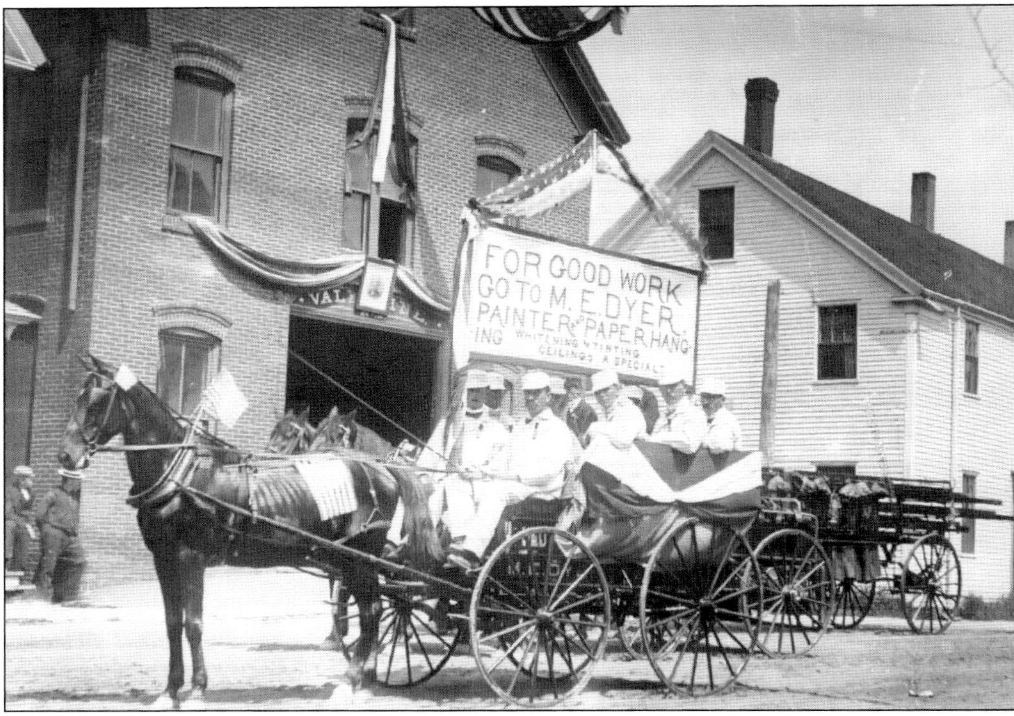

M. E. Dyer "float" ready for the parade, 1914. The Valentine Hose Company is at the rear. Paint and paperhanging was their specialty.

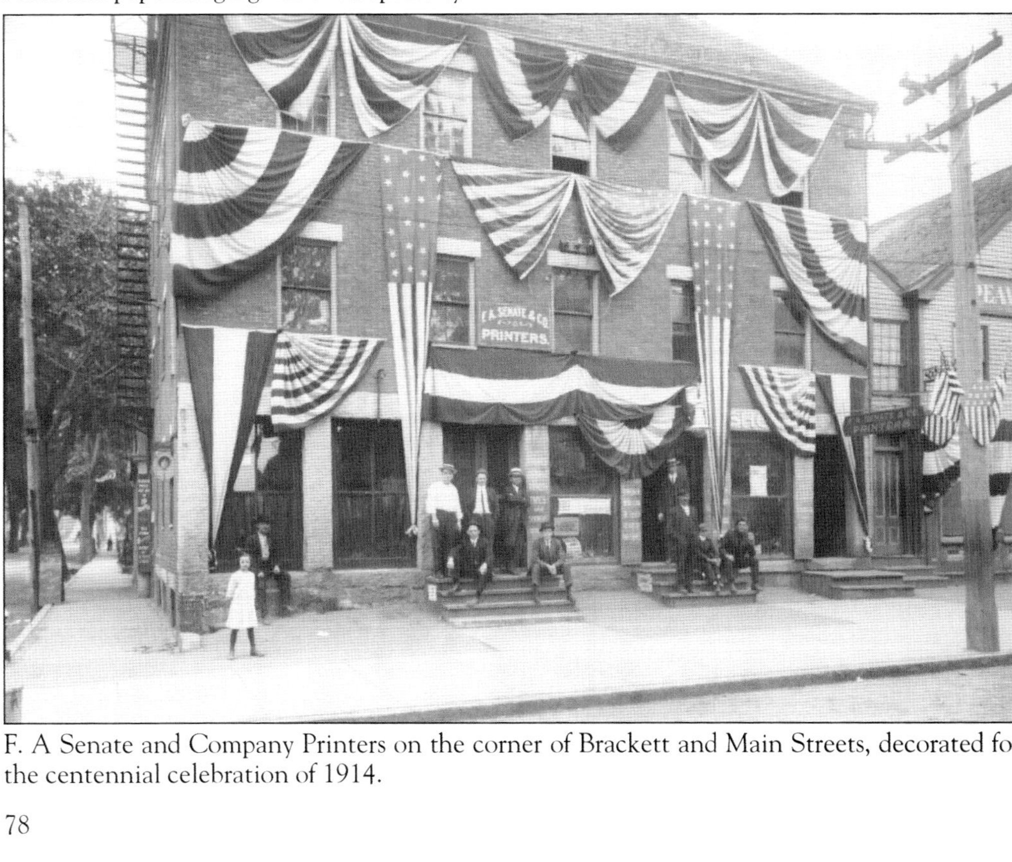

F. A Senate and Company Printers on the corner of Brackett and Main Streets, decorated for the centennial celebration of 1914.

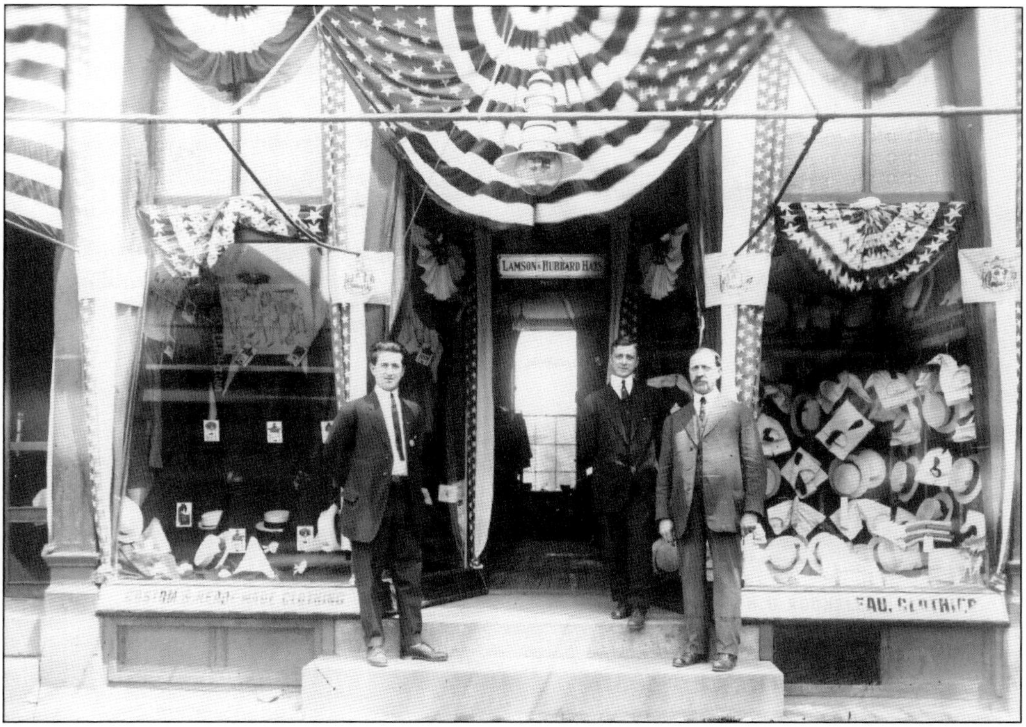

Rocheleau's Clothing Store at 861 Main Street was also decorated with style for the centennial in 1914.

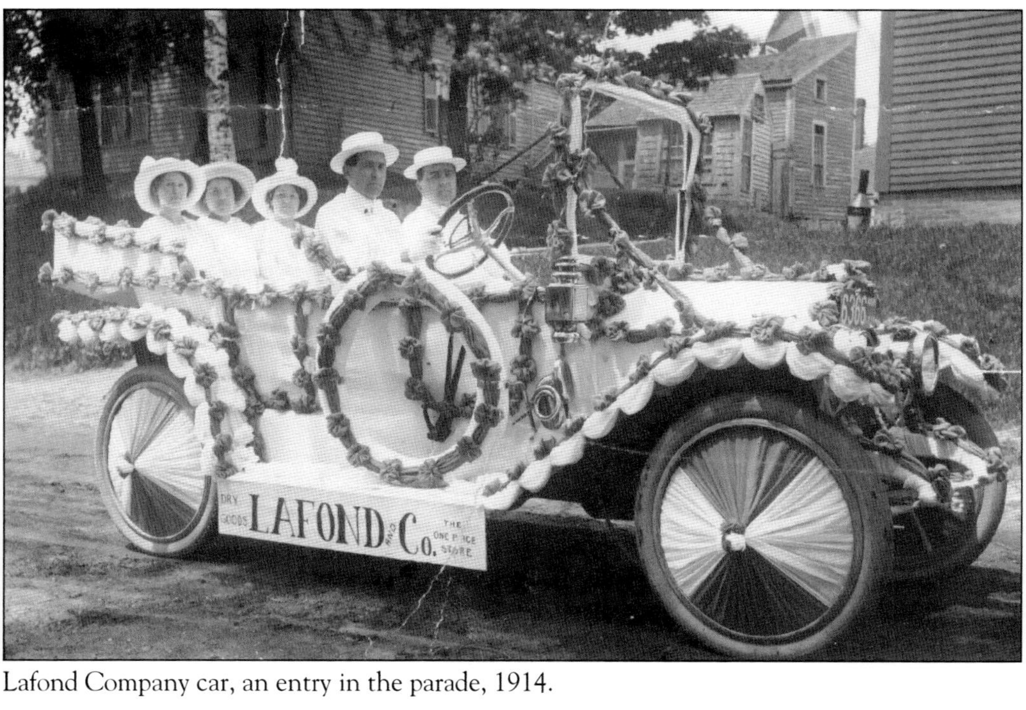

Lafond Company car, an entry in the parade, 1914.

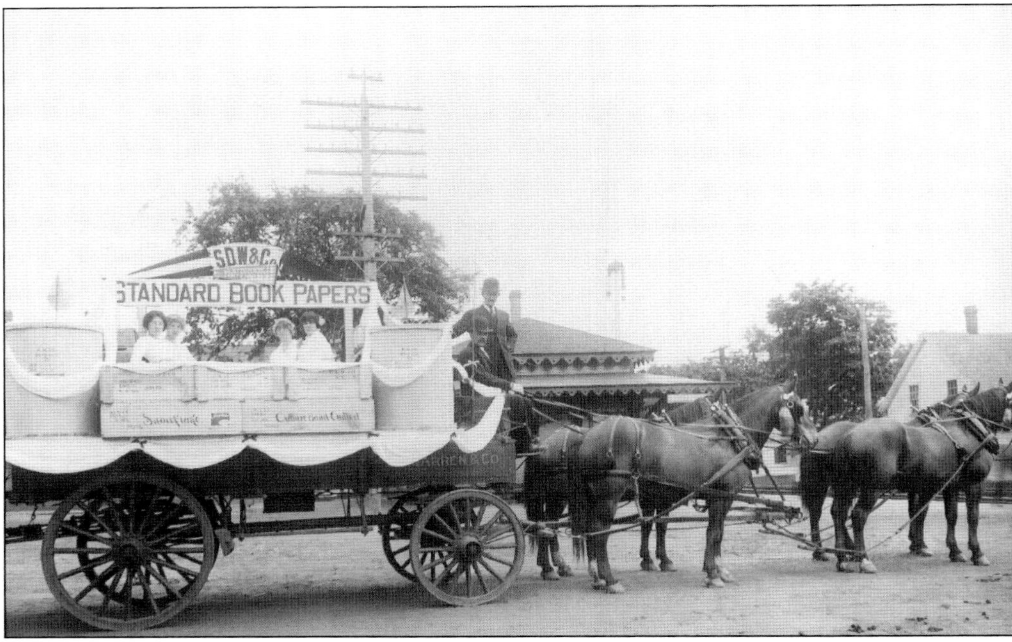

S. D. Warren Company parade float, 1914. The driver is Ed Hulit, and Mr. Tondreau is standing. Seated, from left to right are: Dora Sullivan, Mina Mickelson Paradis, Hattie Johnson Mayberry, and Marion Shaw Goff.

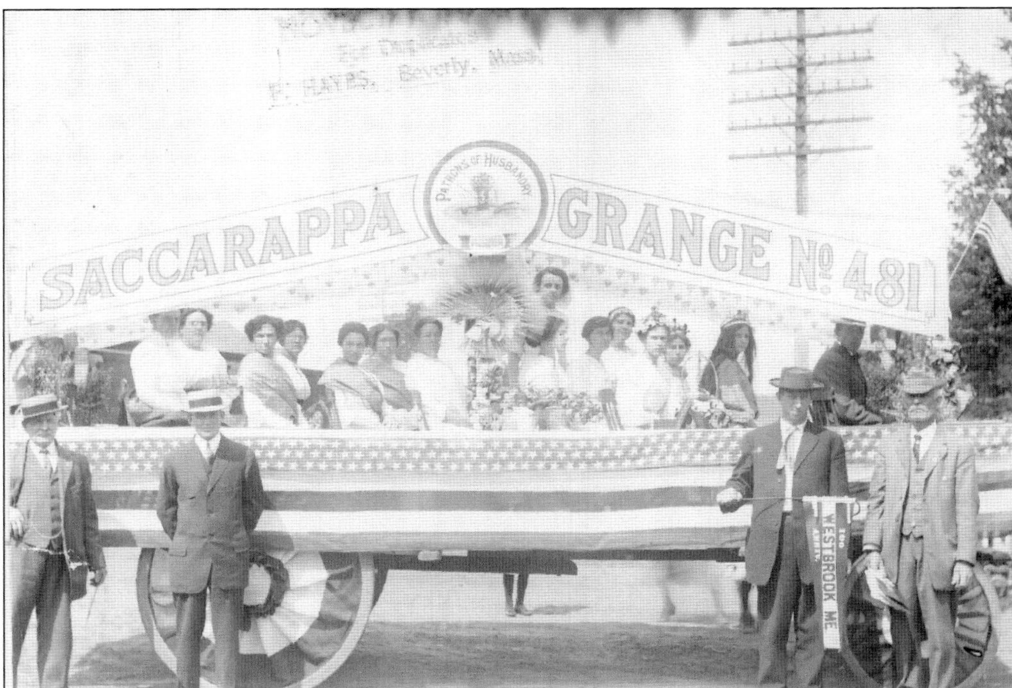

Saccarappa Grange #481 float. Among those identified are: Mrs. Holich, Ruben Holston, W. Metcalf, Mrs. Morris, Joseph Winship, F. O. Dolley, McFarland, George Pike, and Edson Holston.

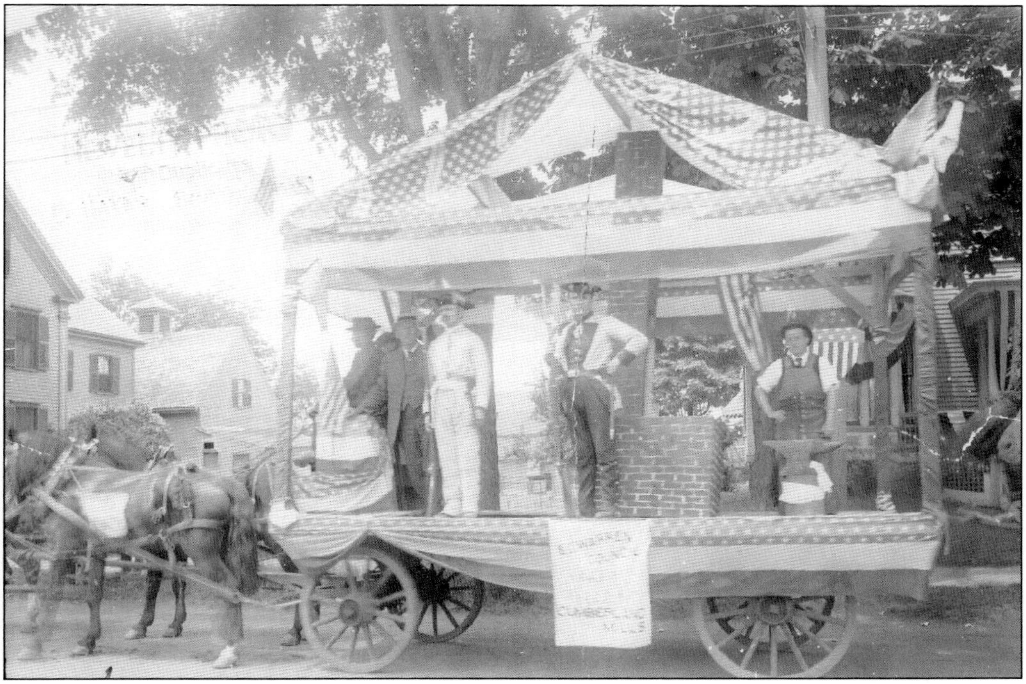

S. D. Warren Council #4, Order of United American Mechanics float, June 9, 1914. Pictured, from left to right, are: Newell Lowell, Frank Porter, Calvin Porter, and Arthur Wood.

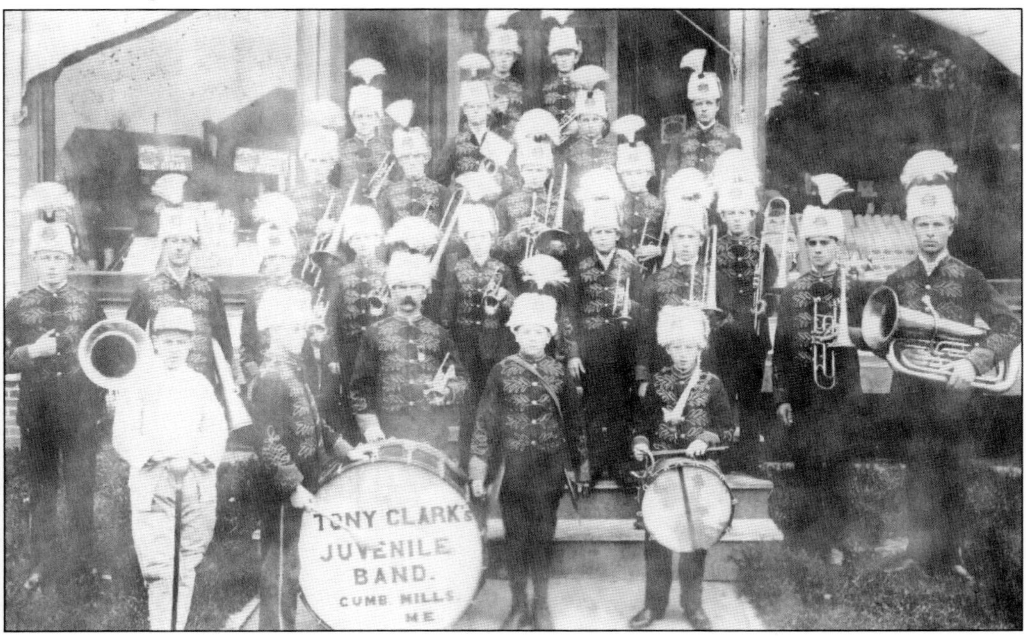

Tony Clark's Juvenile Band, 1894. Pictured, from left to right, are: (first row) Drum Major Butterfield, Arthur Leighton, Tony Clark, Joe Labeau, Albert Gilman; (second row) P.J. Masabyll, Joe Graham, Charles Hinrickson, Jed Watson, Nela Nelson, ? Labeau, ? Labeau, John Snow;. (third row) G. Hinrickson, Al Graham, Peter Peterson, John Davis, John Crowley; (fourth row) Thomas Smith, Percy Elder, Harry Barbour, Roy Leighton; (back) ? Ferguson, and Len Abbott.

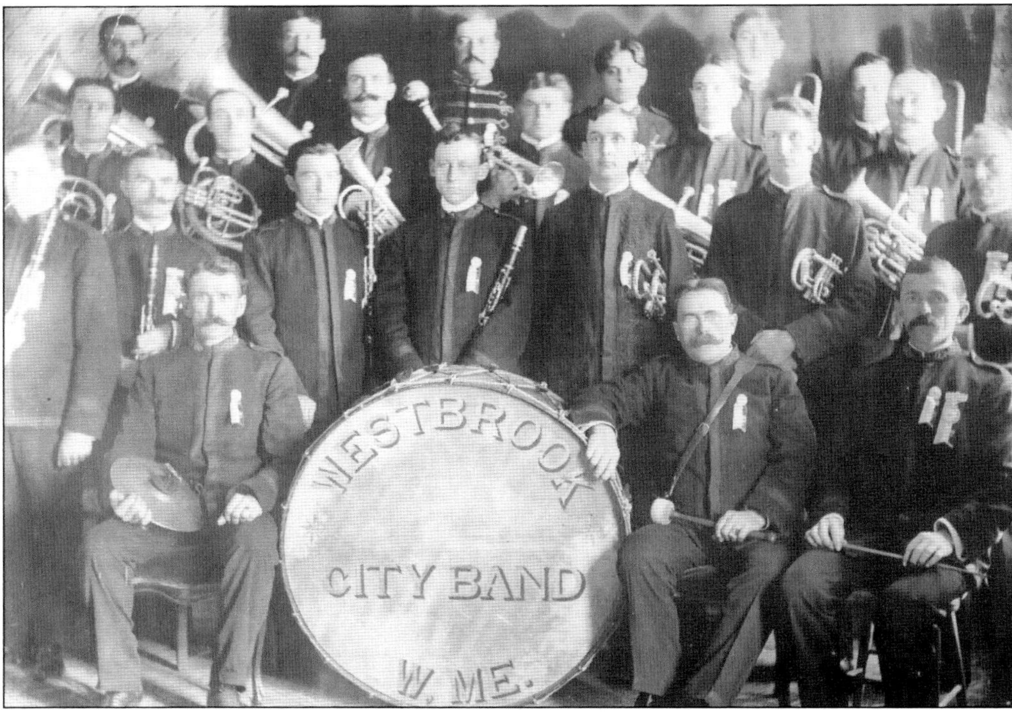

The Westbrook City Band. Howard Babb was the leader of this group, which disbanded in 1894.

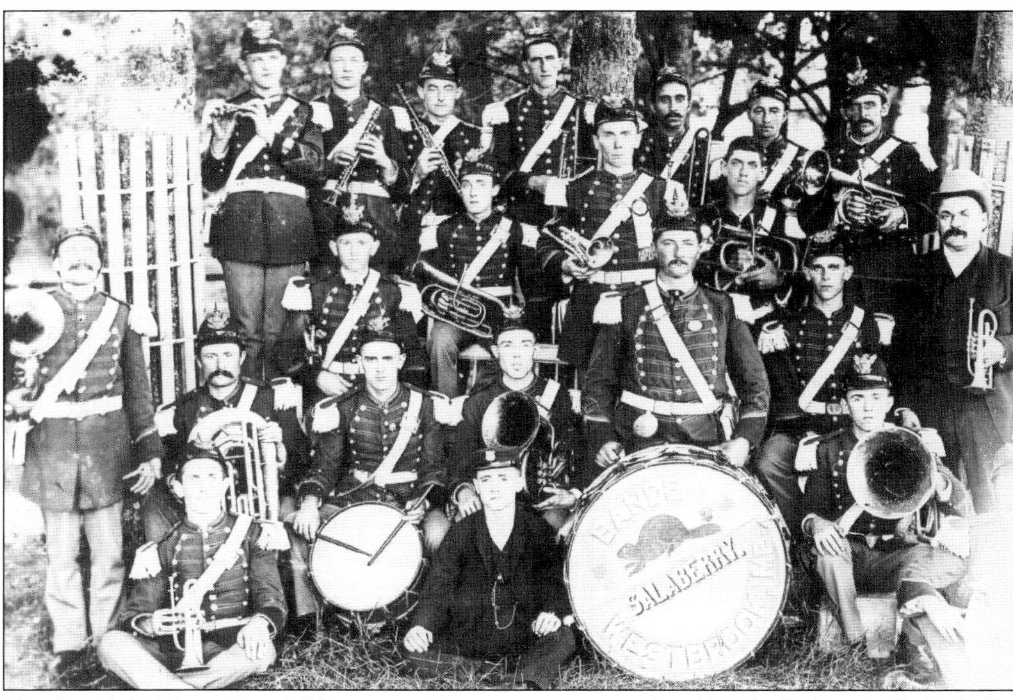

Westbrook Salaberry Band. This musical group was organized in 1884 by Father A. D. DeCelles of St. Hyacinthe's Parish.

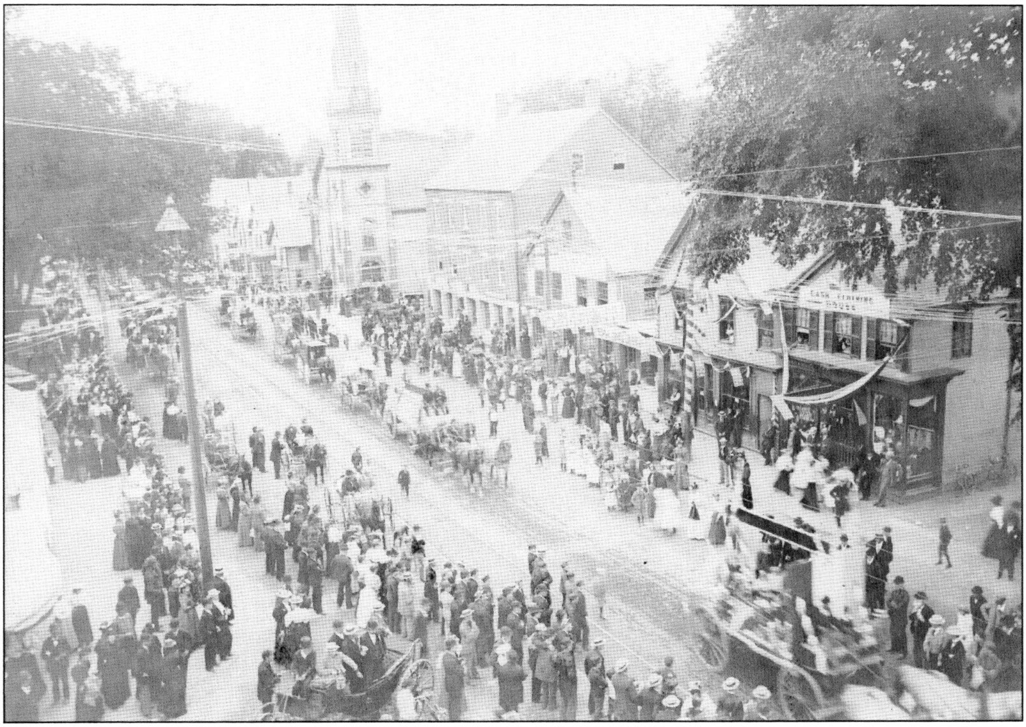
Main Street parade, July 4, 1895.

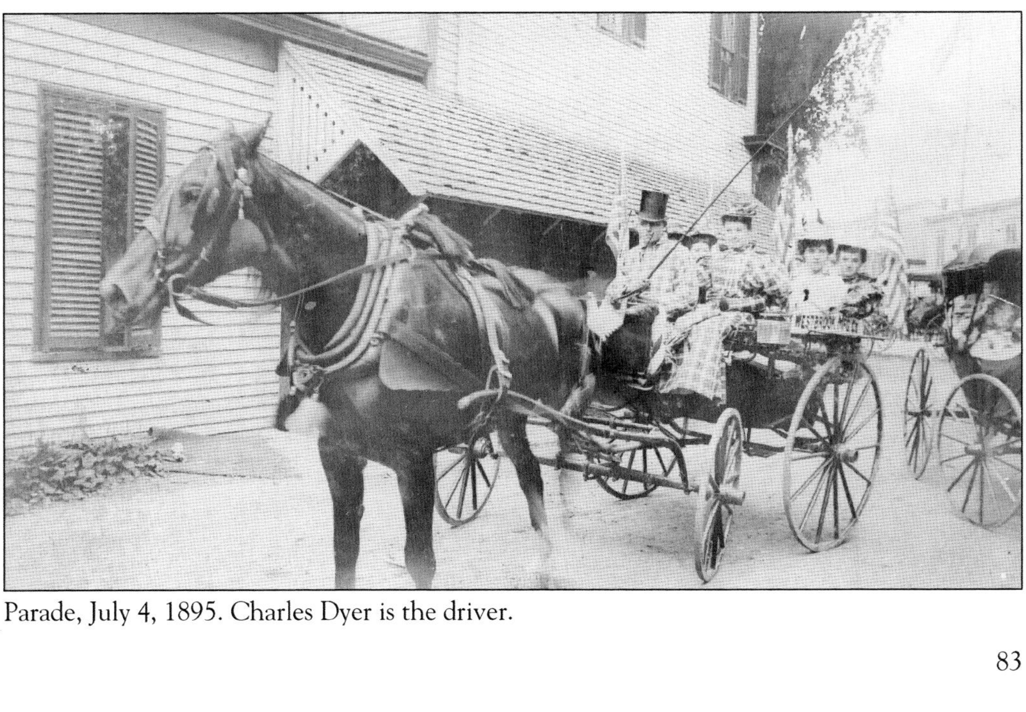
Parade, July 4, 1895. Charles Dyer is the driver.

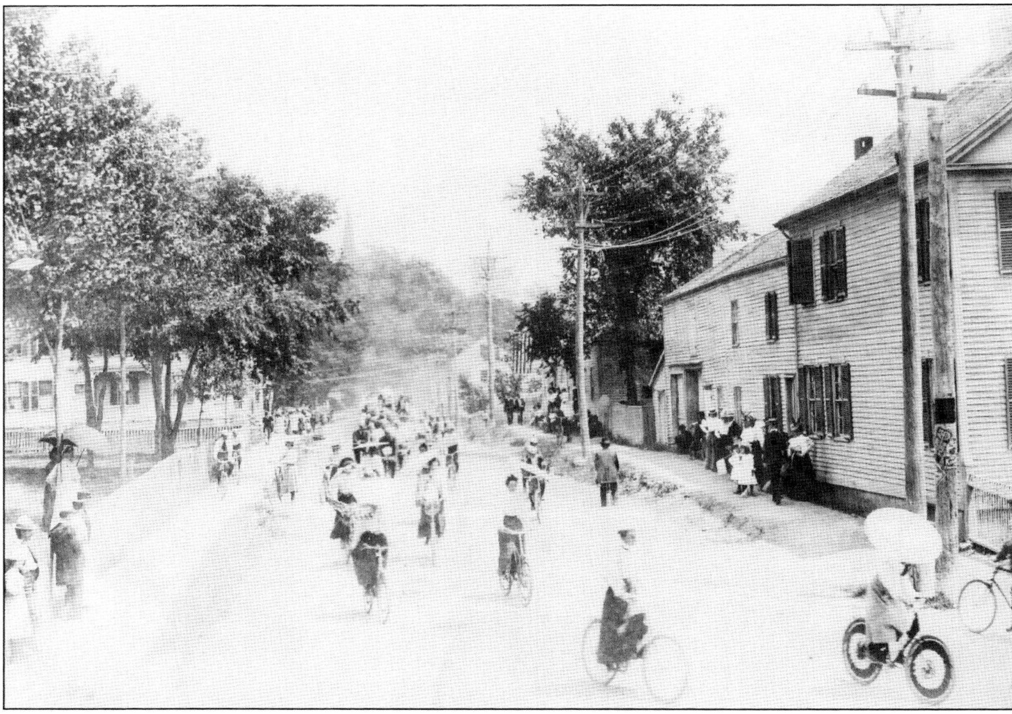

Fourth of July parade, 1899.

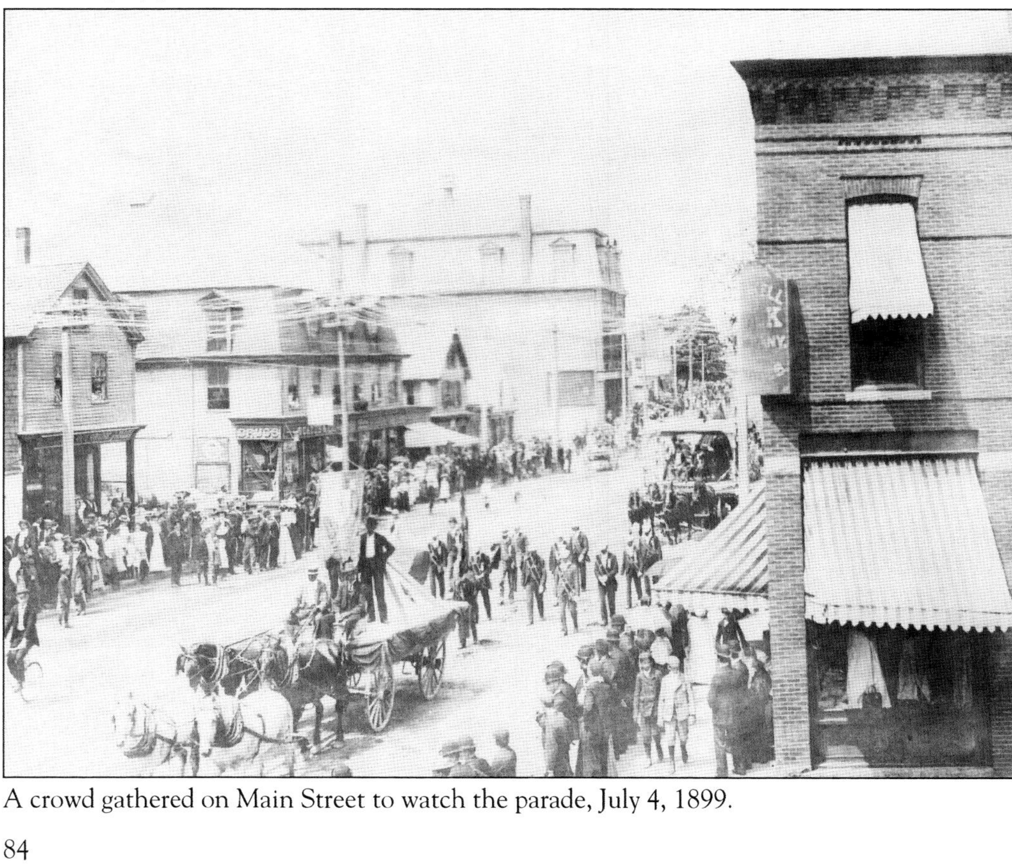

A crowd gathered on Main Street to watch the parade, July 4, 1899.

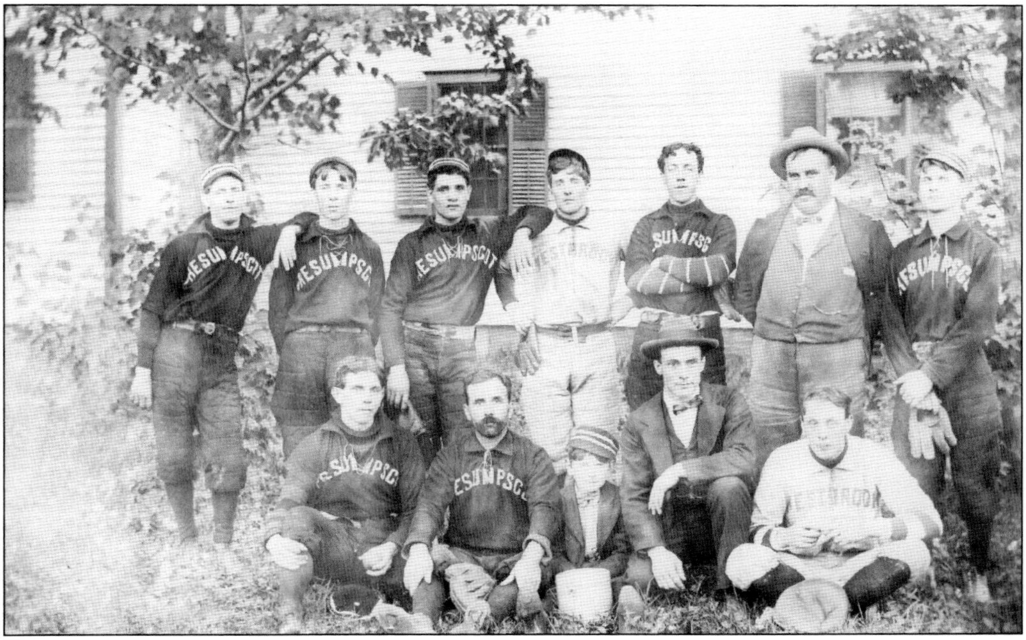

Presumpscot Baseball Team. We were unable to find information about these sporty fellows. Perhaps you can help!

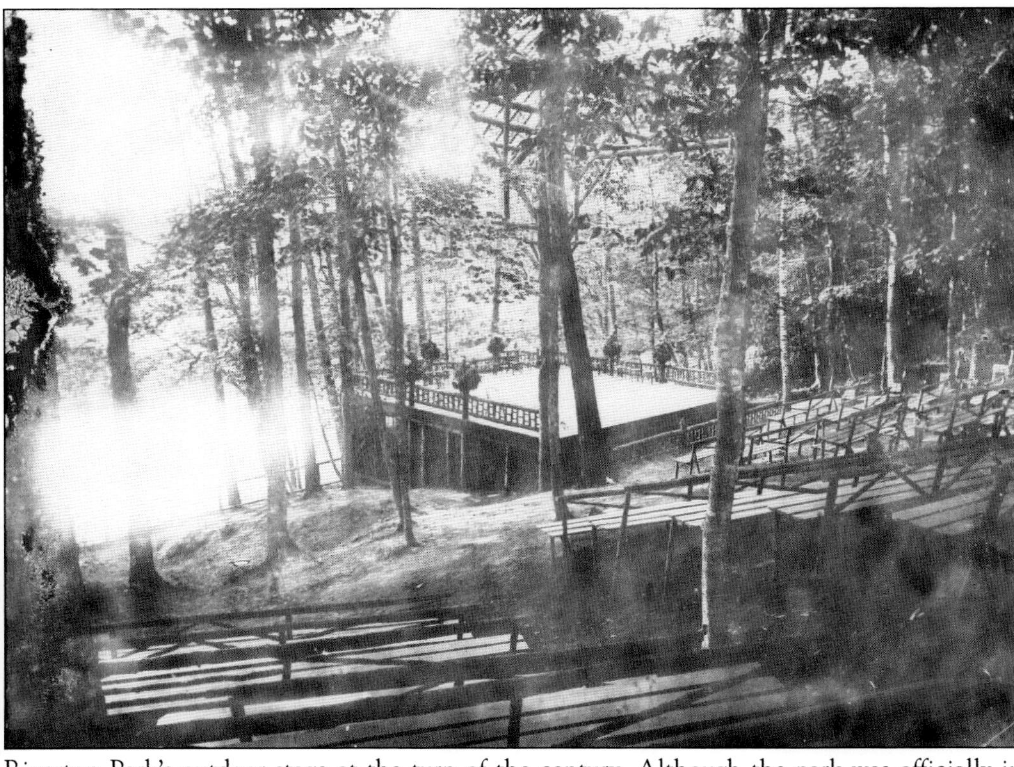

Riverton Park's outdoor stage at the turn of the century. Although the park was officially in Portland, the river provided not only the towns' boundary line, but great access by boat from Westbrook. It was considered an entertainment spot for Westbrook people.

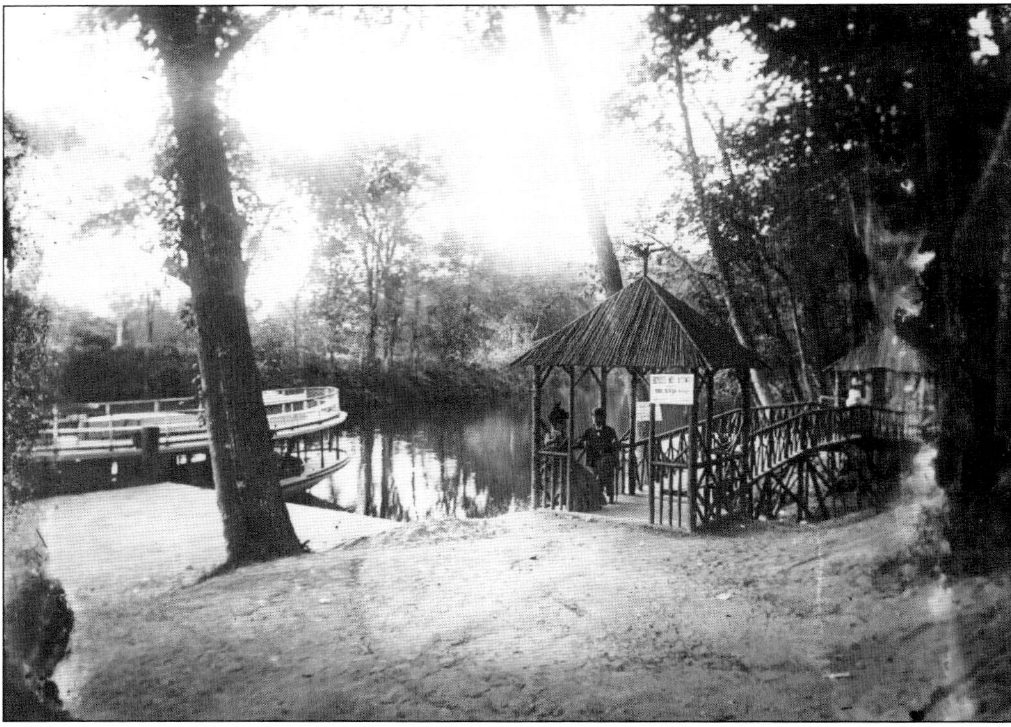

Riverton Park, c. 1900. The little bridge and gazebo are on the right, and the riverboat is docked on the left.

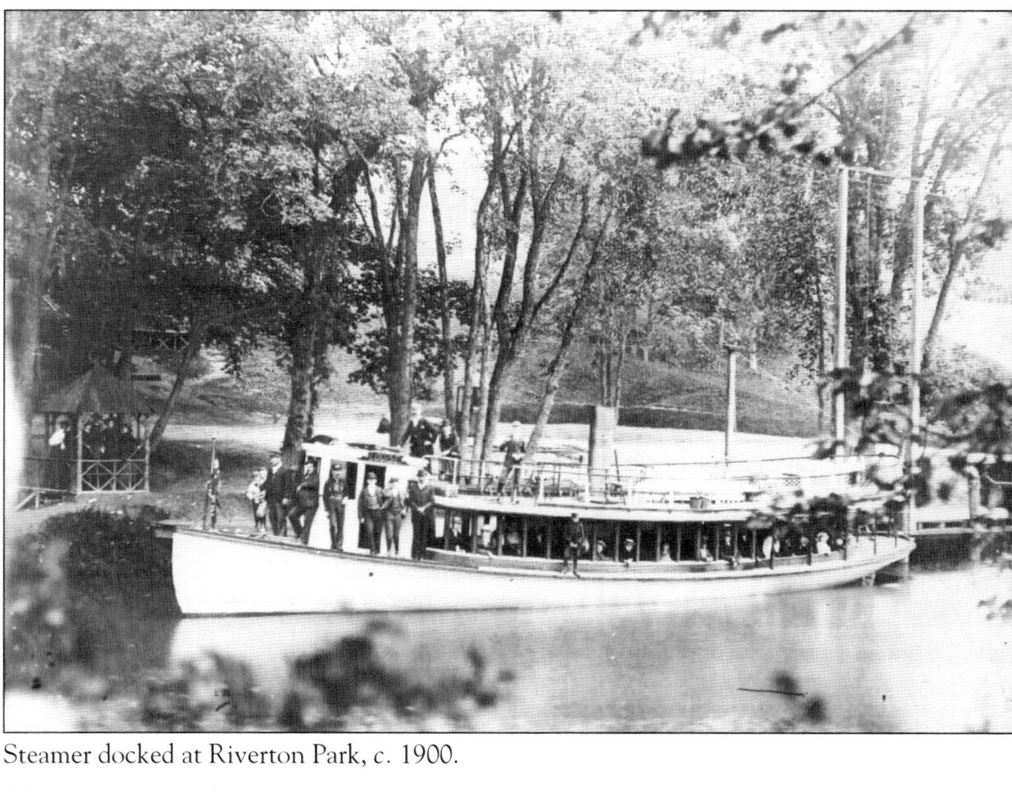

Steamer docked at Riverton Park, *c.* 1900.

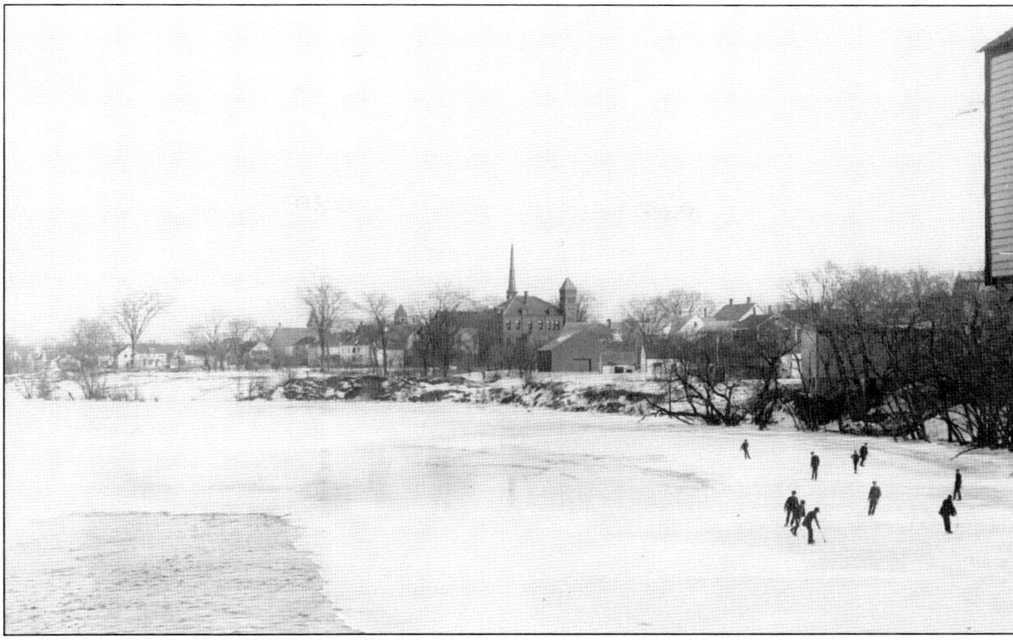

Presumpscot River as seen from the Bridge Street Bridge, *c*. 1910. The high school can be seen in the background. The people are playing hockey on the river near what appears to be open water!! (Berg Family Collection.)

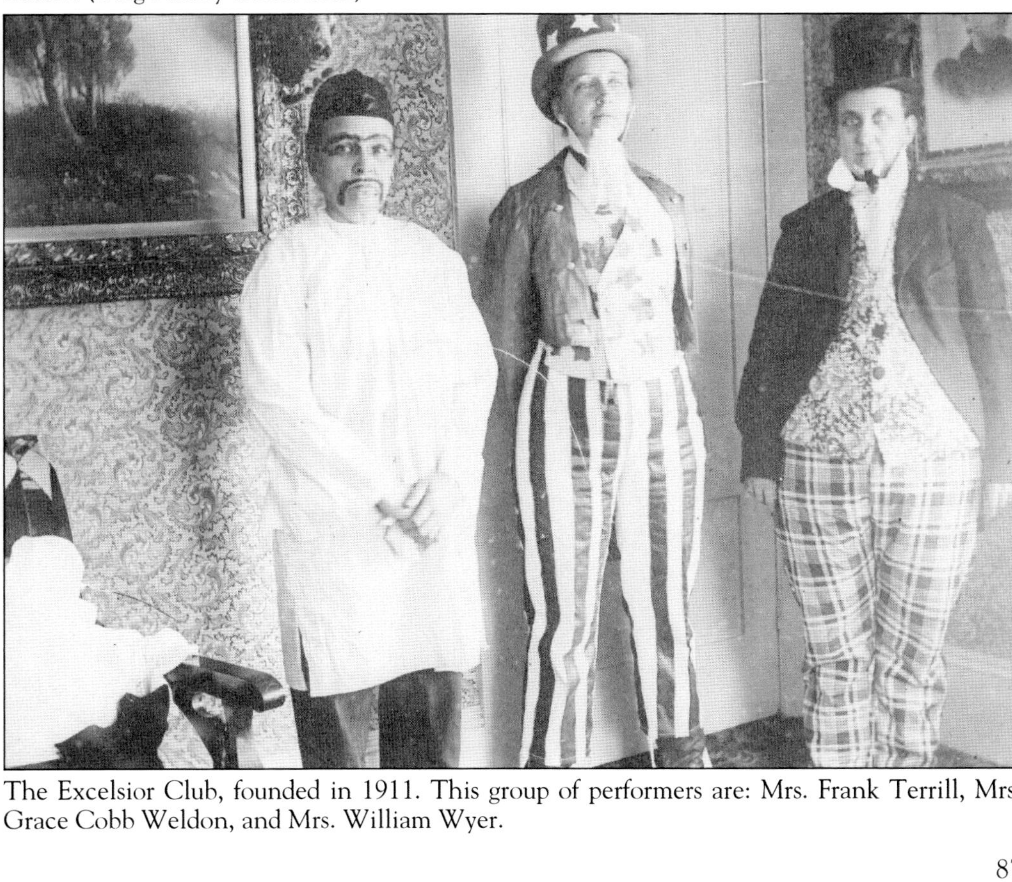

The Excelsior Club, founded in 1911. This group of performers are: Mrs. Frank Terrill, Mrs. Grace Cobb Weldon, and Mrs. William Wyer.

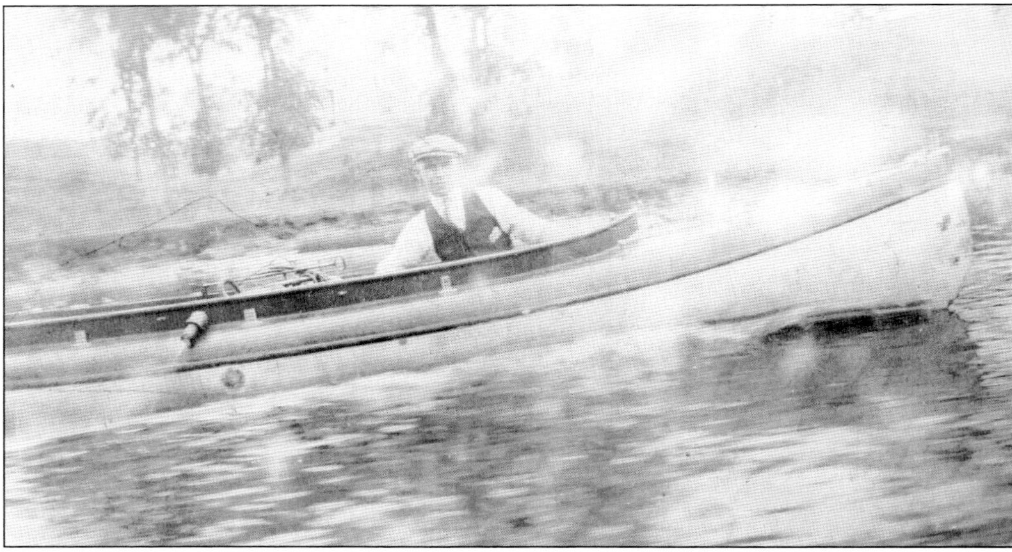

Henry Pednault, who built his own boats, enjoys a ride on the Presumpscot, *c.* 1913. (Curtis Family Collection.)

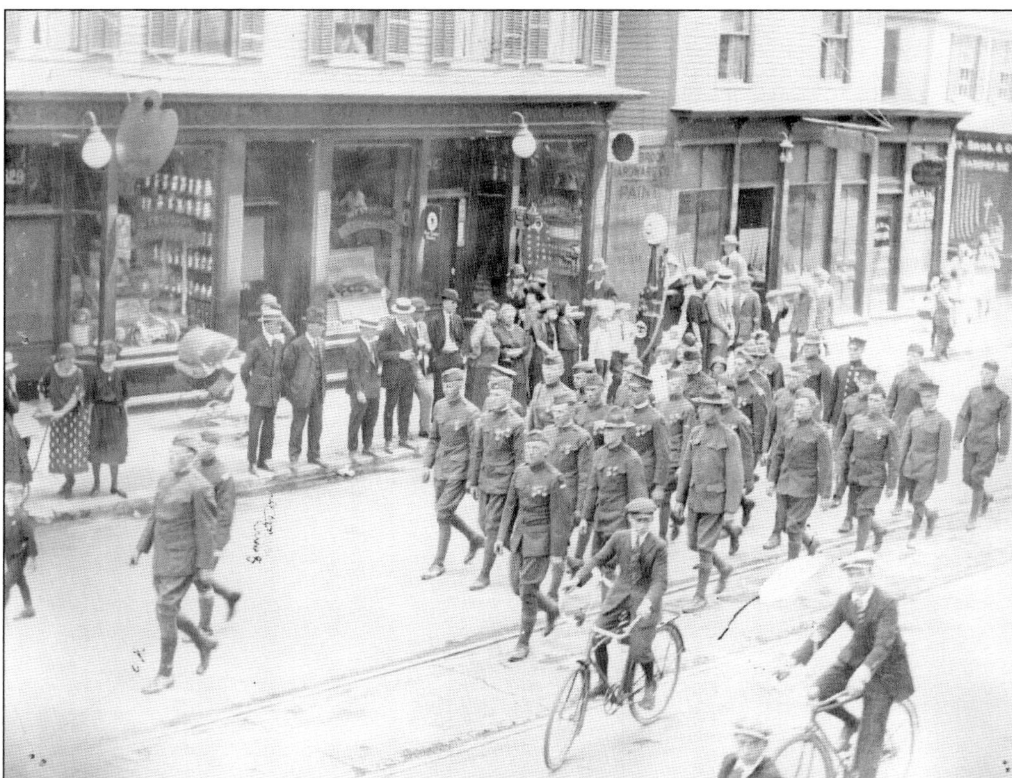

An unknown military unit on parade on Main Street after World War I, c. 1919. Westbrook Hardware Store is in the background.

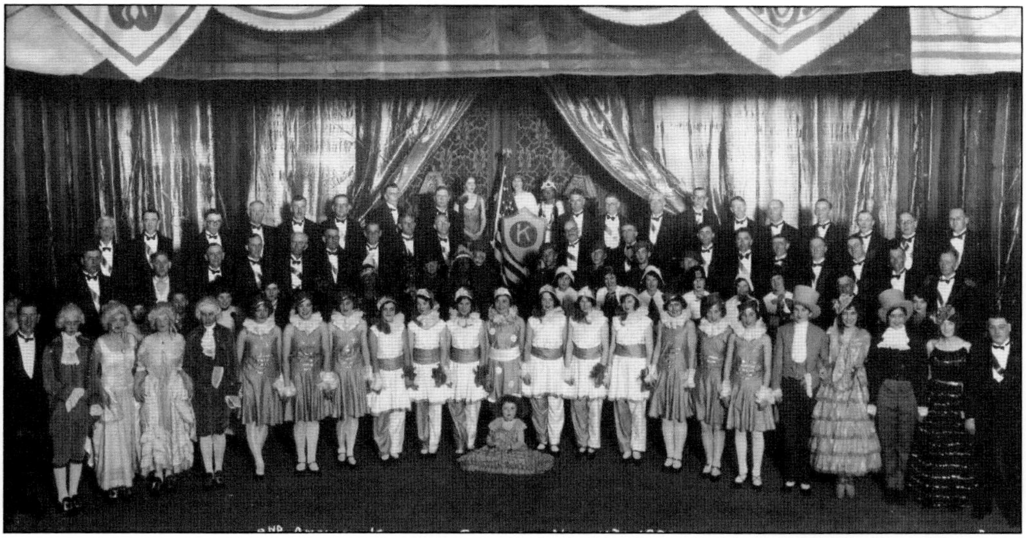

The second annual Kiwanis Club Circus, November 10, 1927. (Westbrook Historical Society Collection.)

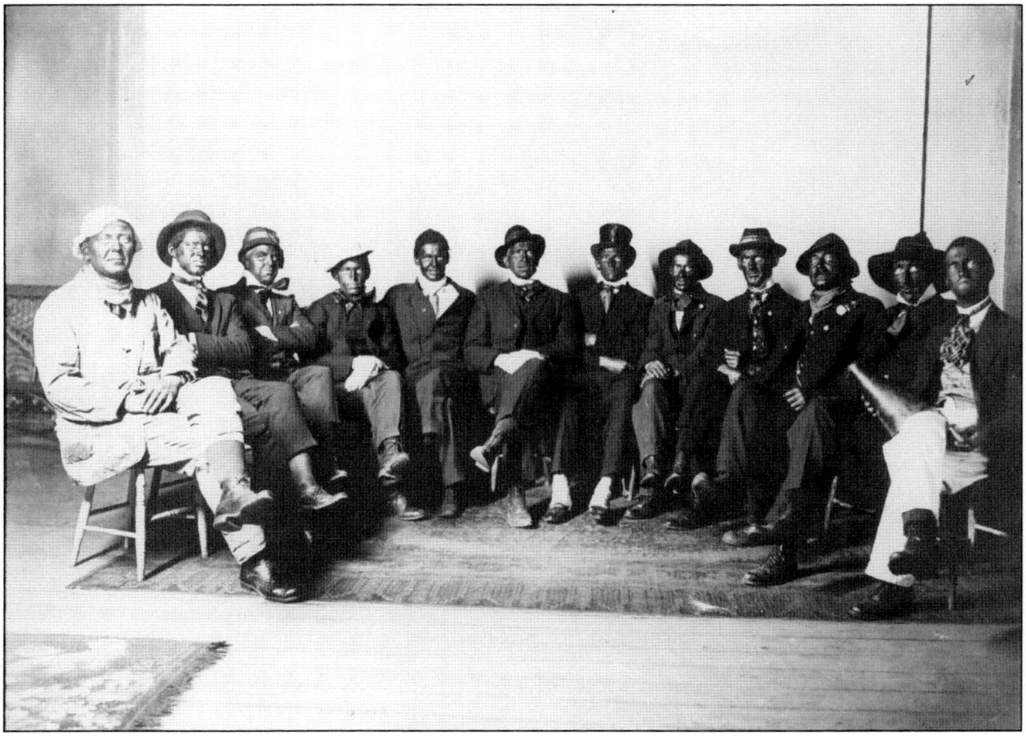

Lion's Club Minstrel Show, *c.* 1940. Blackface was typical feature of minstrel shows at the time.

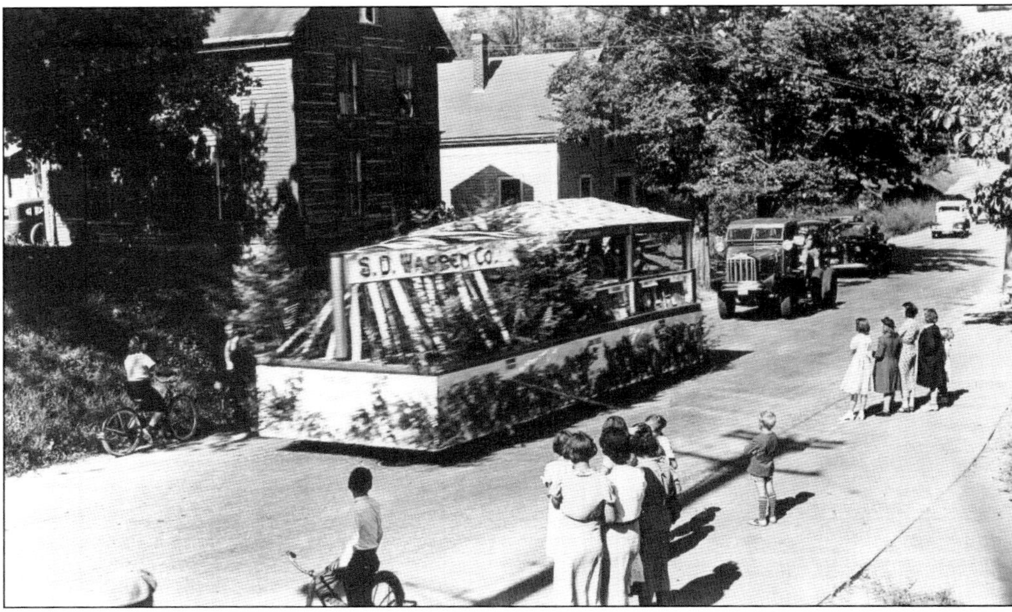

National Recovery Act parade, 1933. This is the S. D. Warren Float on Brown Street. (Westbrook Historical Society Collection.)

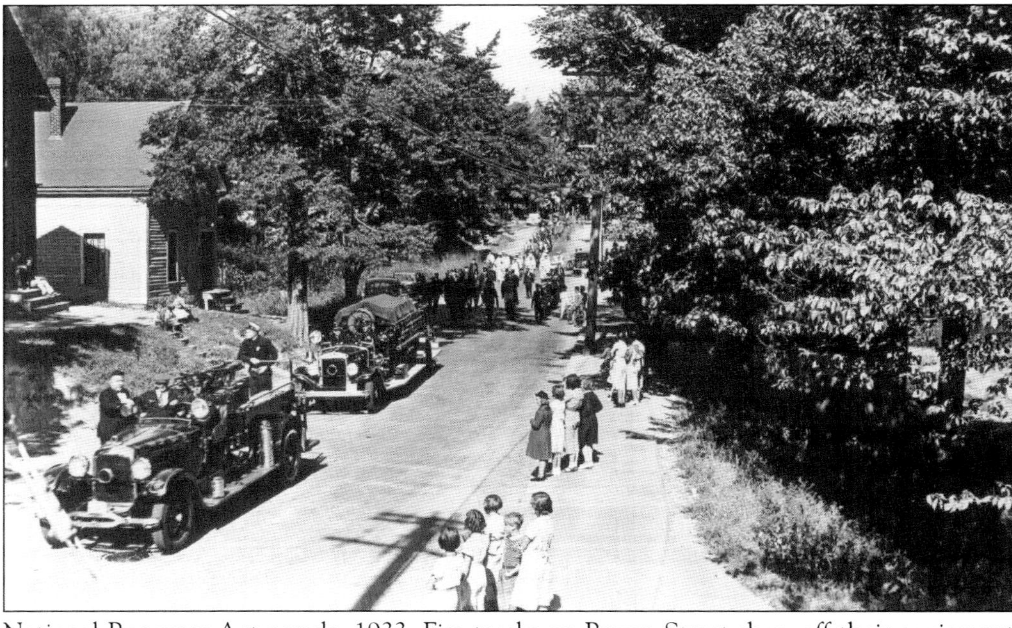

National Recovery Act parade, 1933. Fire trucks on Brown Street show off their equipment. Identified are: Maurice Parker (standing) and Harry Sproul (seated). (Westbrook Historical Society Collection.)

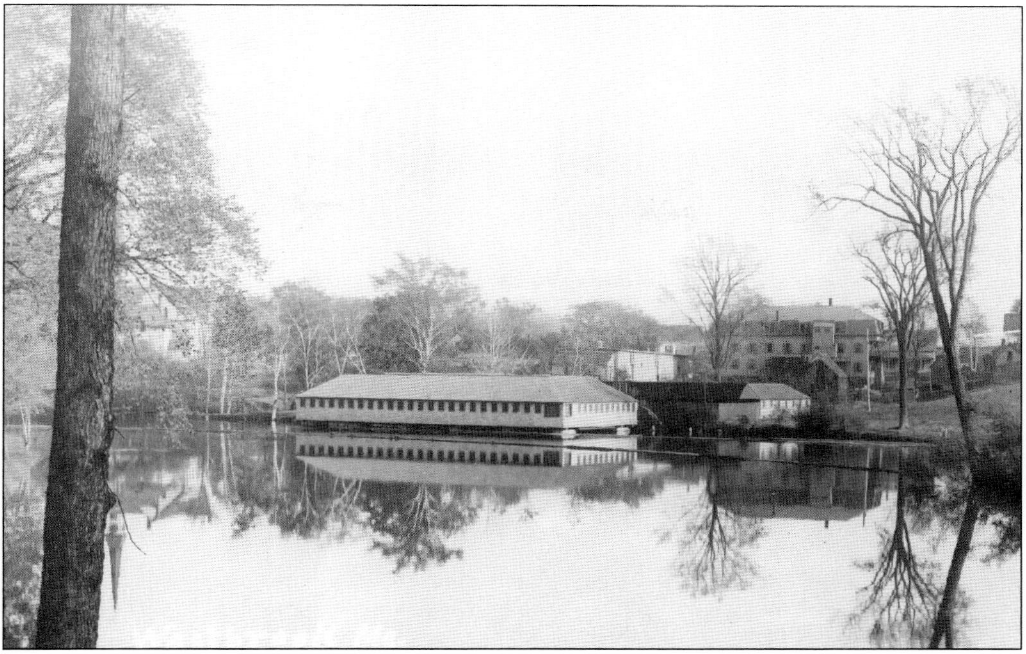

The "old swimming tank." Several generations cooled off in this tank that was built both in and next to the bank of the river, behind what is now Fraser Field.

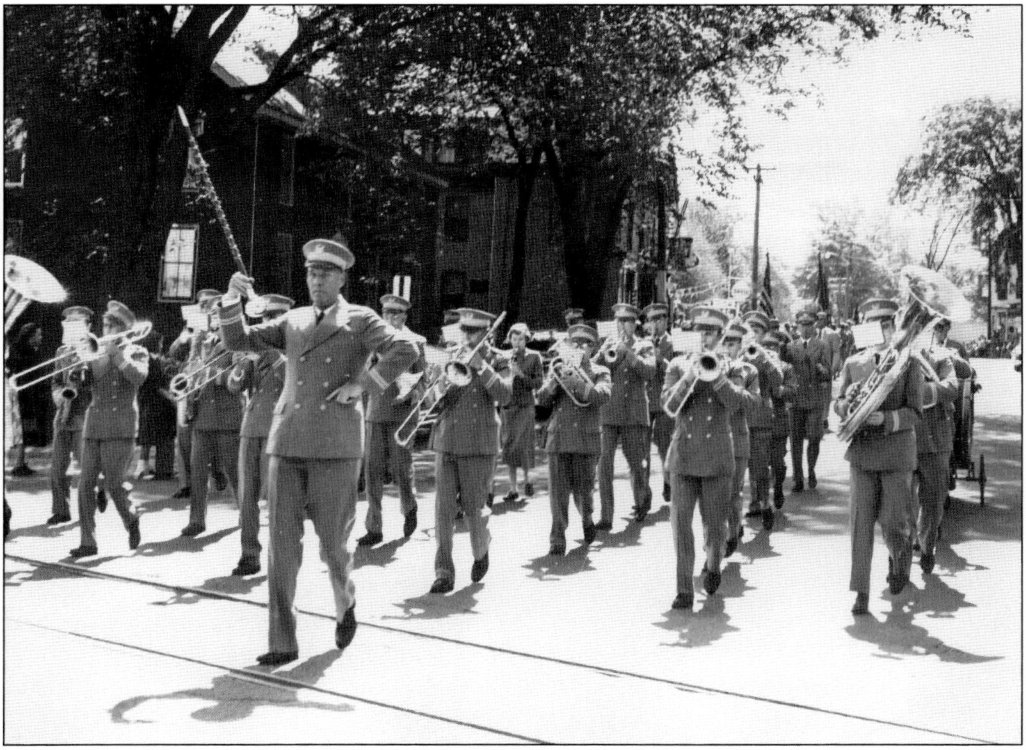

The S. D. Warren Band. John Gooch was the director and leader of this group that was a mainstay of Westbrook parades for many years. Here they are shown crossing the railroad tracks in Cumberland Mills. (Westbrook Historical Society Collection.)

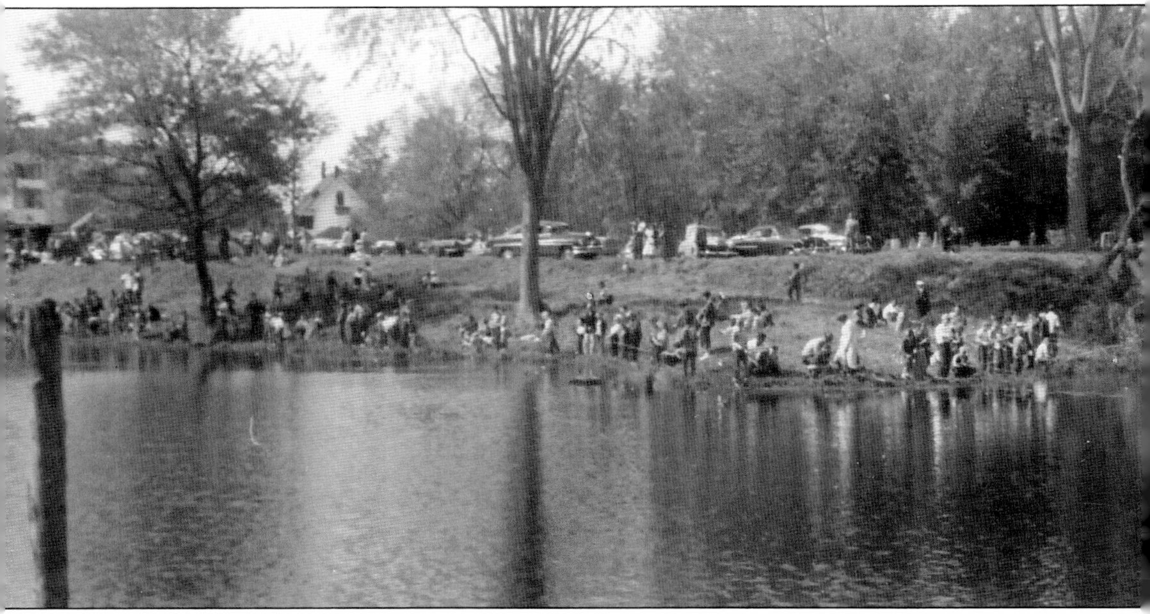

The fishing derby at Beaver Pond, 1948. A total of 1,192 young fishermen participated in this event. Westbrook's Rod and Gun Club stocked the pond with trout. The pole sticking up out of the water is the only remains of the Cumberland and Oxford Canal, which used the pond as part of its journey from the Atlantic to Sebago Lake.

Beaver Pond

An ancient rite of spring occurred, I've seen it here today.
They're fishing on the Beaver Pond; the ice just went away.

March winds are still blowing cold, but its April third today.
The trees are bending from the wind and water's rippling spray.

They're fishing off the point of land where tow path bridge did cross,
and canal boats were towed along by the plodding of the horse.

It seems the Rod and Gun Club would stock the pond with trout,
and a thousand kids with fishing poles went scurrying about.

They called it "the Fishing Derby" and prizes were to be won.
the people came from miles around, just for a day of fun.

Close by is Saccarappa hill, a cemetery by the pond,
where lovely ancient ferns did grow with long and pointed fronds.

And Sunday's picnic baskets brimmed with delights galore,
spread out on the banking along the Beaver's shore.

Yes, they're fishing on the Beaver Pond, the ice just went away,
and memories, and thoughts of youth come back for one more day.

—William Jacobs, April 3, 1996.

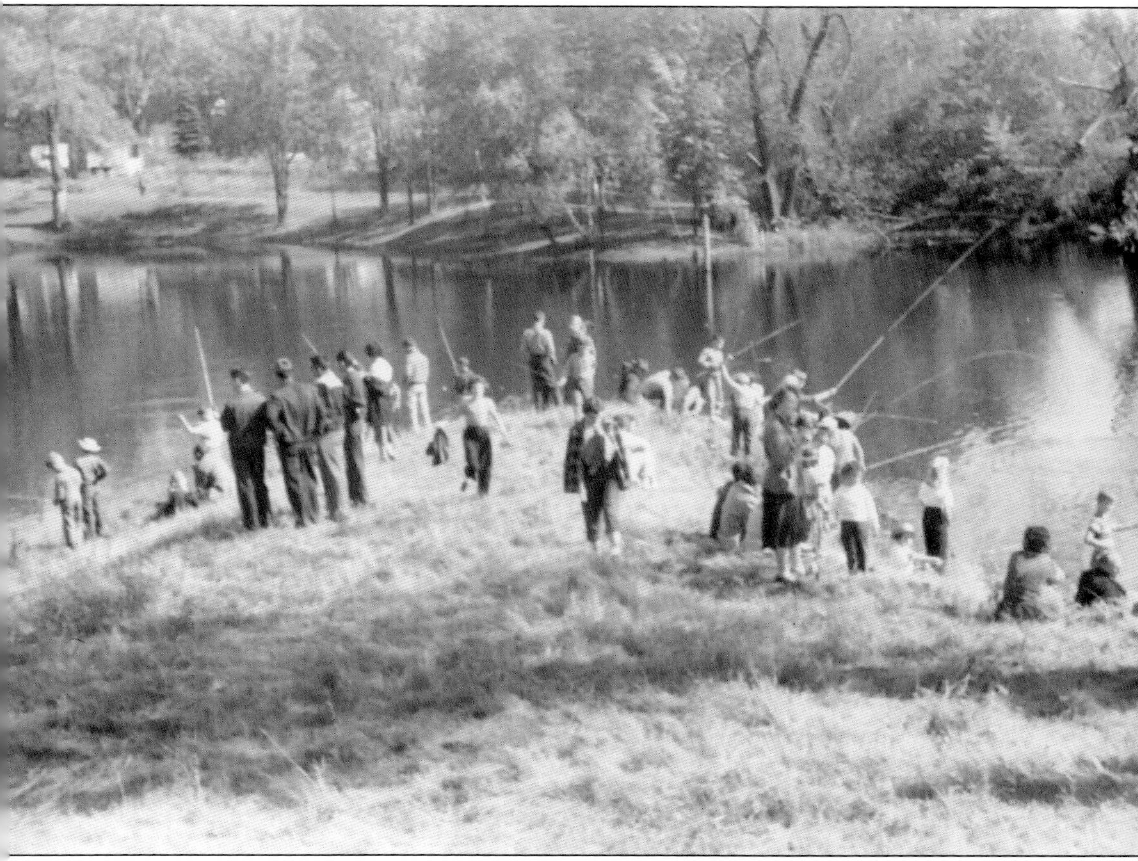
The fishing derby, 1948. Children crowd the banks of Beaver Pond hoping to snag the biggest trout and win a prize. (William Jacobs Collection.)

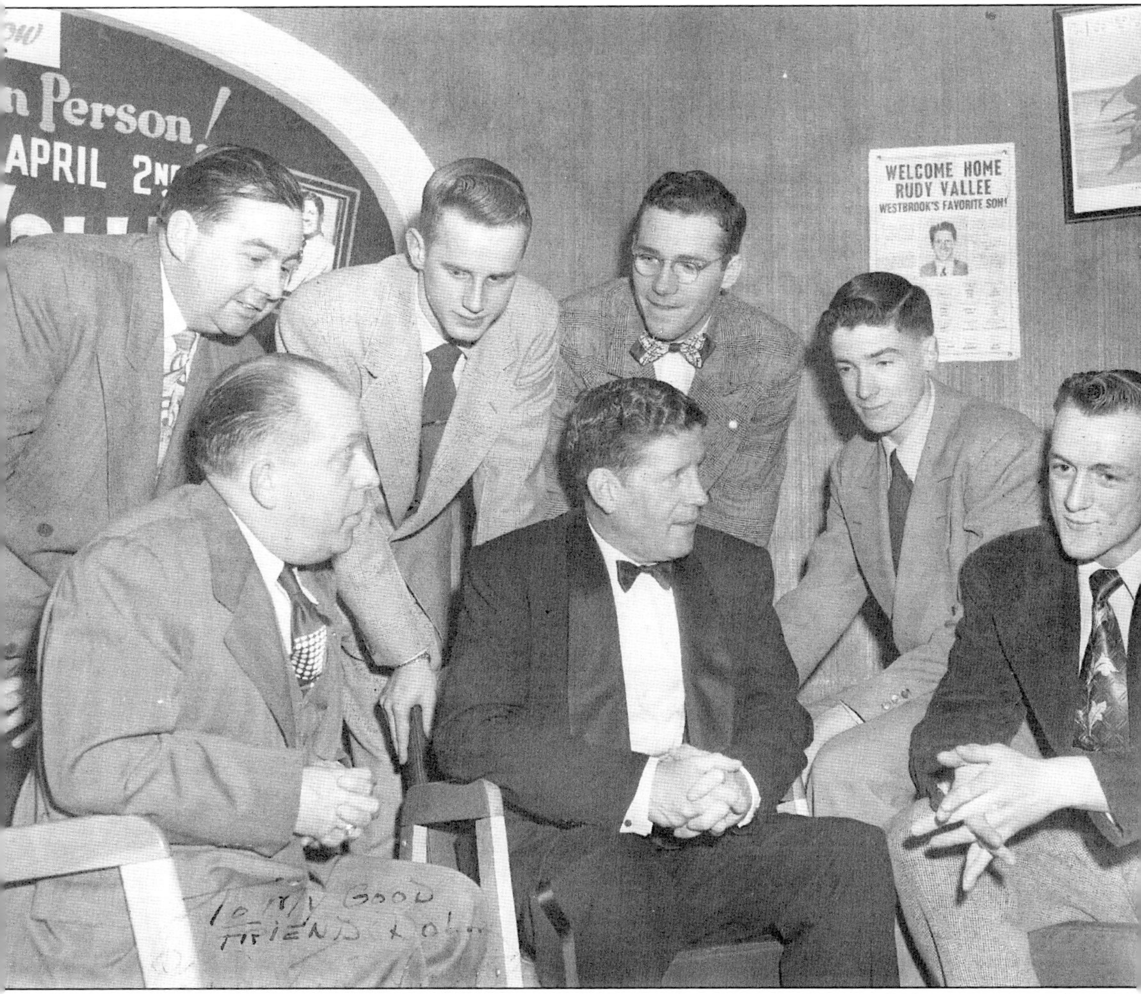

April 3, 1951. Rudy Vallee (center) is chatting with some members of the 1951 Westbrook High School State Champion Basketball Team and the mayor of Westbrook, Ernest O. Porell (at left, seated). Robert "Bob" MacHardy is on the right. In the back row are: George Russell, Robert "Bob" Morton, William "Bill" Cary, and Anthony "Tony" Wedge.

Six

Street Scenes

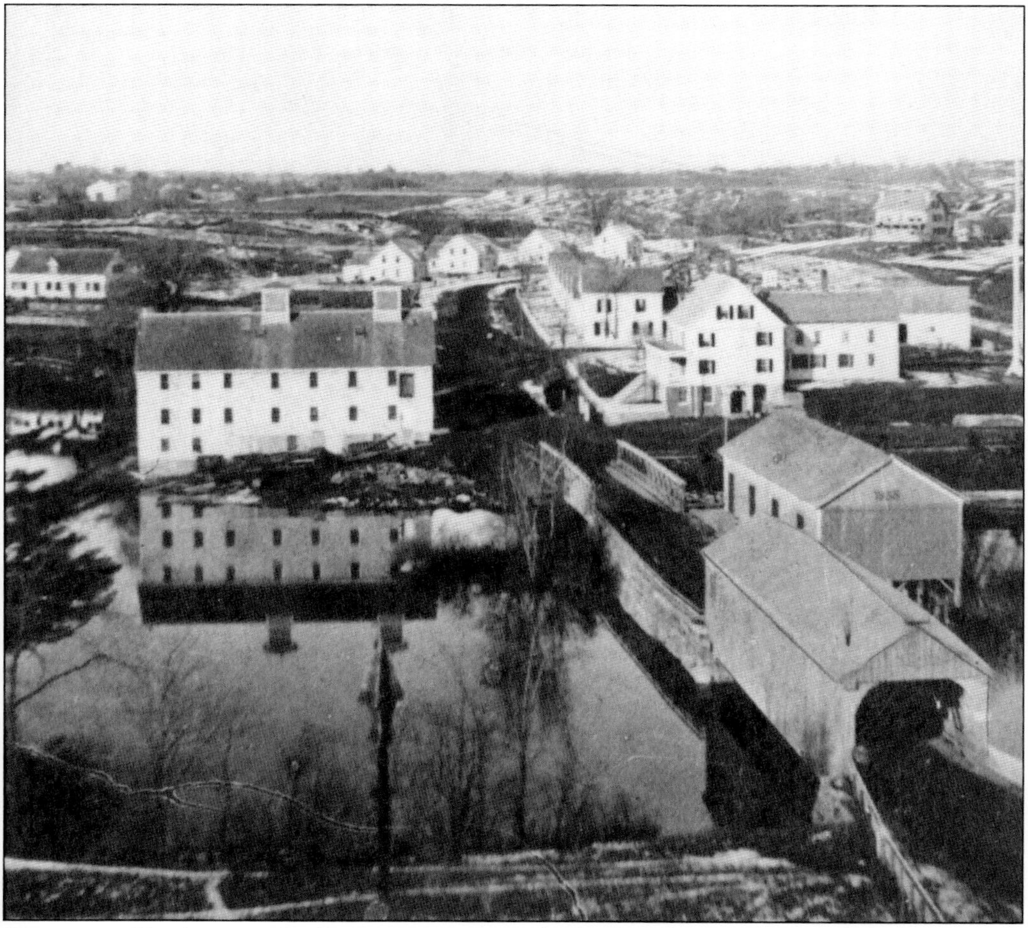

The covered bridge over the Presumpscot at Cumberland Mills. This structure was replaced by an iron bridge in 1879.

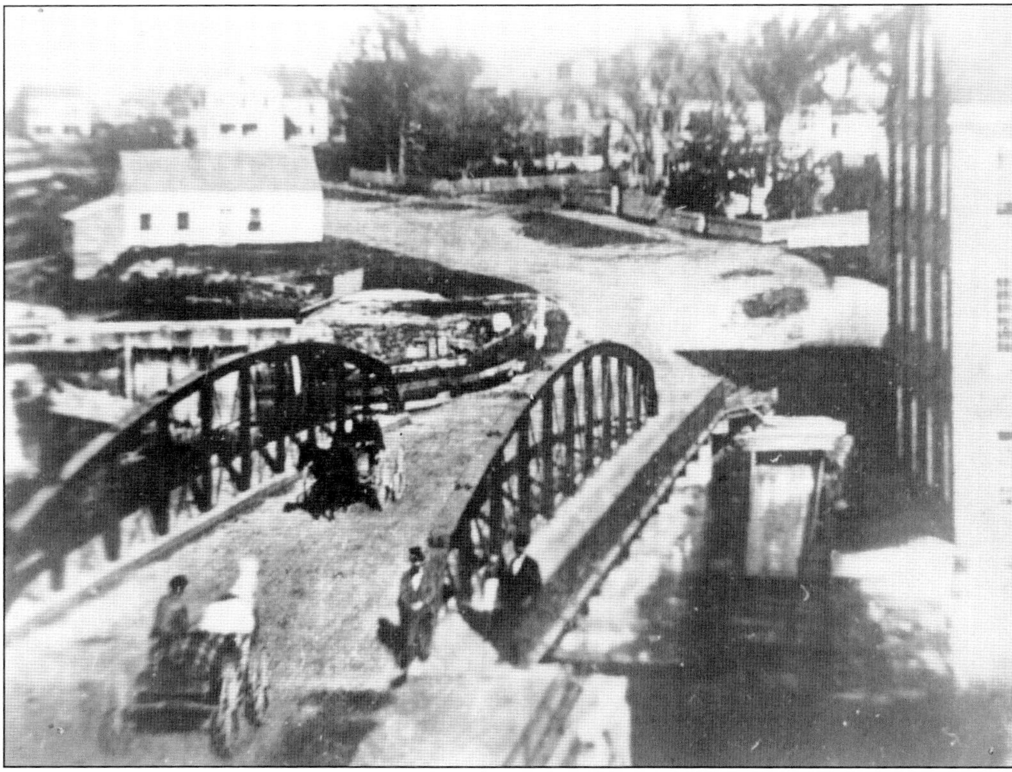

The iron bridge over the Presumpscot at Bridge Street, mid-1800s.

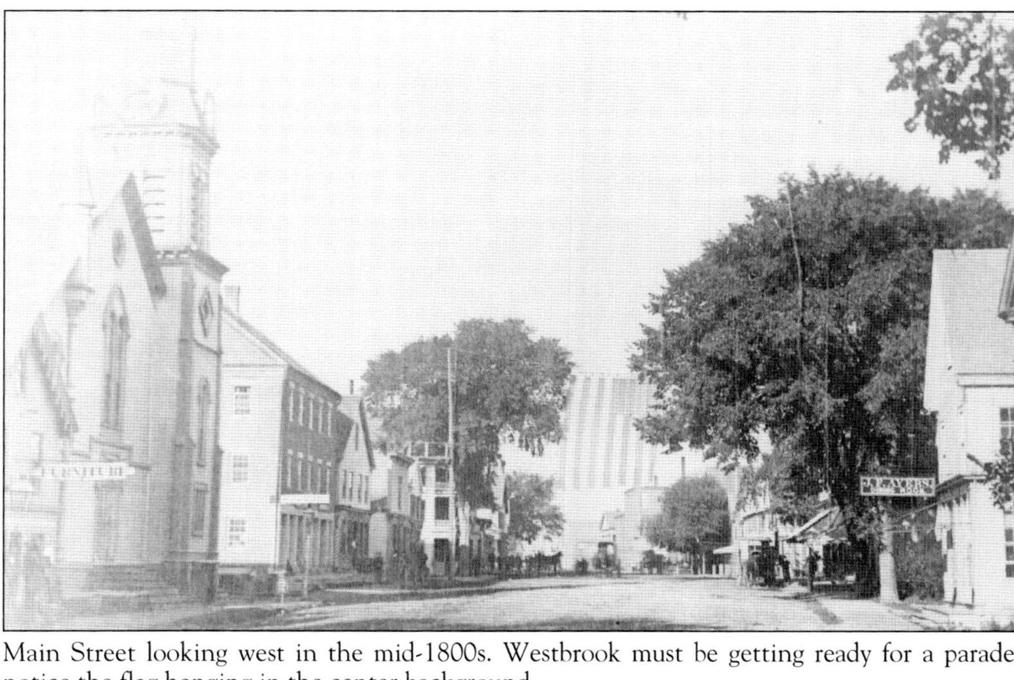

Main Street looking west in the mid-1800s. Westbrook must be getting ready for a parade; notice the flag hanging in the center background.

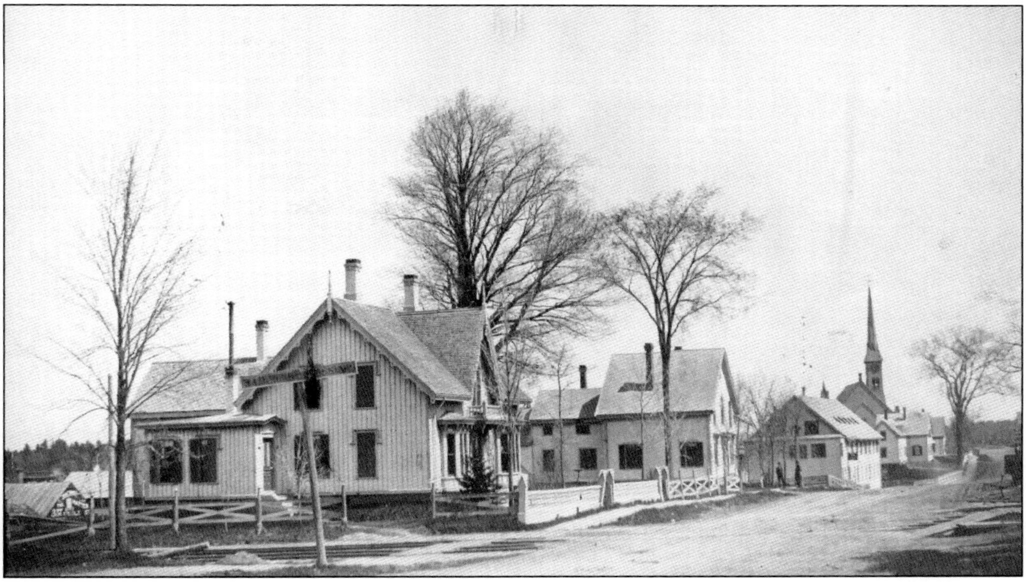

Cumberland Mills, 1882. This view was taken from the Cumberland Street railroad crossing, looking toward the paper mill.

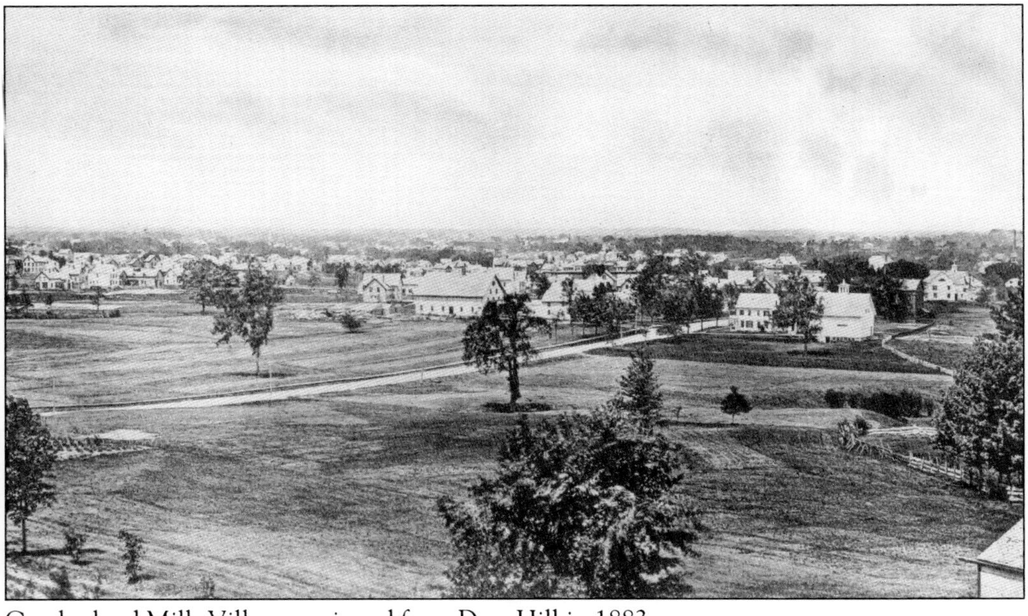

Cumberland Mills Village as viewed from Deer Hill in 1883.

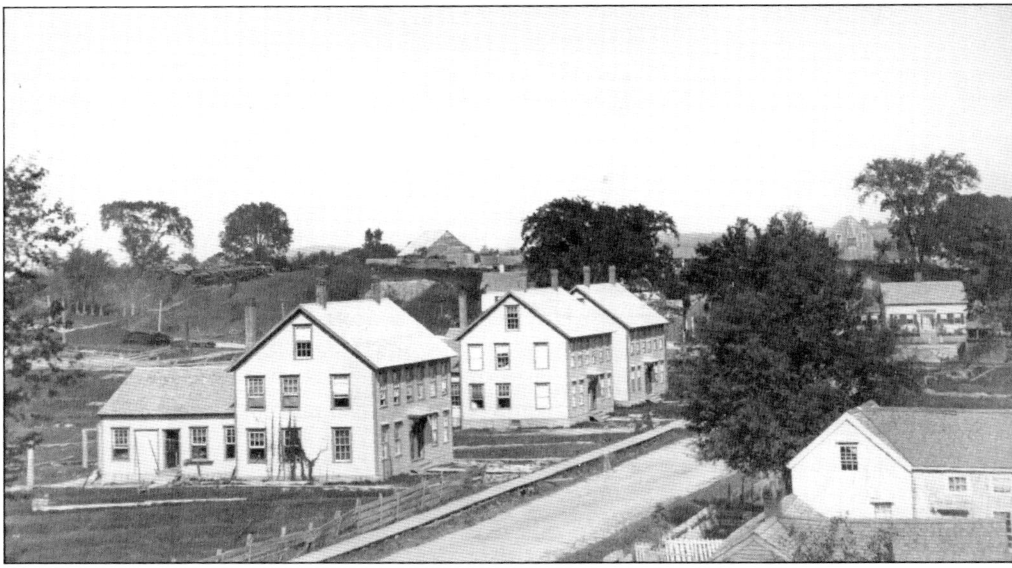

Lower Saco Street, late 1800s. The hill in the background is Pork Hill (Park Hill). Some of the homes in this picture still stand.

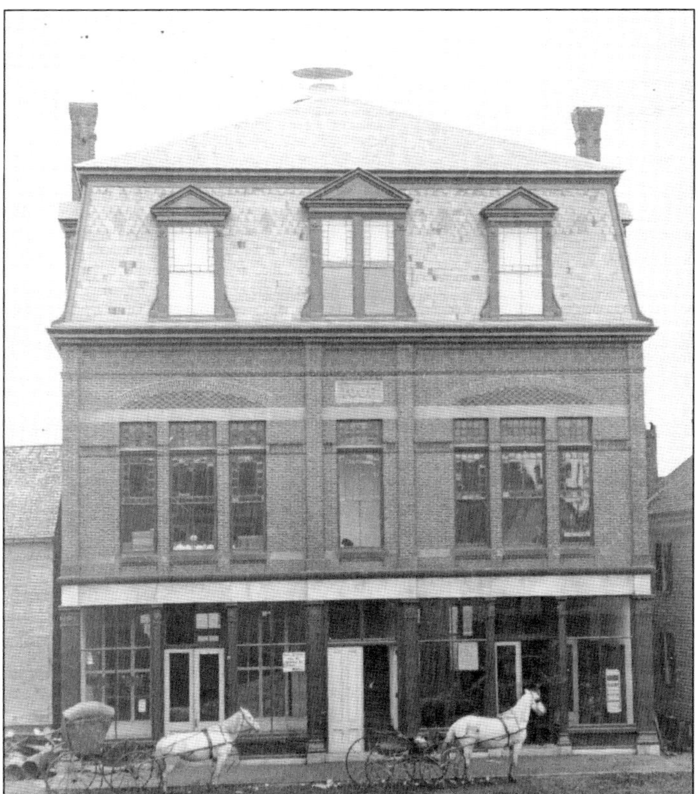

Odd Fellows Hall, 1883. This building stood on Main Street between Central and Mechanic Streets. It was demolished in 1975.

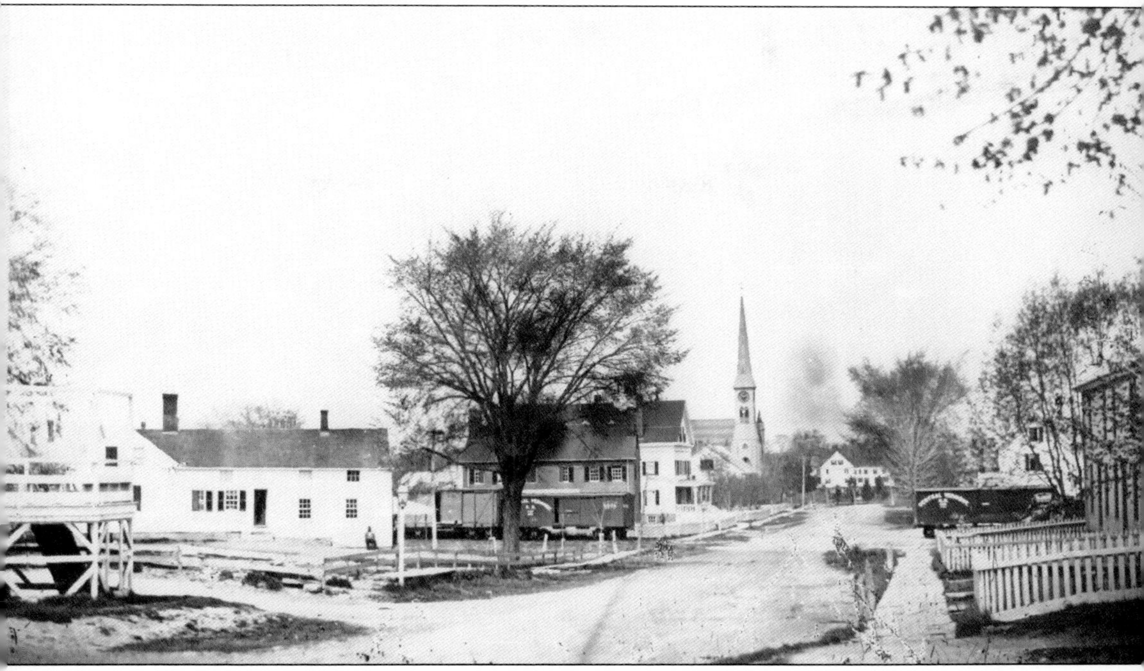

Cumberland Mills Village. The bandstand on the left is the site of the present Warren Block. The white cape with the ell still stands on Main Street, along with "the inn" at the center on Cumberland Street. Warren Congregational Church rises in the background.

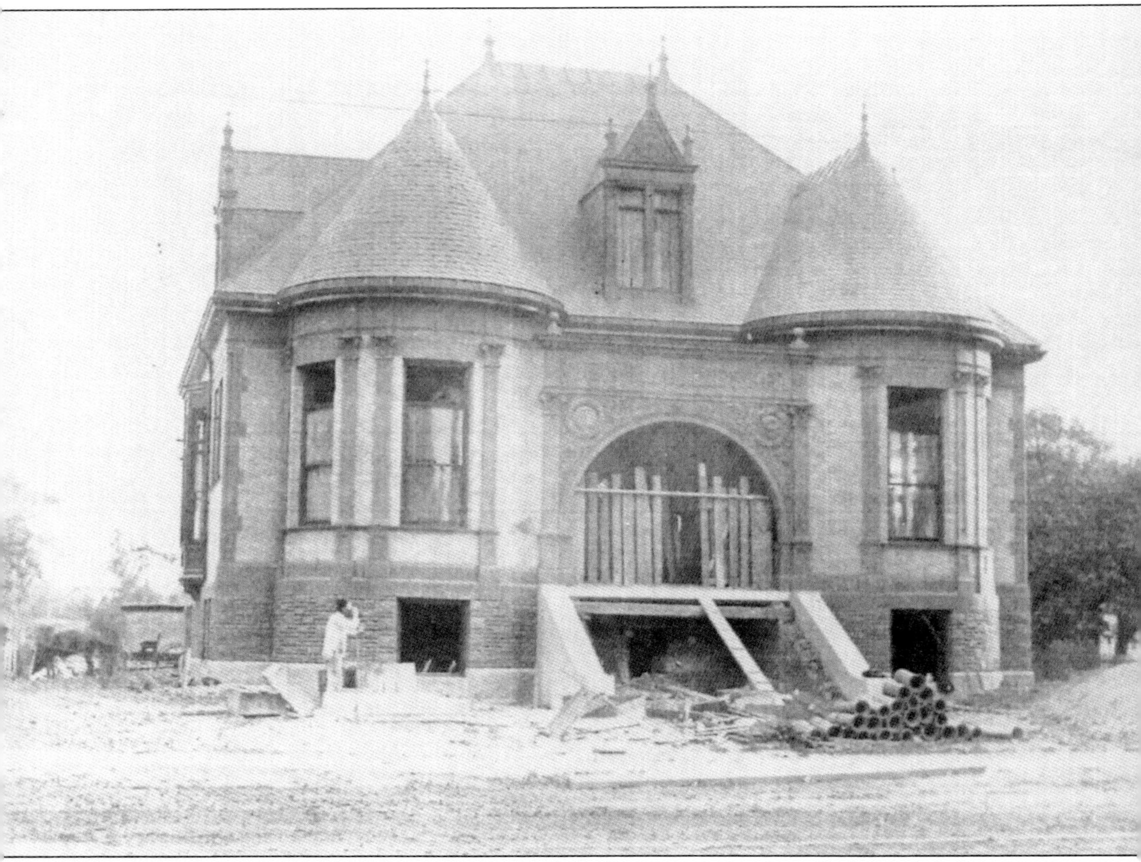

Walker Memorial Library, 1894. This public library was built with funds left for this purpose in the will of Joseph Walker. The library was then turned over to the City of Westbrook. An addition was built in 1989, making it one of the most attractive and functional buildings in the city.

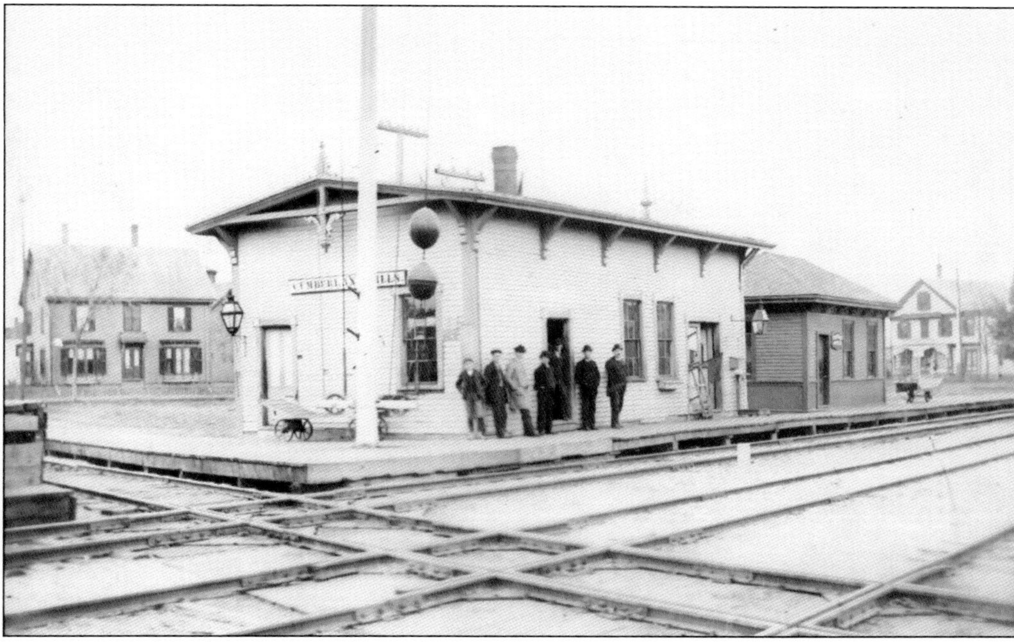

Maine Central Railroad Depot, located at Main and Rochester Streets, 1894.

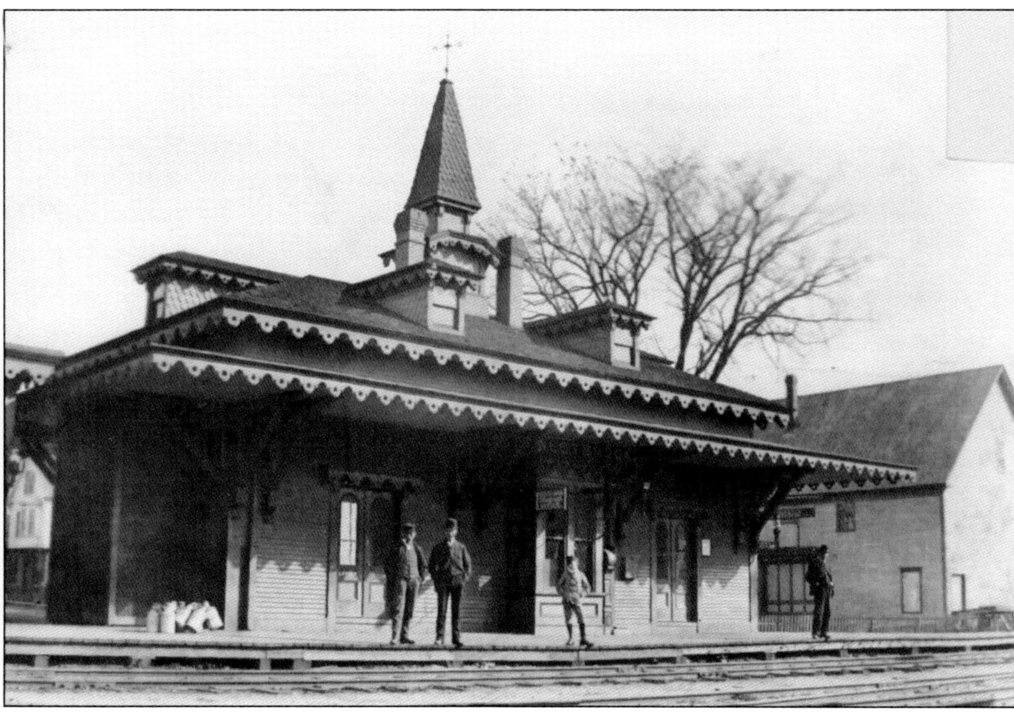

Boston & Maine Railroad Station, c. 1900. This important hub of transportation was located at the end of Fitch Street, between Brackett and Central Streets.

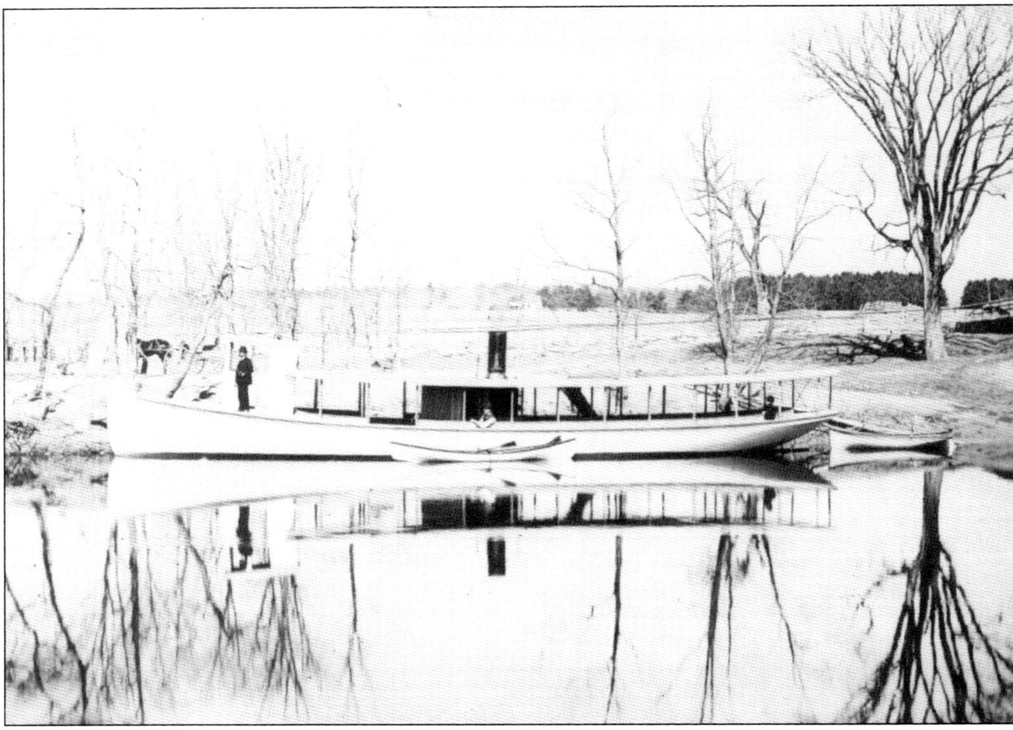

River Steamer, early 1900s. The vessel was stopped at Pride's Bridge. Perhaps it was waiting for passengers?

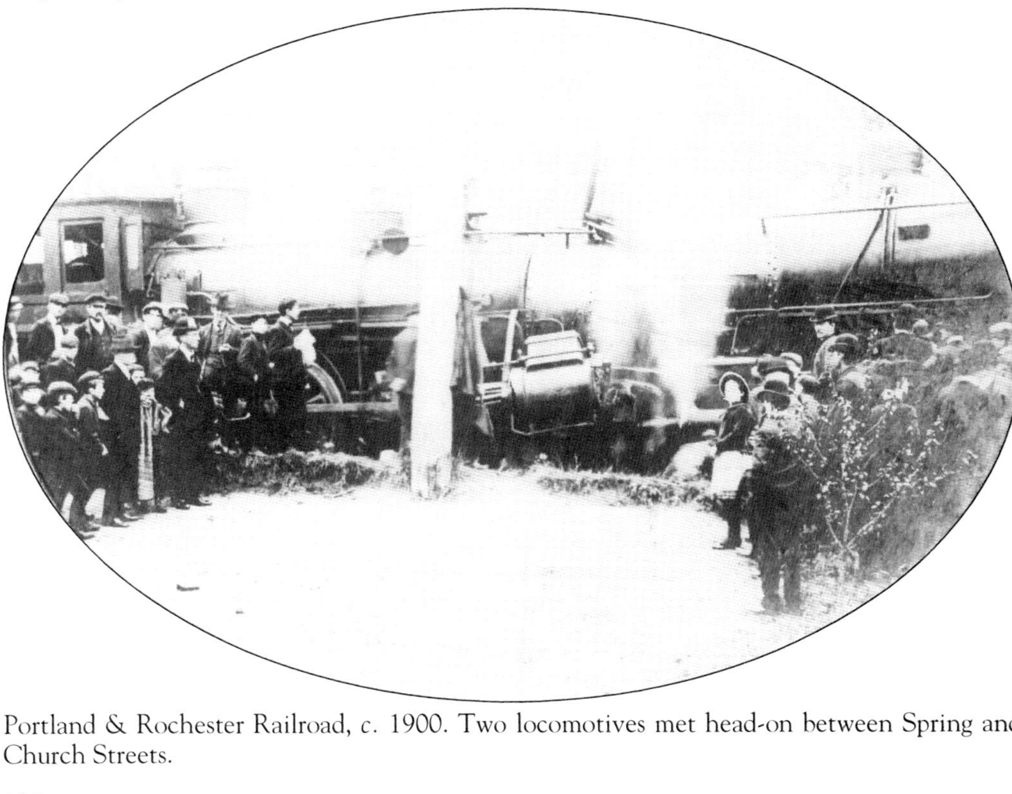

Portland & Rochester Railroad, *c.* 1900. Two locomotives met head-on between Spring and Church Streets.

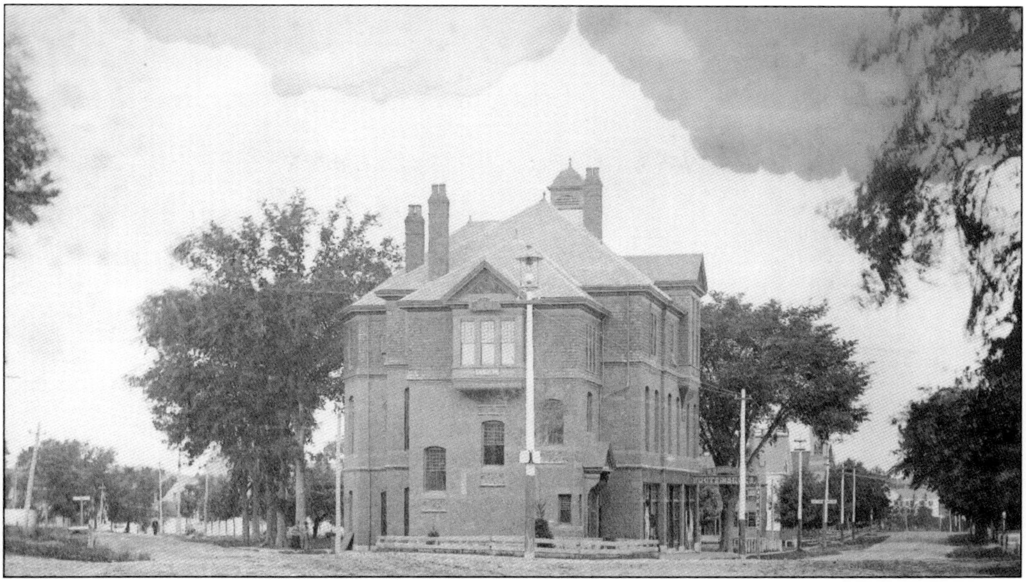

Warren Block, located at the junction of Main and Cumberland Streets, *c.* 1900. Built by the Warren family, this block housed a gymnasium, lodge rooms, and several retail stores.

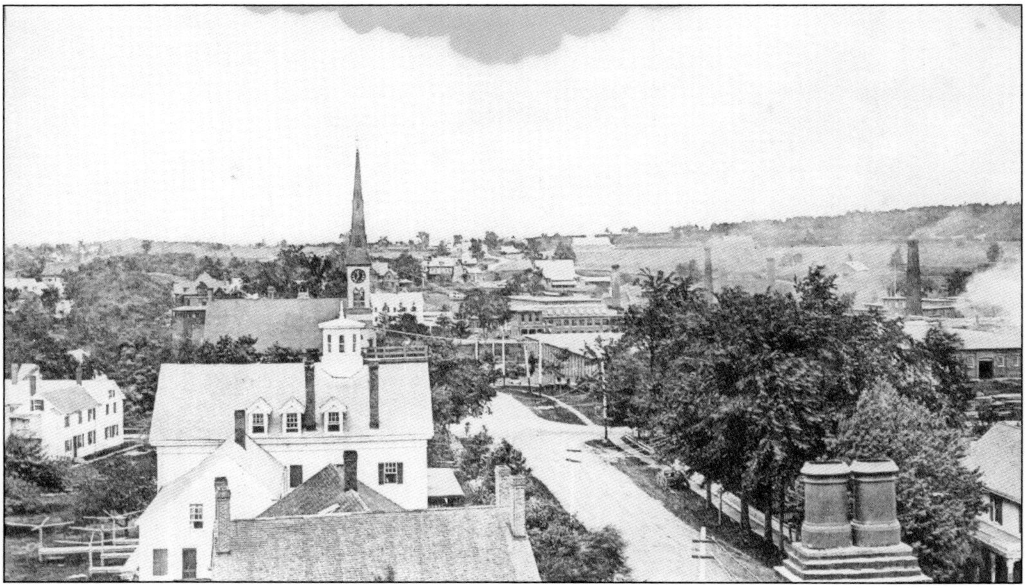

Cumberland Street, *c.* 1900. This view from the Warren Block looks down Cumberland Street to the river, with Congregational Church on the left and S. D. Warren Paper Mill on the right.

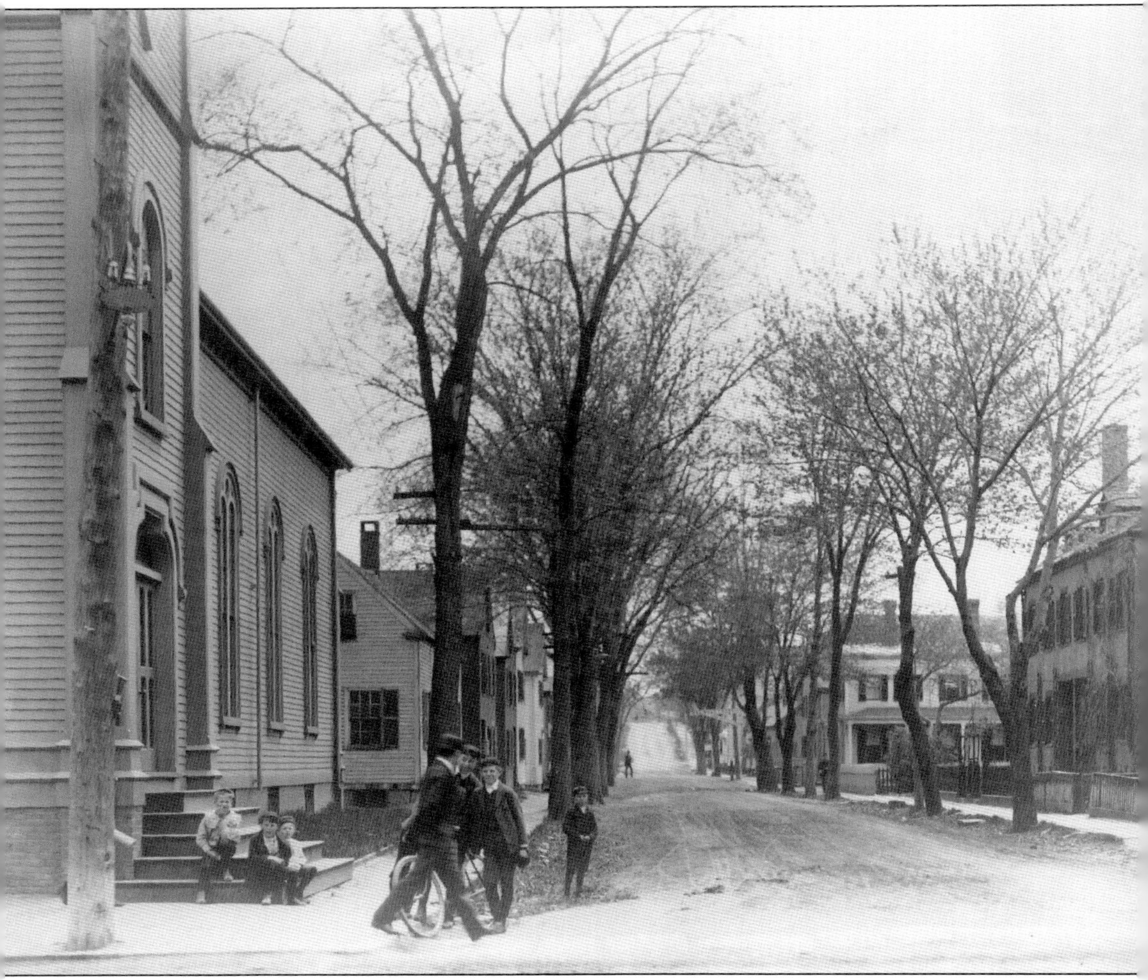

Brackett Street, 1910. Looking up from Main Street, we can see Westbrook Congregational Church on the right. For over one hundred years, young people enjoyed congregating on the church steps in order to watch the goings-on in town. It was the perfect spot to while away a lazy afternoon with your friends. (Berg Family Collection.)

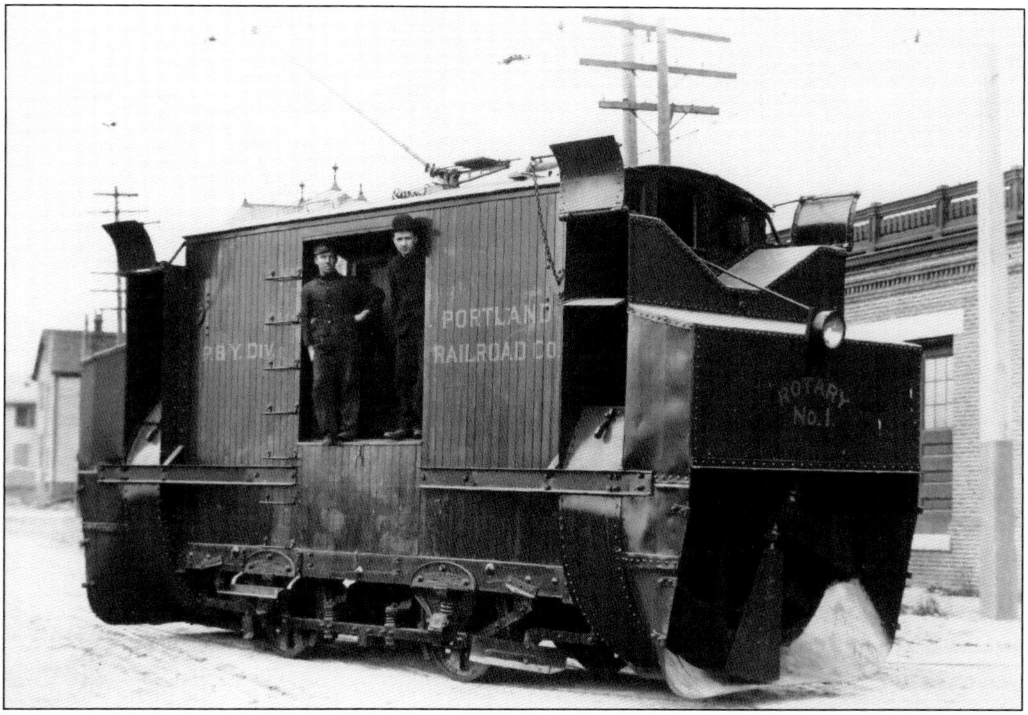

Portland Railroad Company. This rotary #1 snowblower was often used to clean off the railroad tracks.

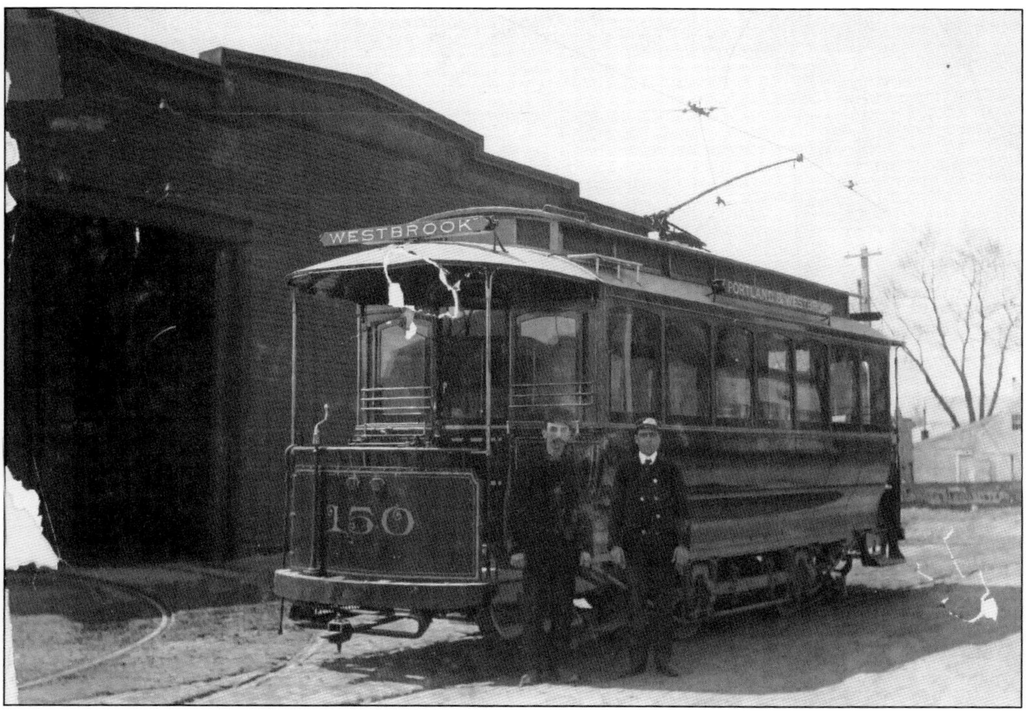

Westbrook trolley car. George Barbour and Frank Spring stand beside their trolley.

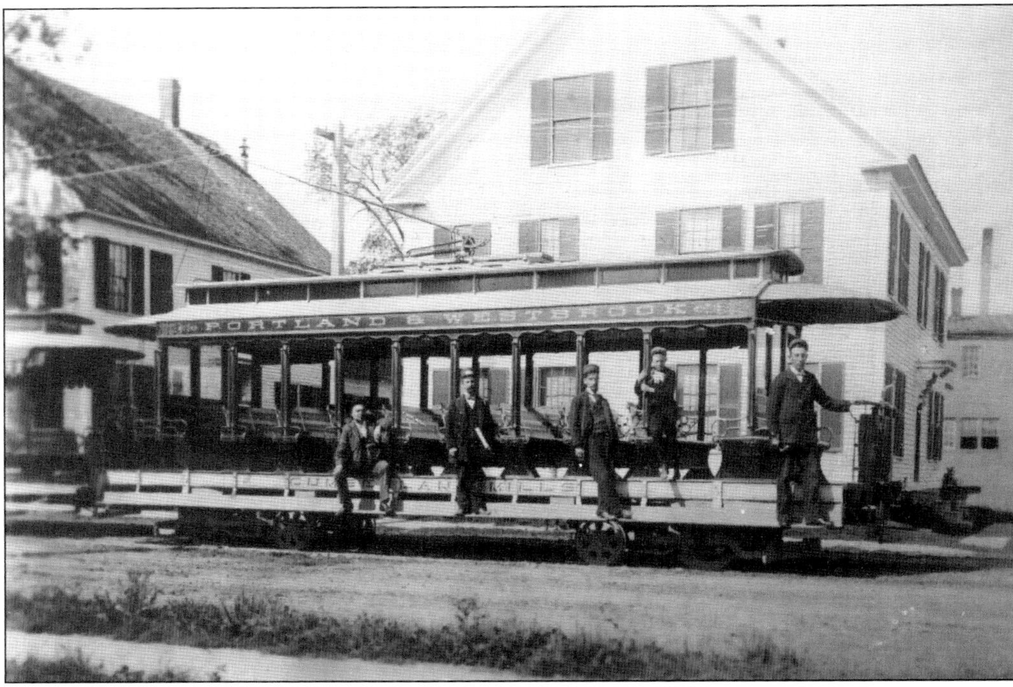

Portland and Westbrook Trolley on Main Street at the turn of the century.

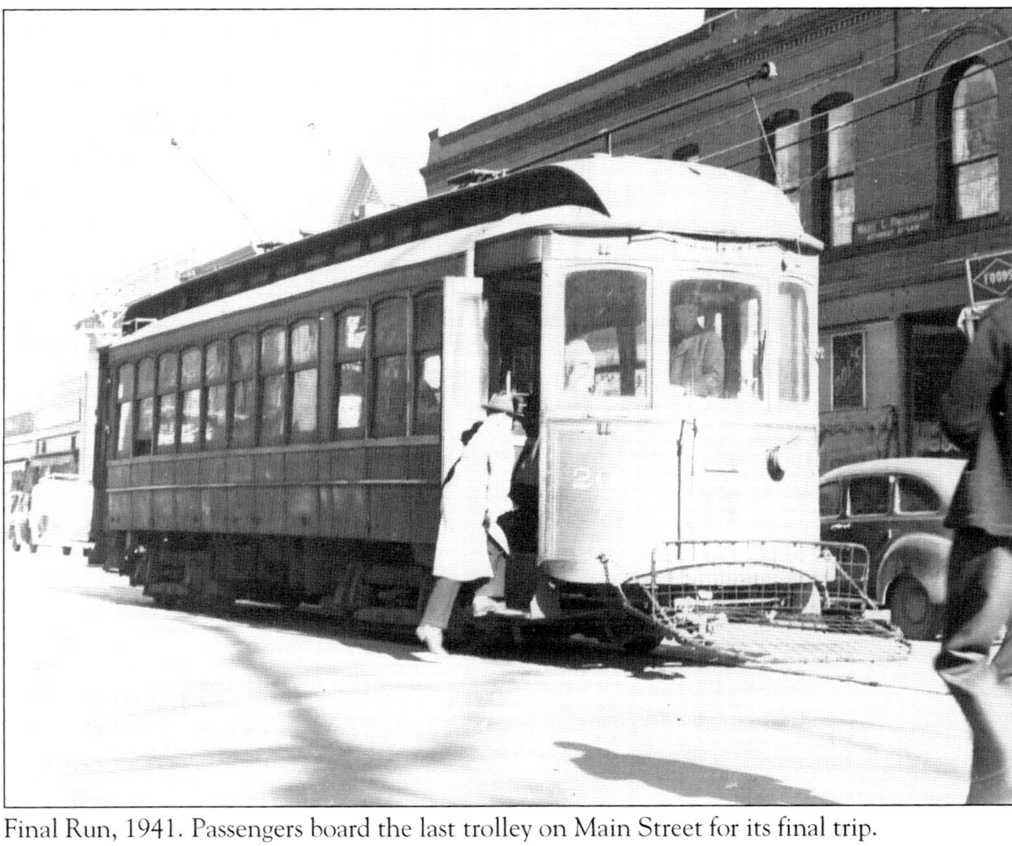
Final Run, 1941. Passengers board the last trolley on Main Street for its final trip.

Seven

Faces of Nature

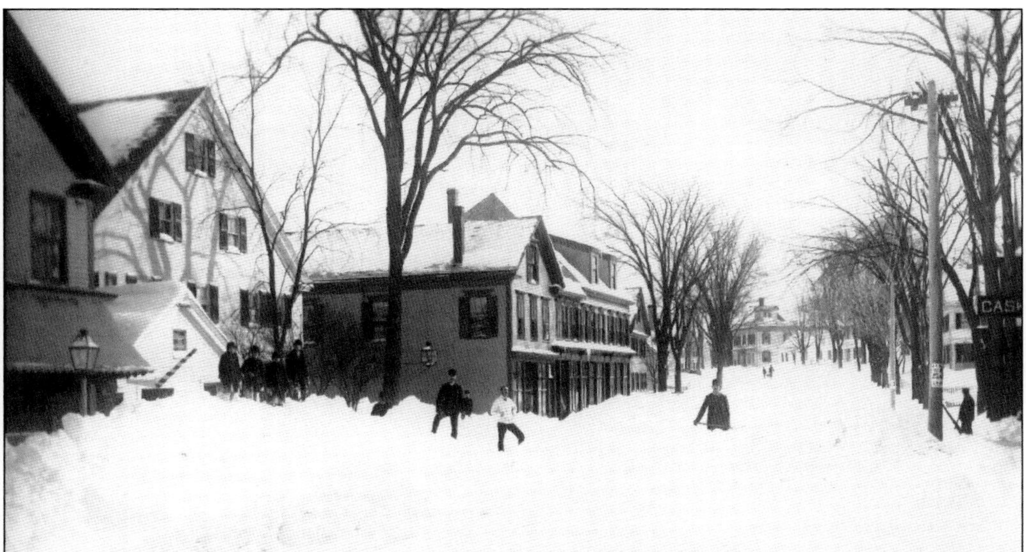

Saccarappa, during the winter of 1885. Westbrook, like most of the northeast, hosted some rugged winter storms. Much hand shoveling was done, as snow removal equipment was scarce and limited. This photograph was taken on Main Street looking east toward the future site of the Walker Memorial Library.

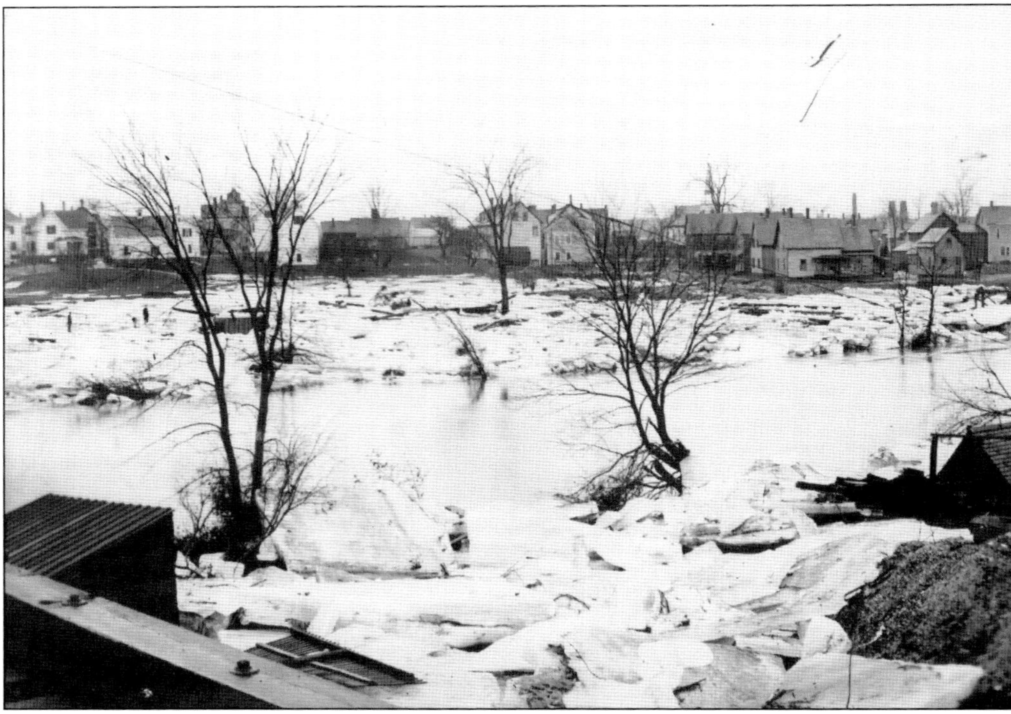

The flood of 1896. This view looks from Brown Street across the river above the Maine Central Railroad crossing.

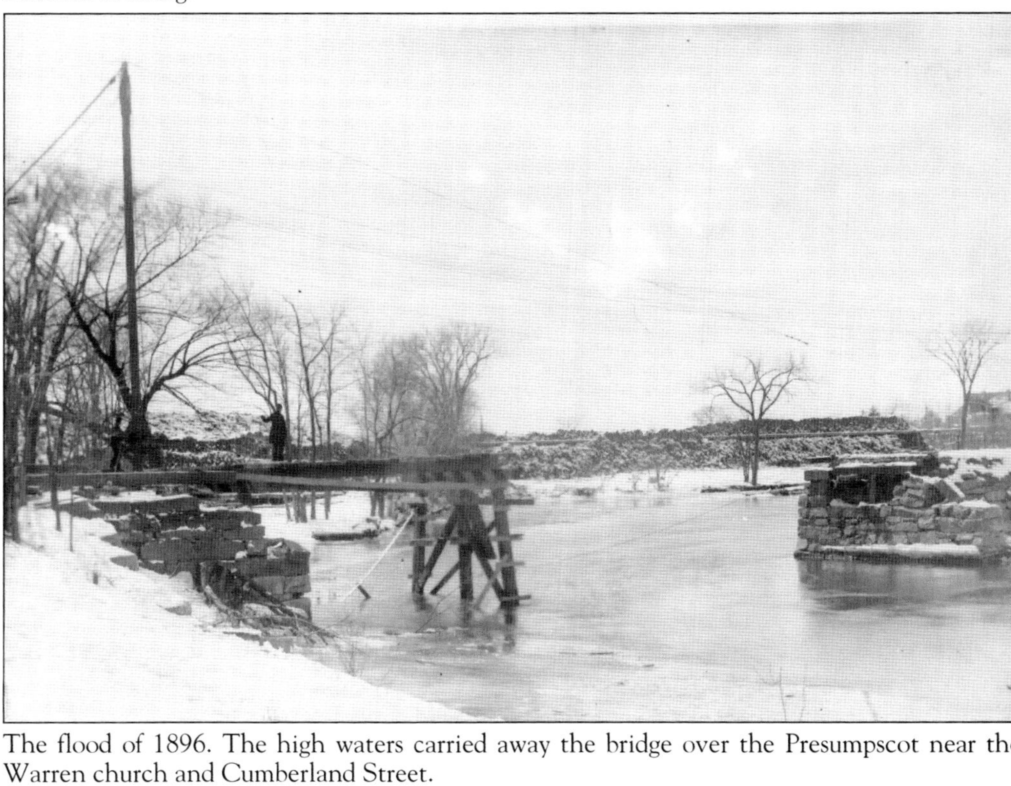

The flood of 1896. The high waters carried away the bridge over the Presumpscot near the Warren church and Cumberland Street.

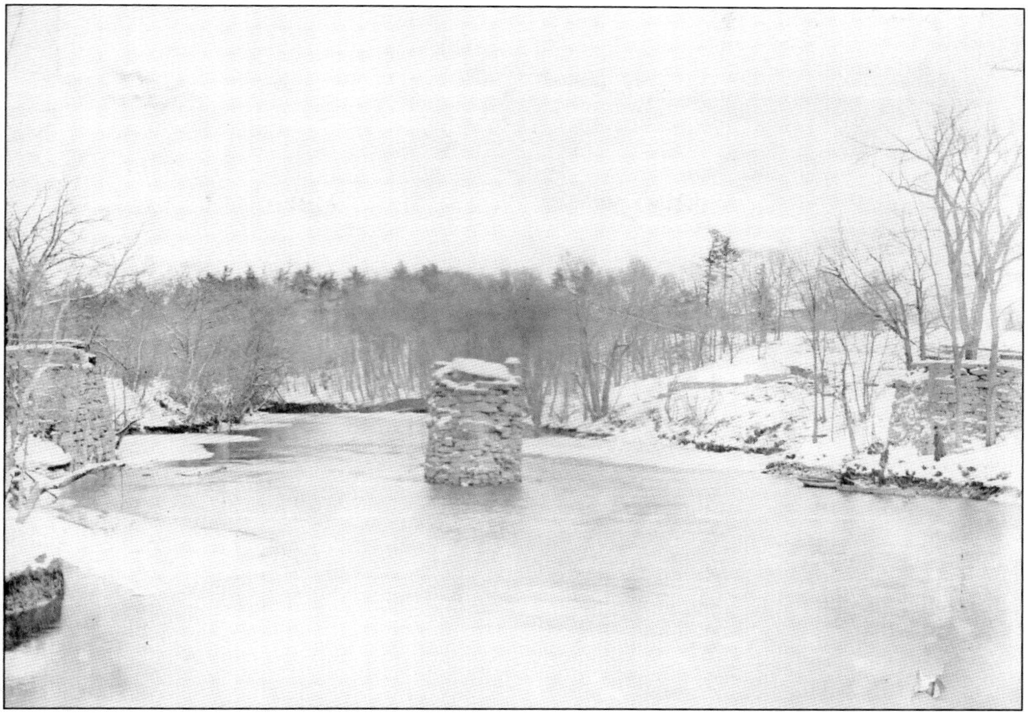

The flood of 1896. In its flight to the ocean, the mighty Presumpscot River washed away the Riverton bridge.

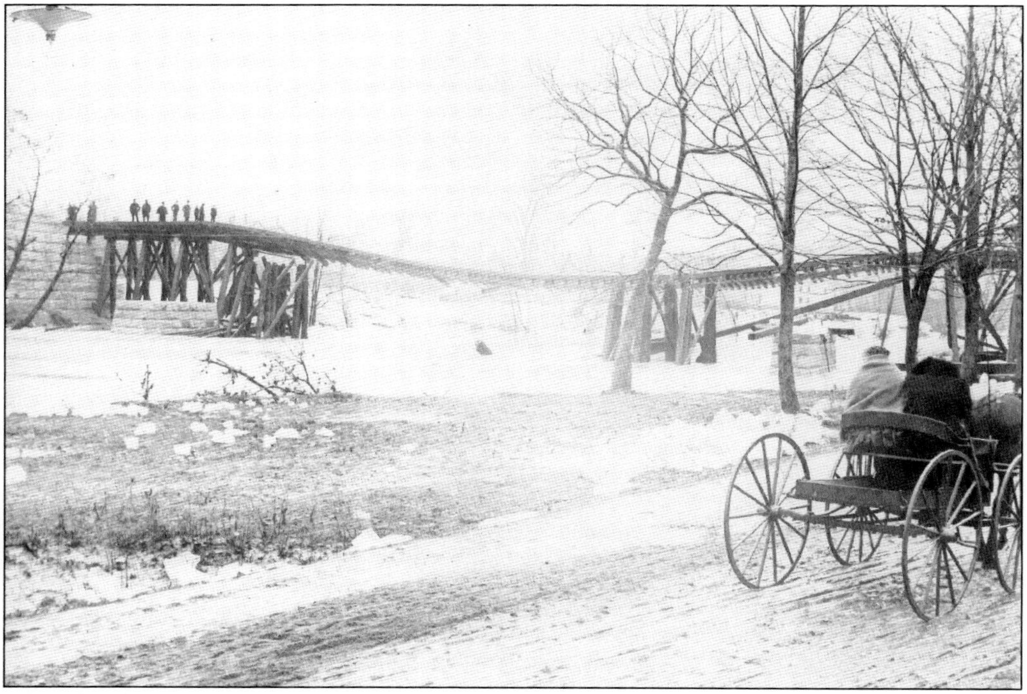

After the flood of 1896. Curiosity seekers survey the damage wrought by the river. Some are standing on the railroad bridge and some are pausing their buggy to have a look. (Westbrook Historical Society Collection.)

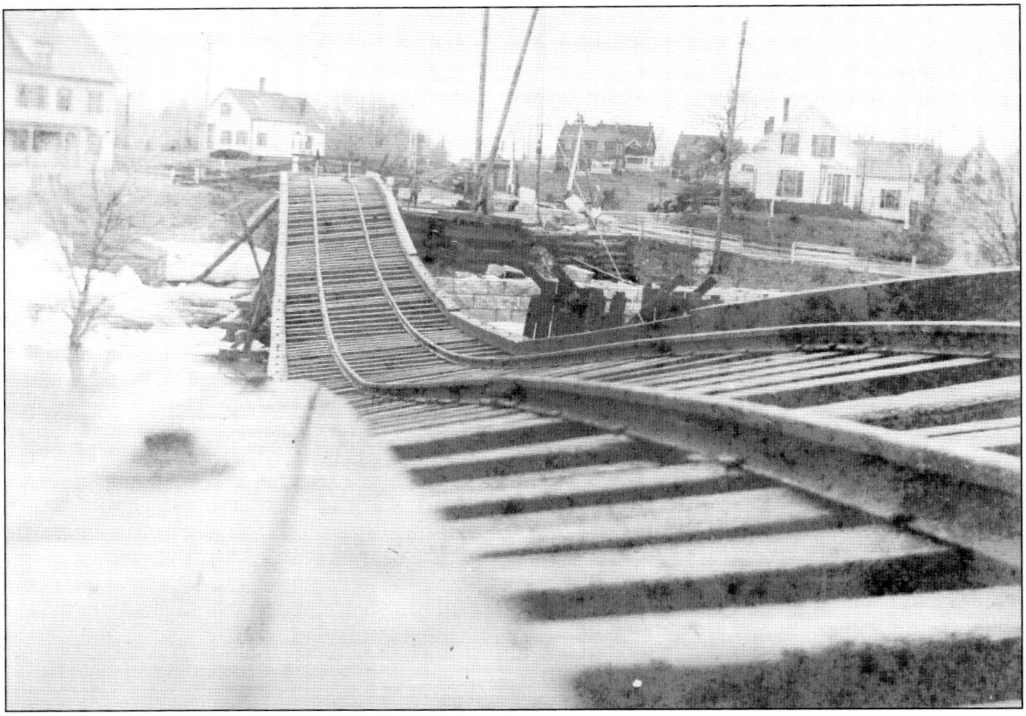

After the flood of 1896. Another view of the Brown Street railroad bridge from the east bank.

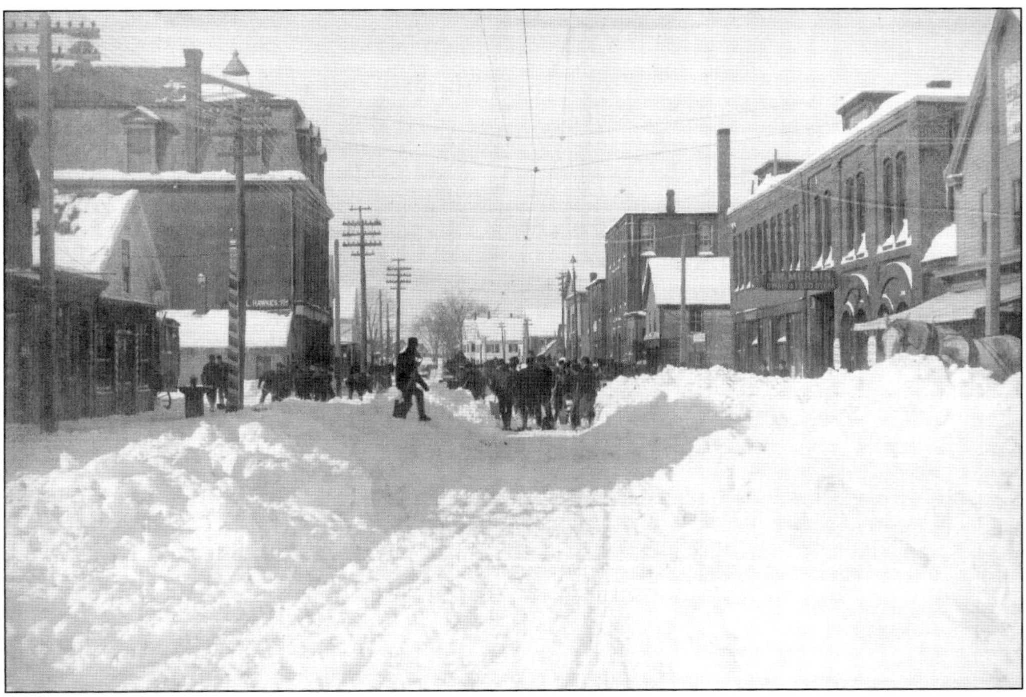

Upper Main Street, c. 1910. "Plowing" after a big winter storm. (Berg Family Collection.)

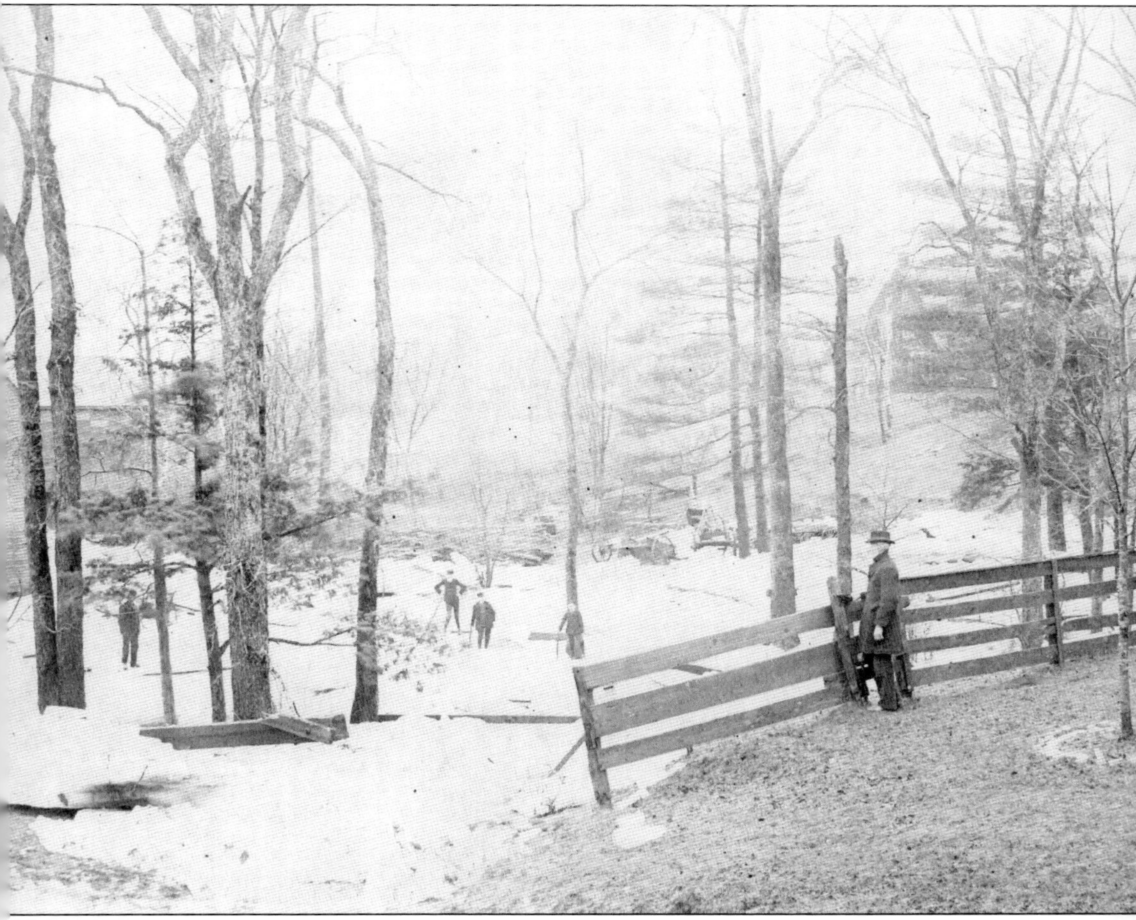

Ice in Brown Street Ravine, March 2, 1896. Pictured, from left to right, are: A. Hooper, Herbert Herman, Lem Babb, Grover Hooper, and Jacob Brydon. The barn on the left belonged to Michael O'Neil. The barn behind it was Daniel Cressey's. The house on the right is in "Hotten Tot."

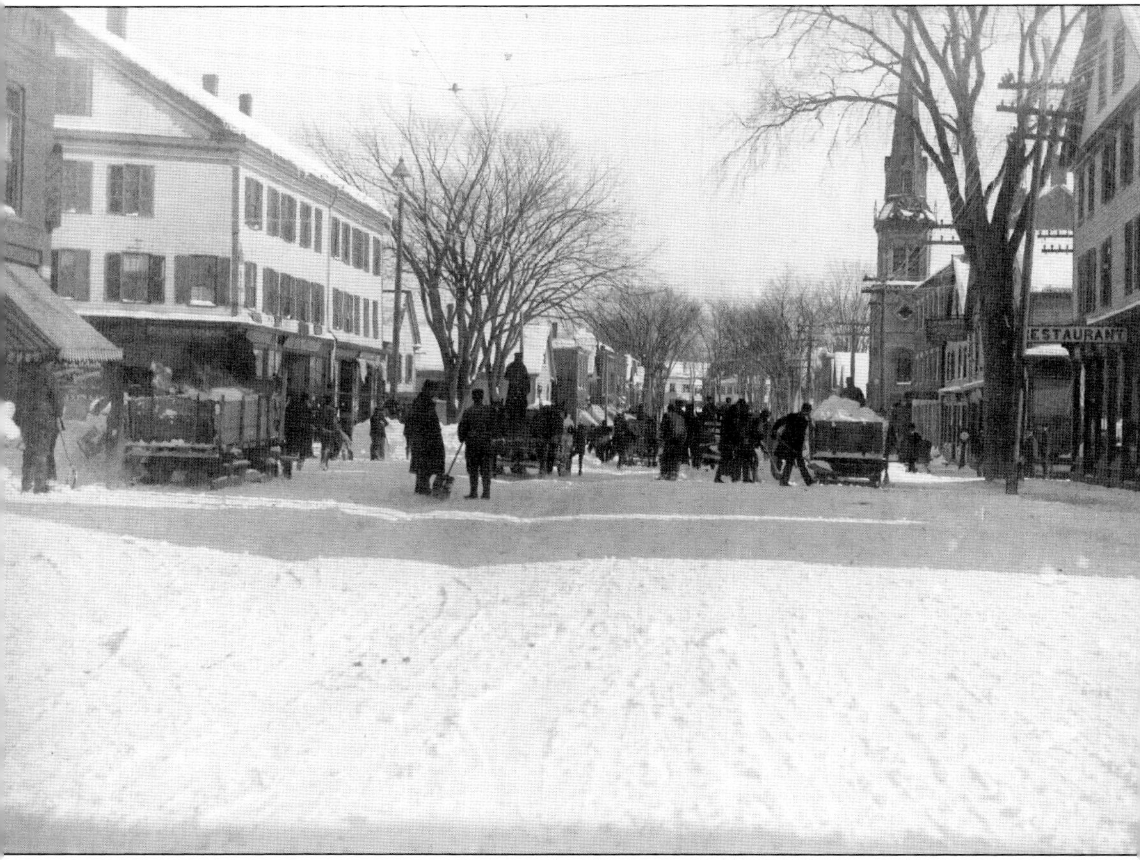

Snow Removal. This is another great photograph of group snow removal on Main Street. Store owners are clearing their storefronts, wagons are piled high with snow, and streets are being rolled to pack them down. (Berg Family Collection.)

Eight

Monuments to Our History

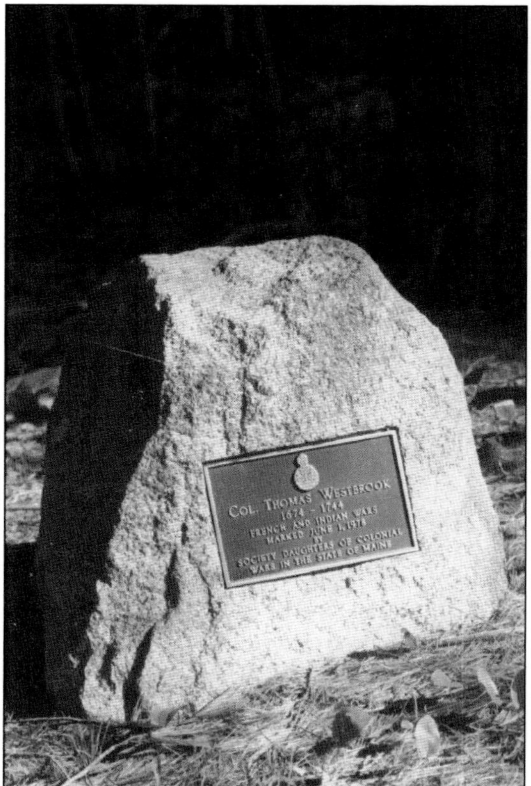

Grave of Colonel Thomas Westbrook (1674–1744). Our city's namesake was an Indian fighter, a mast agent for the king of England, a civic leader, and businessman. He built and operated the first paper mill in Maine, damming the Presumpscot River. When his health declined and his business began to suffer, his partner sued him and took much of his property to partially satisfy the debts. When he died, the family, fearing that the body might be confiscated for non-payment of his debts, secretly arranged to have him buried in an unmarked plot on his sister Mary Knight's property. Roger Knight, the present owner and descendant of Mary and Nathan Knight, remembered family talk about the stones in the woods being where "Colonel Westbrook was buried." He encouraged the historical society to excavate the site as a bicentennial project in 1976, and the unmistakable remains of the colonel were found. A dedication ceremony was held and the site was recovered with a proper marker placed on the grave. (Ketover Collection.)

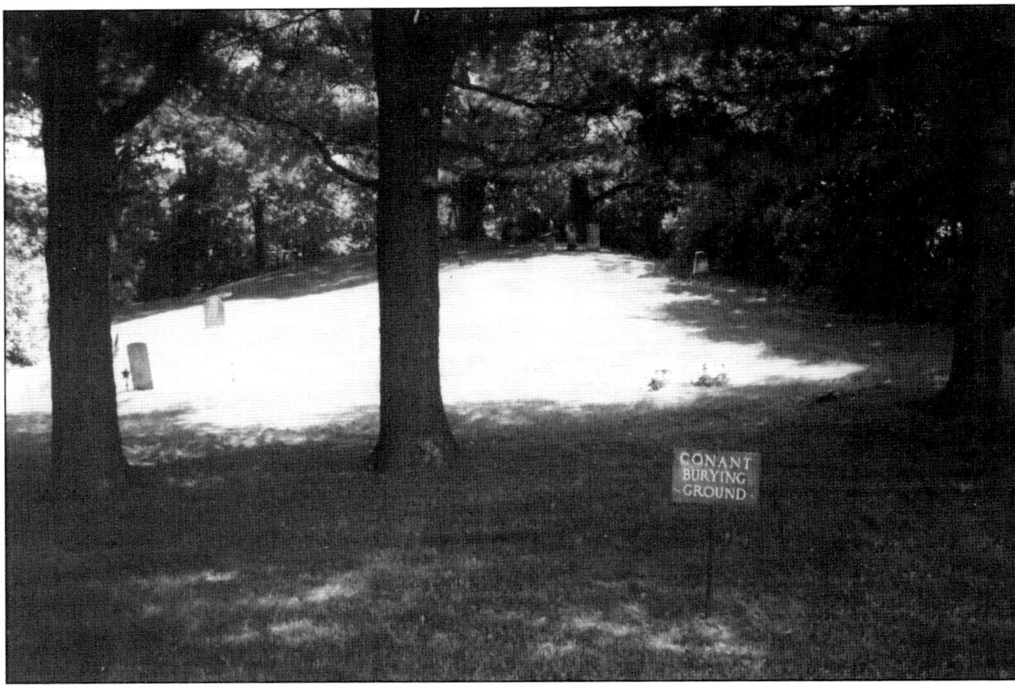

The Conant burying ground, Conant Street, Westbrook. This cemetery was named for Joseph Conant, who was believed to be the first permanent settler in the town.

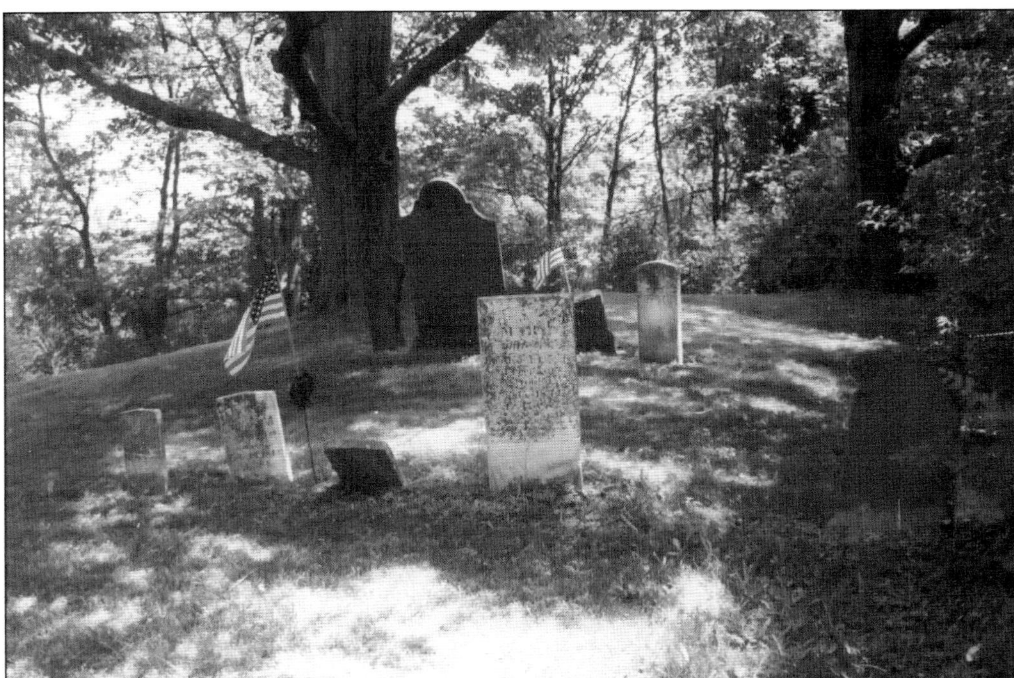

A closer look at the Conant burying ground, showing some very old family stones.

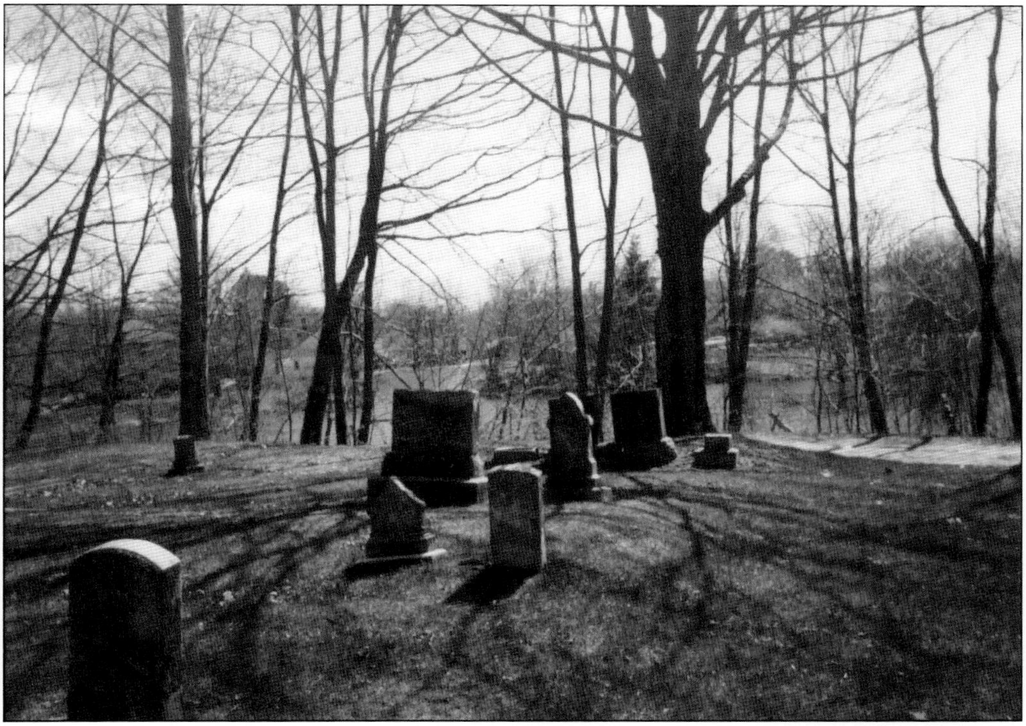

Two images of Saccarappa Cemetery, a burying ground containing very old Westbrook graves. Located off upper Church Street, it abuts Beaver Pond. (Both images from Ketover Collection.)

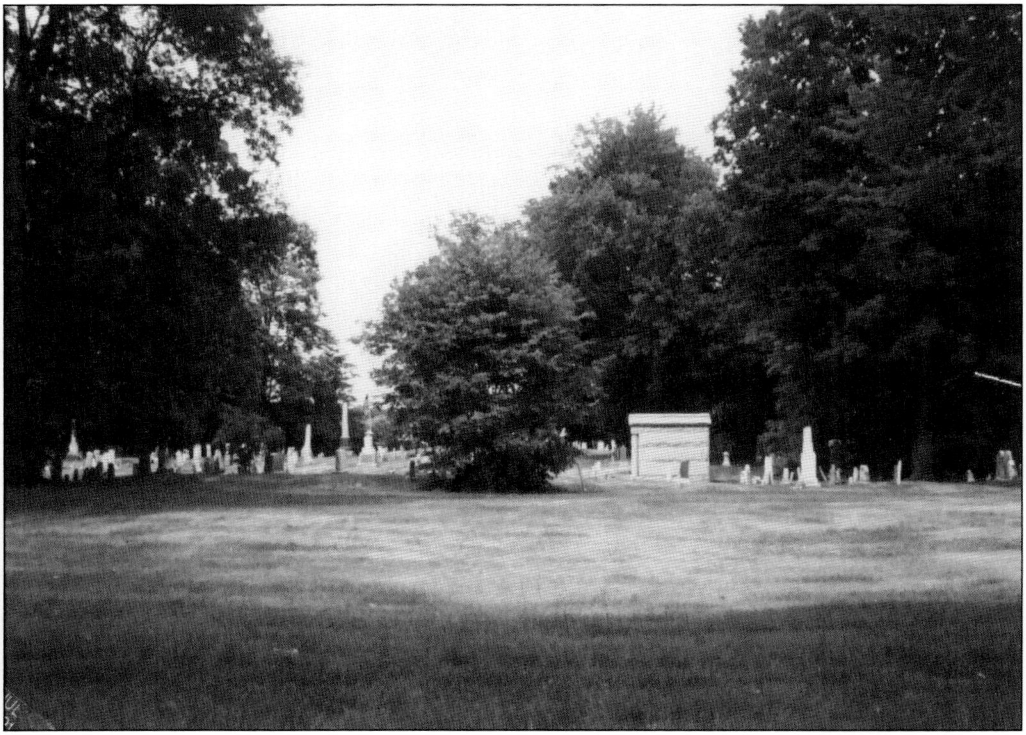

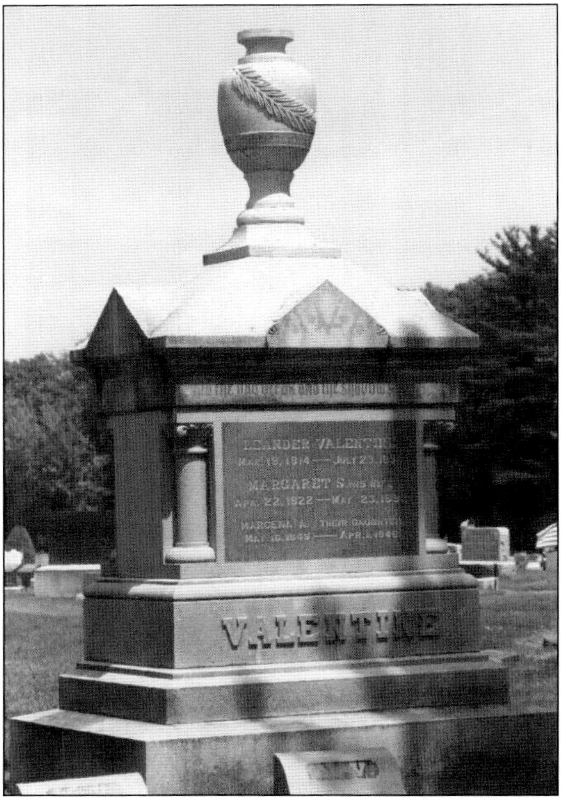

The grave of Leander Valentine (1814–1895) in Woodlawn Cemetery. Valentine was the first mayor of Westbrook in 1891. (Ketover Collection.)

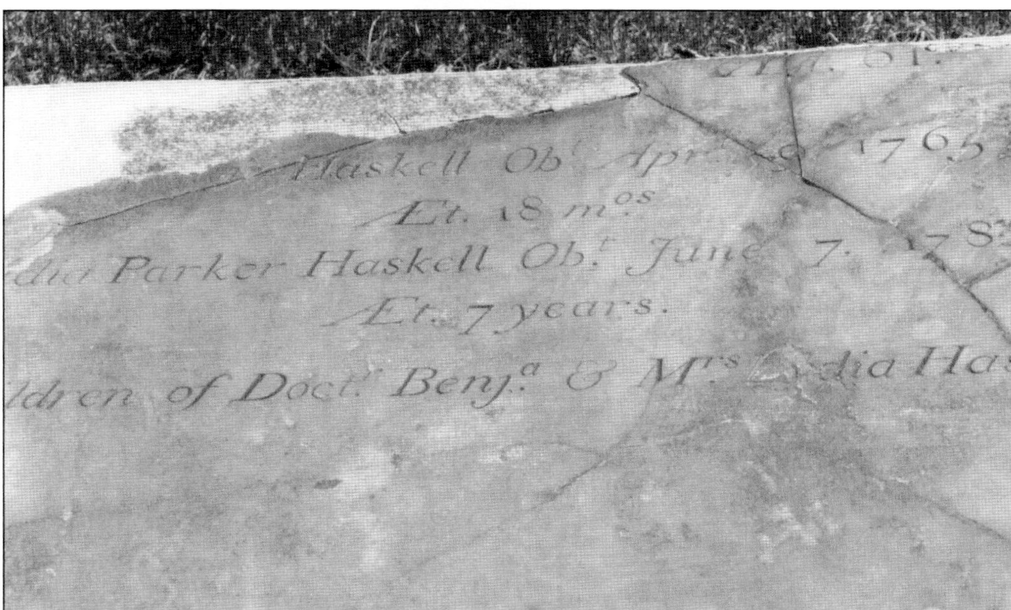

An early settler's grave. One of the graves that was removed from the Pike Street lot and transferred to Woodlawn Cemetery was this one of Dr. Benjamin and Lydia Freeman Haskell and their children. Dr. Haskell was one of Saccarappa's earliest settlers. He died in 1785. (Ketover Collection.)

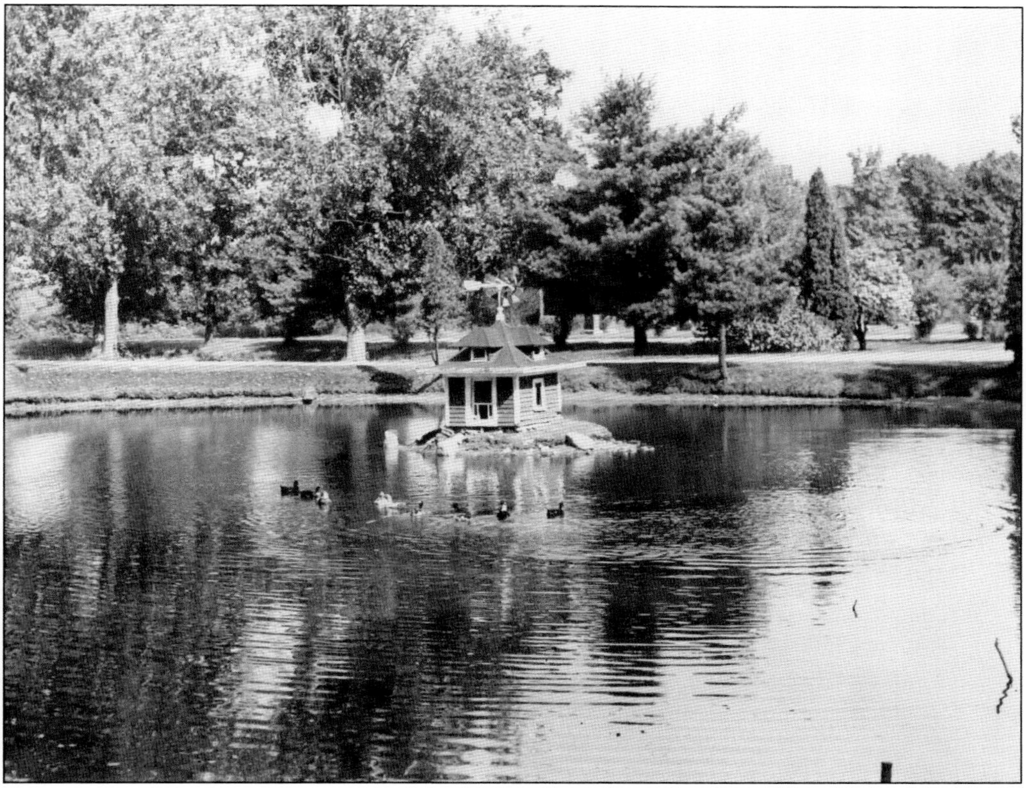

The duck pond at Woodlawn Cemetery. This is still a tranquil and beautiful place to take the children to feed the ducks or to sit and enjoy your lunch.

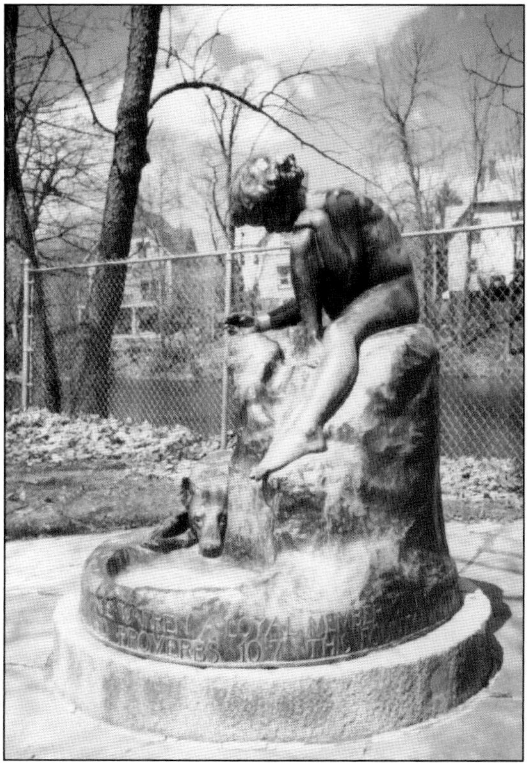

The memorial fountain to John E. Warren. The fountain is located behind the present Westbrook Pool on the bank of the Presumpscot. It was presented on May 29, 1921 as a gift of Miss Cornelia Warren, a cousin. It is designed of bronze and is a creation of Miss Baska Paeff. It is inscribed as follows: "In affectionate memory of John E. Warren, a loyal member of this community, who planned this path by the river, this fountain is placed by his cousin, Cornelia Warren. The memory of the just is blessed. Prov. 107." (Ketover Collection.)

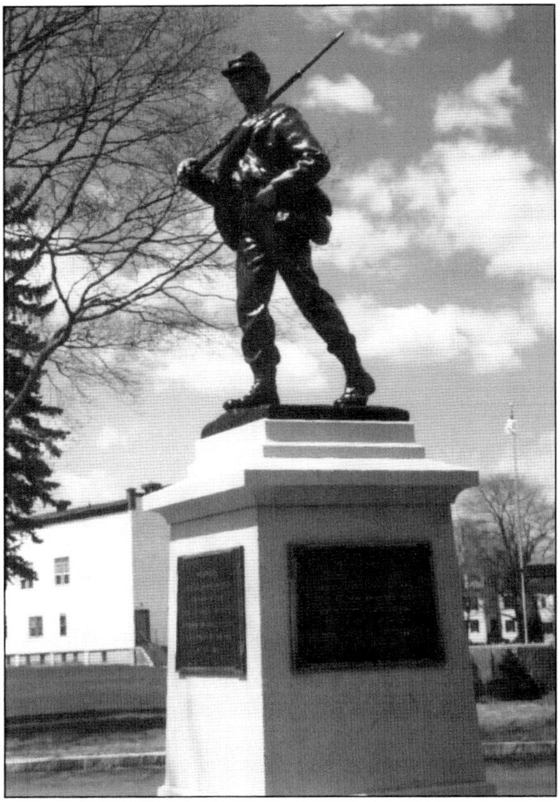

Soldiers' monument at Riverbank Park, dedicated July 4, 1917. Money was raised with the help of Mr. and Mrs. Woodbury K. Dana and the bronze figure was cast by the Gorham Manufacturing Company of Providence and New York. Sculptor was Alice Ruggles Kitson of Quincy, Massachusetts. (Ketover Collection.)

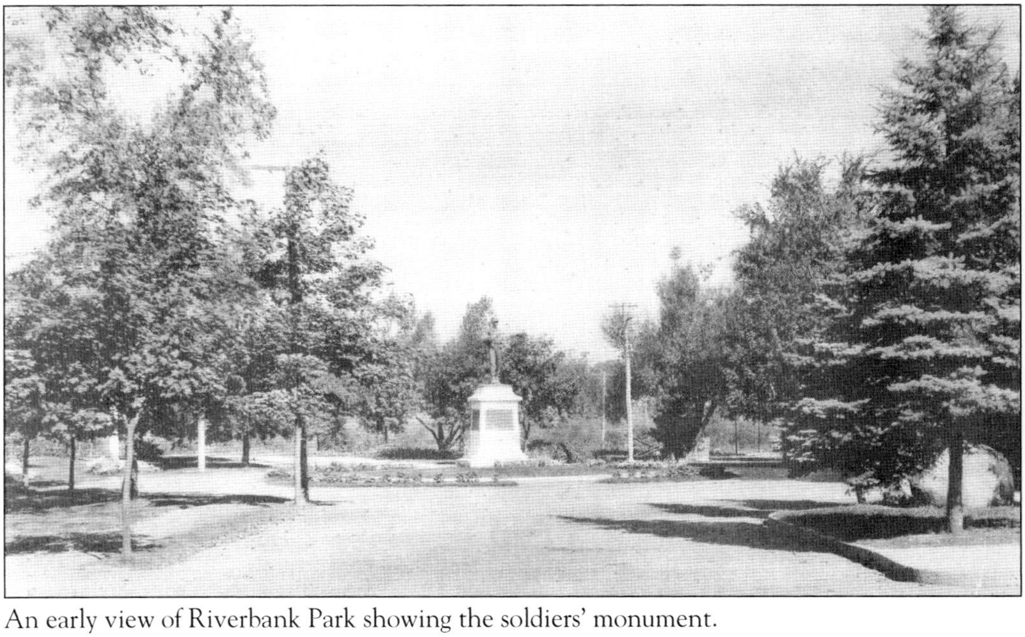

An early view of Riverbank Park showing the soldiers' monument.

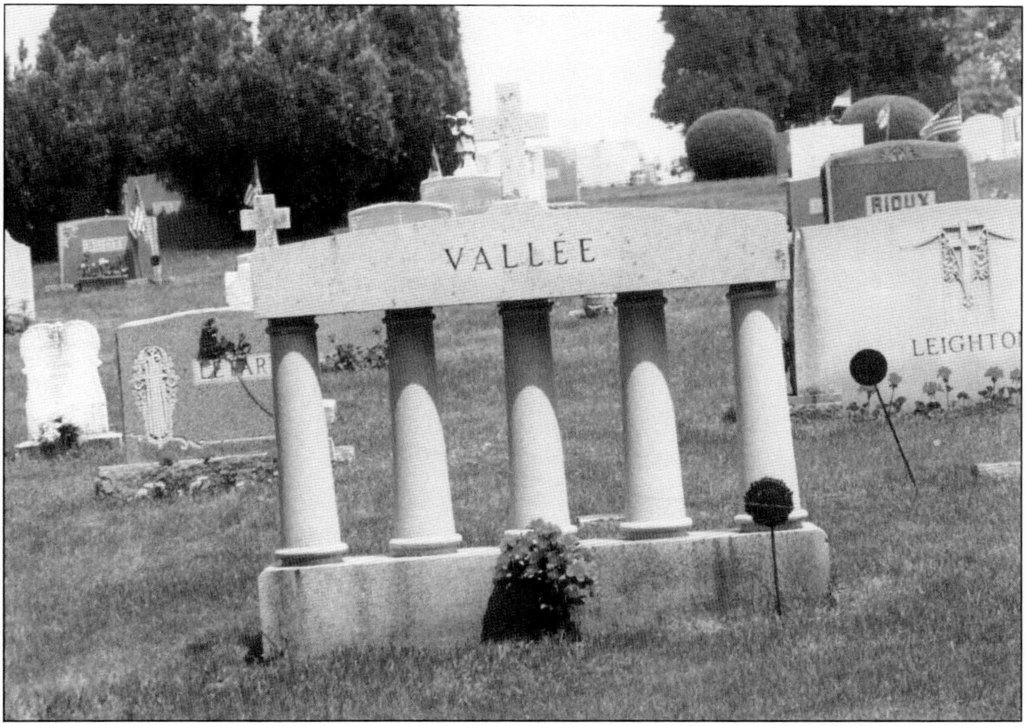

The Vallee family monument in St. Hyacinthe's Cemetery. (Ketover Collection.)

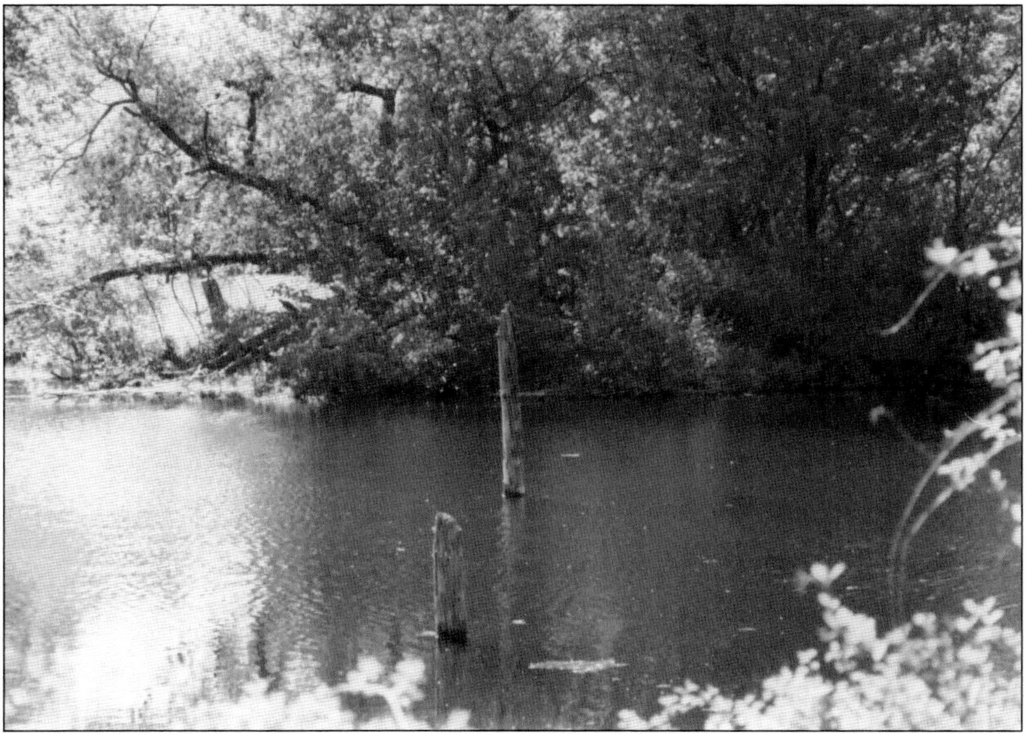
Tow-path crossover at Beaver Pond. The only visible remains of the Cumberland and Oxford Canal are in this spot. (Ketover Collection.)

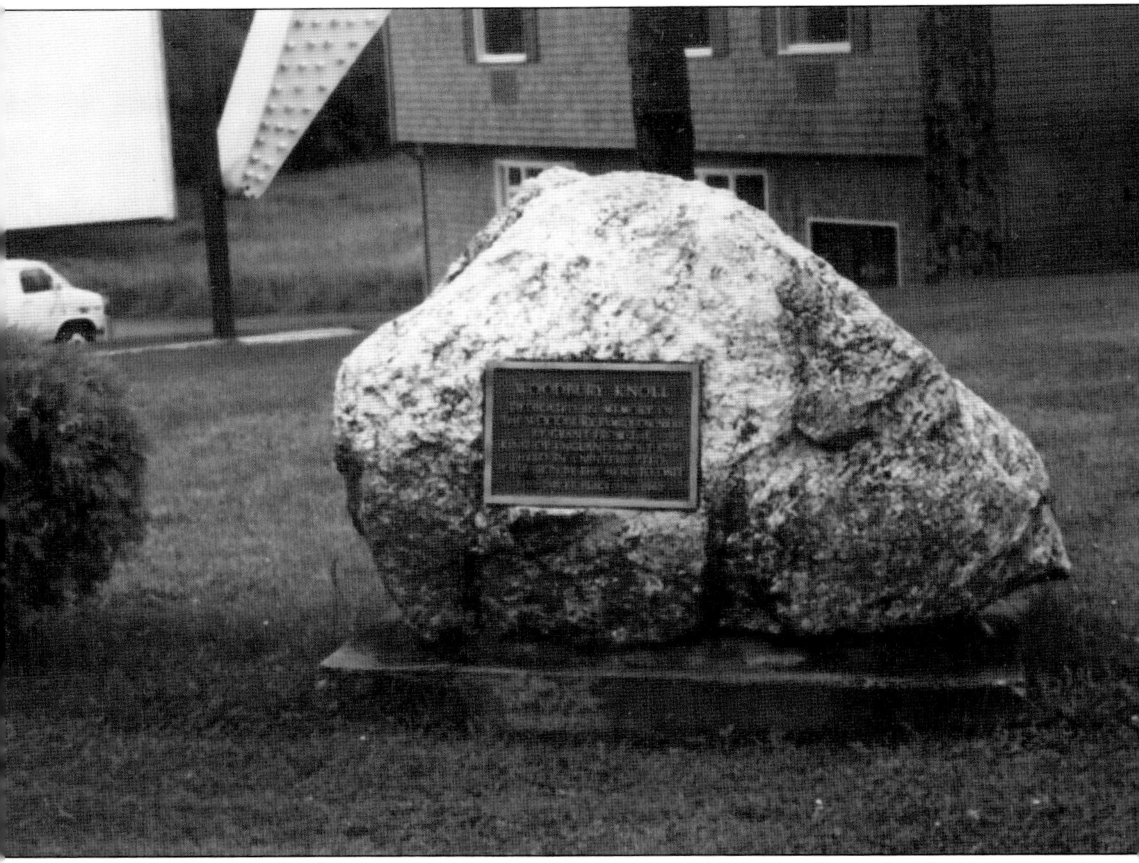

Woodbury Knoll. This area was dedicated in memory of the Woodbury family, by a grant from the king of England about 1700. The land has been held in uninterrupted possession by the heirs to date. This tablet was placed in 1962. (Mike Sanphy Collection.)

Nine

The Later Years

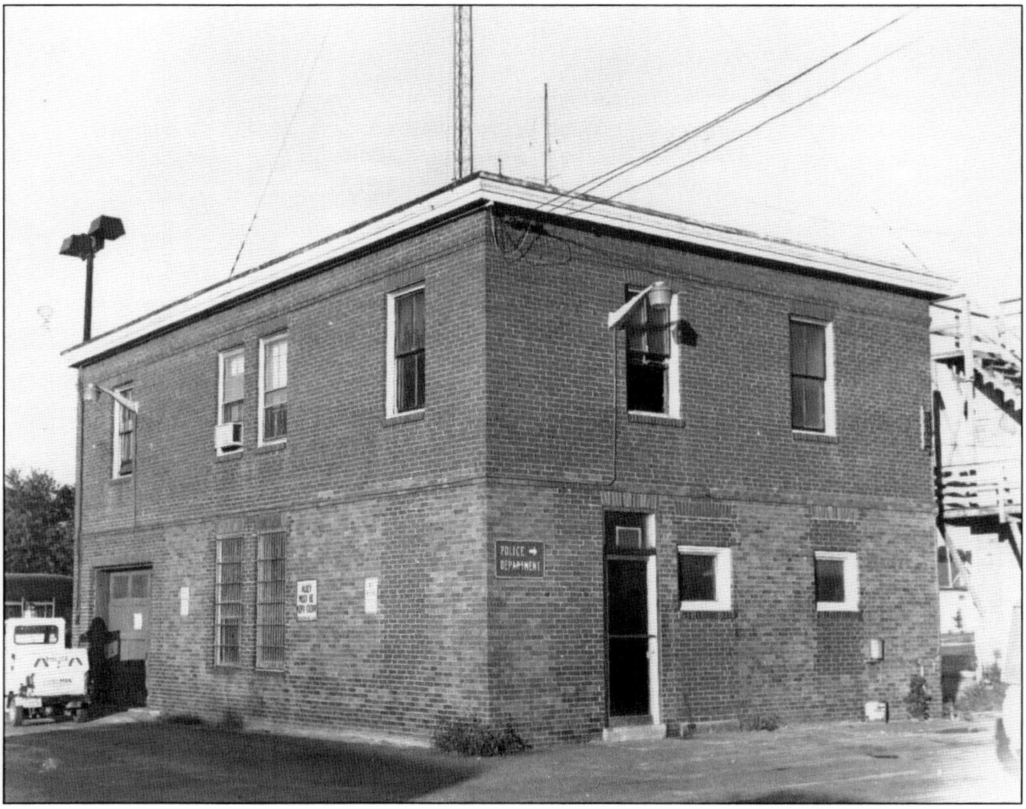

Old Police Station. Located on Carpenter Street, off Main Street, this station was in service from 1914 to 1977. It was demolished as part of Urban Renewal and the police department moved its operations to its present location in Cumberland Mills.

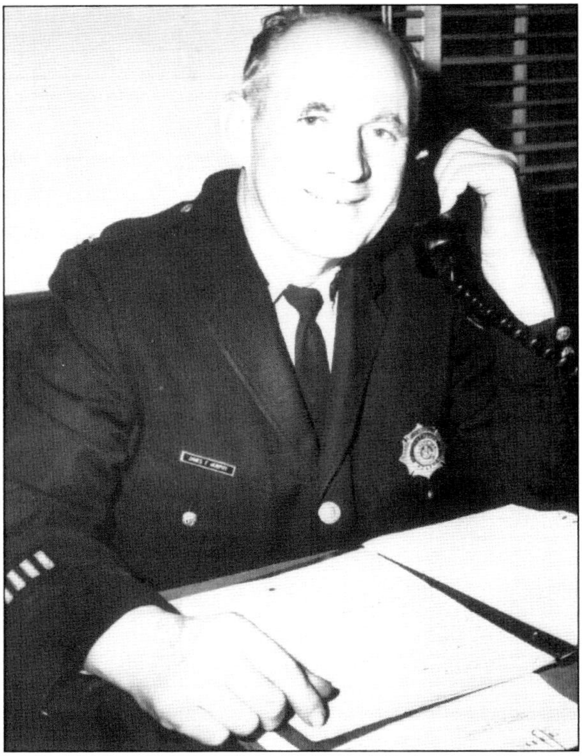

James Murphy, police chief from 1960 to 1970. (Sanphy Collection.)

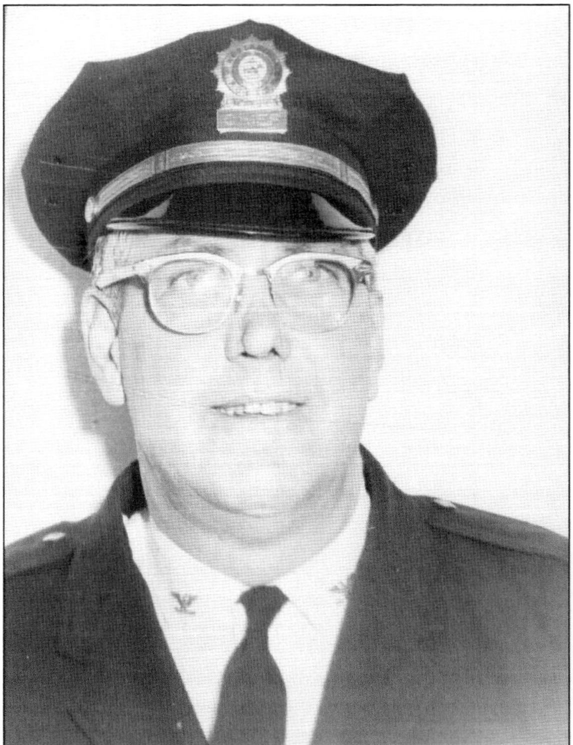

Philip Hansen, police chief from 1970 to 1973. (Sanphy Collection.)

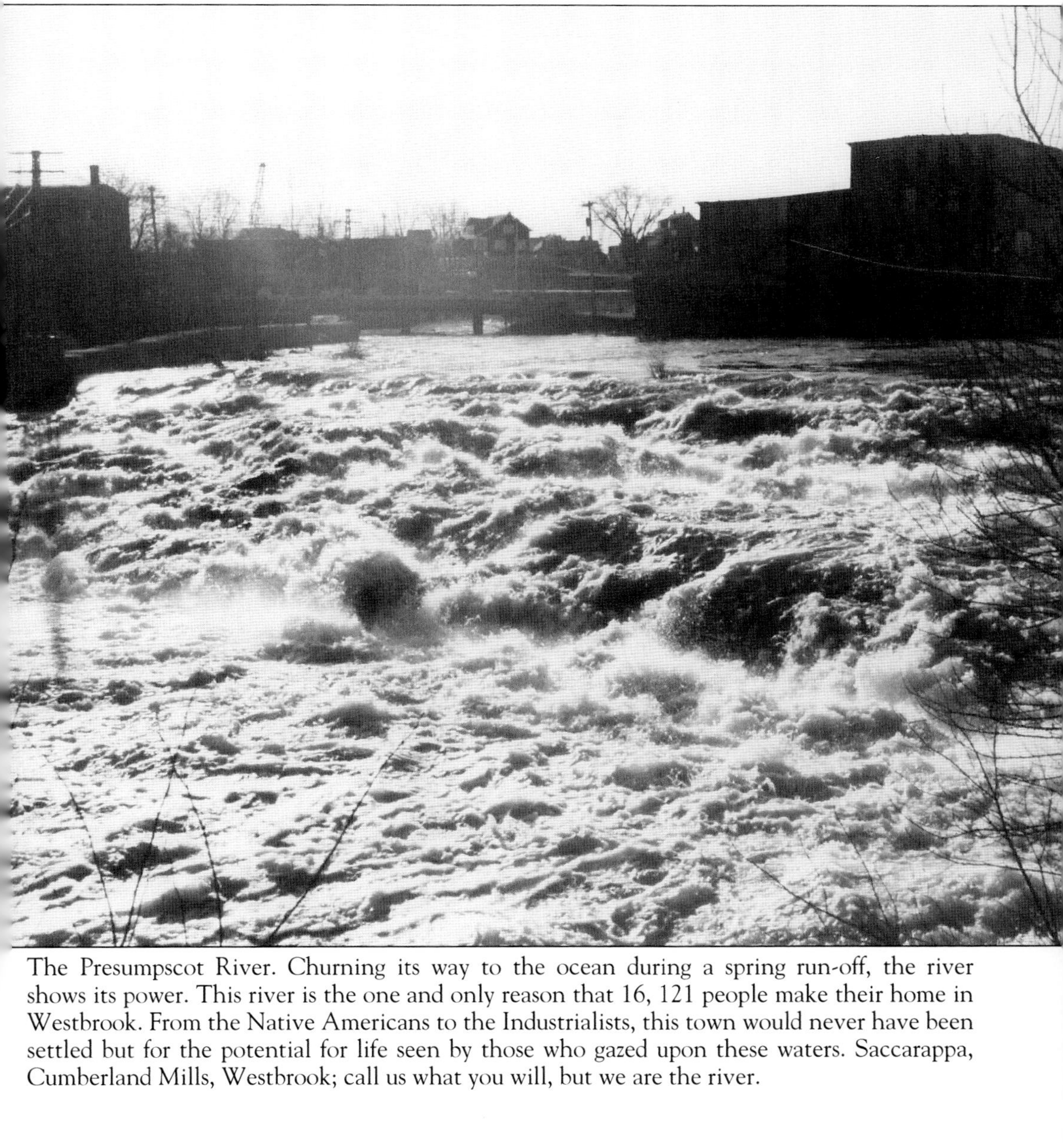

The Presumpscot River. Churning its way to the ocean during a spring run-off, the river shows its power. This river is the one and only reason that 16, 121 people make their home in Westbrook. From the Native Americans to the Industrialists, this town would never have been settled but for the potential for life seen by those who gazed upon these waters. Saccarappa, Cumberland Mills, Westbrook; call us what you will, but we are the river.

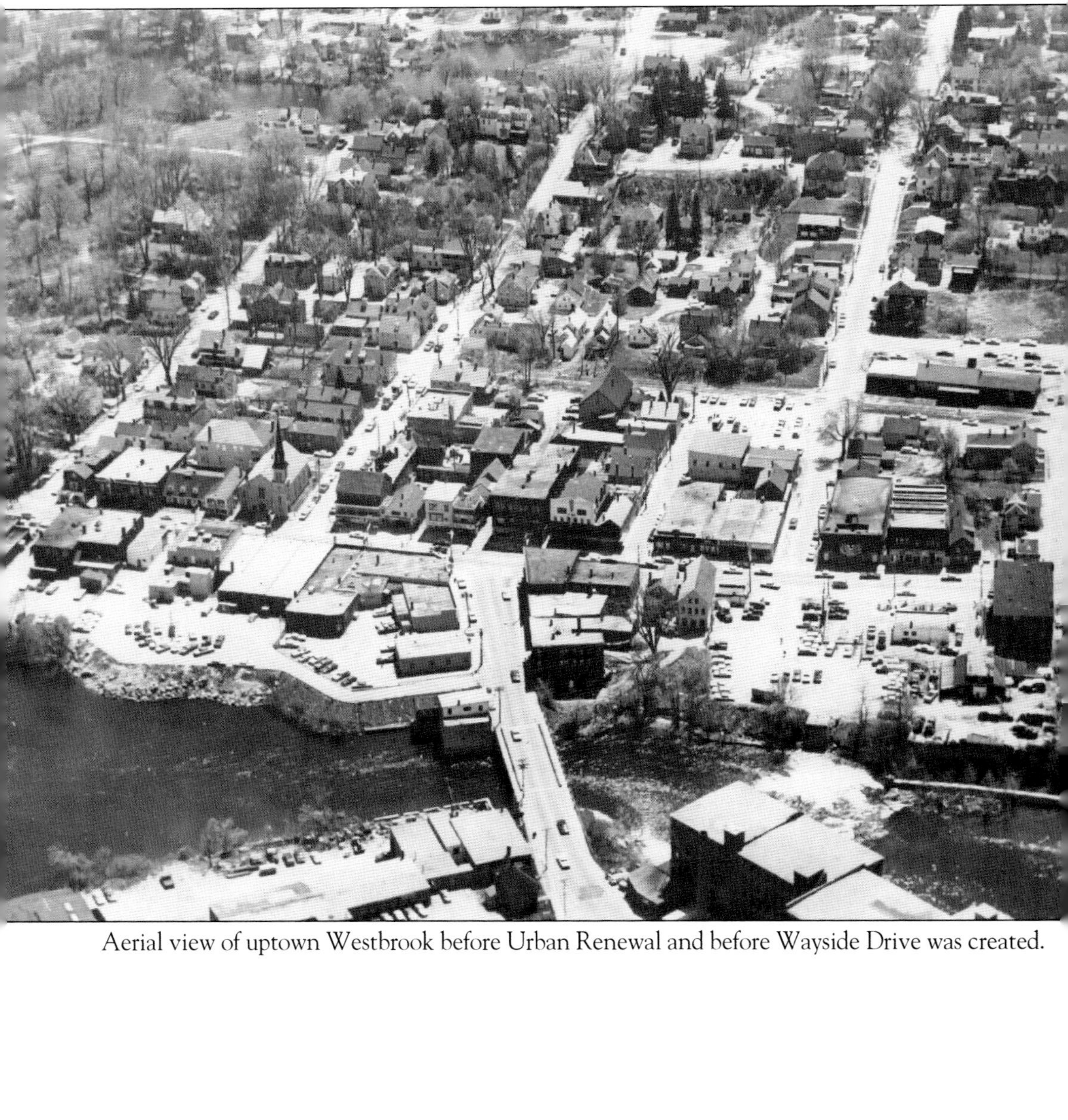

Aerial view of uptown Westbrook before Urban Renewal and before Wayside Drive was created.

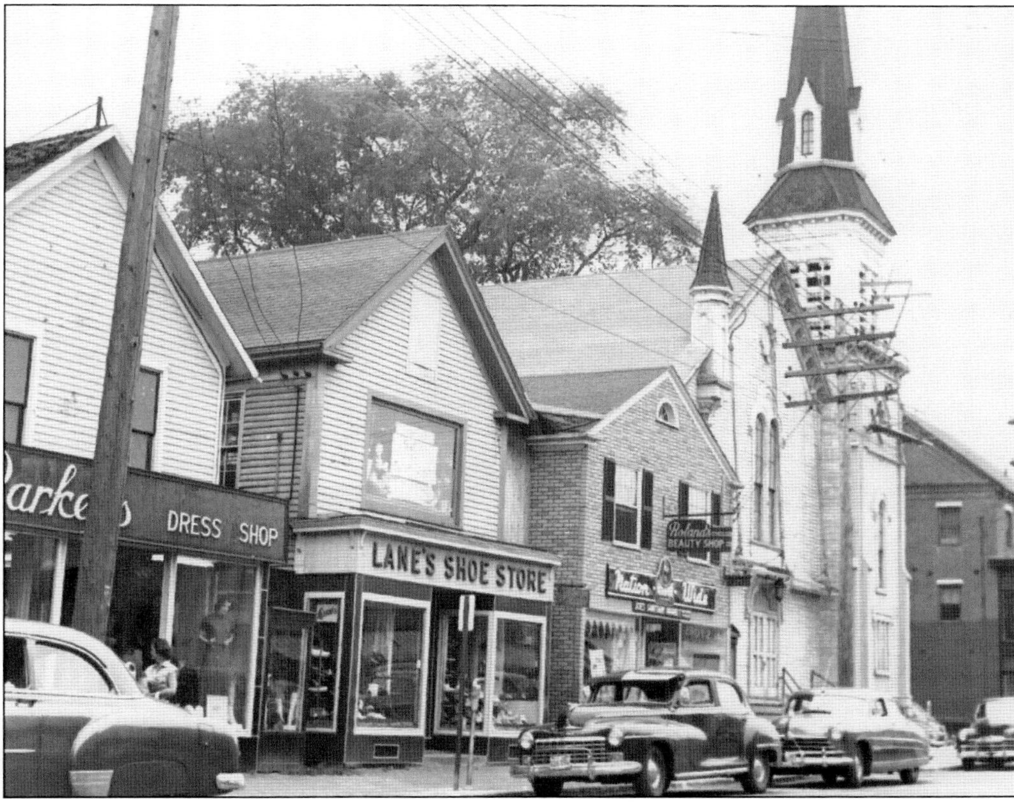

A section of Main Street in the 1950s, showing familiar shops and the Westbrook Congregational Church.

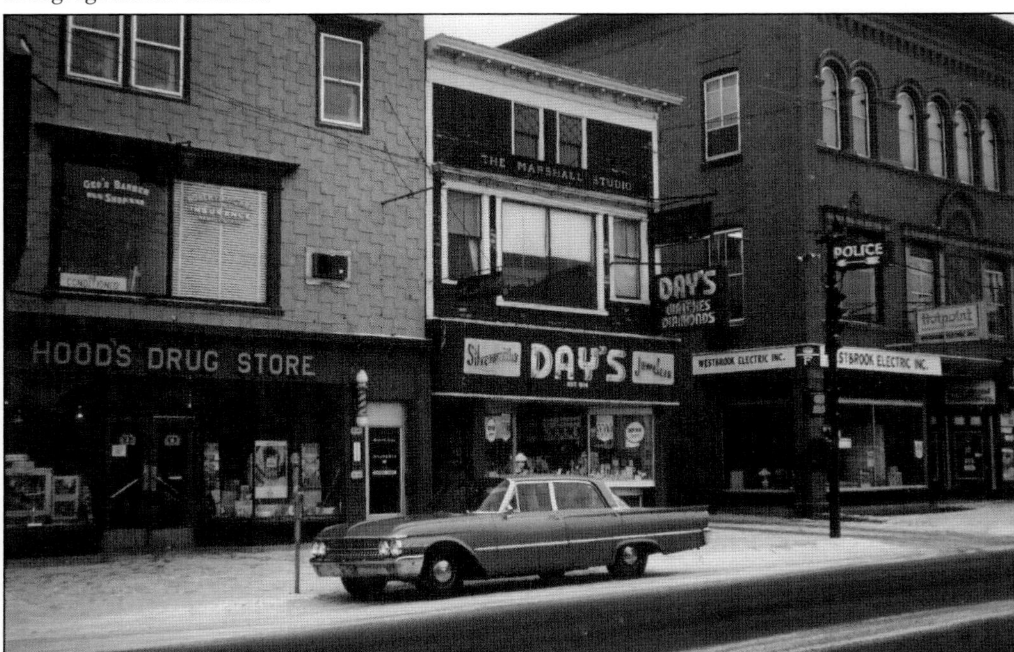

Main Street in the 1960s, further up the street.

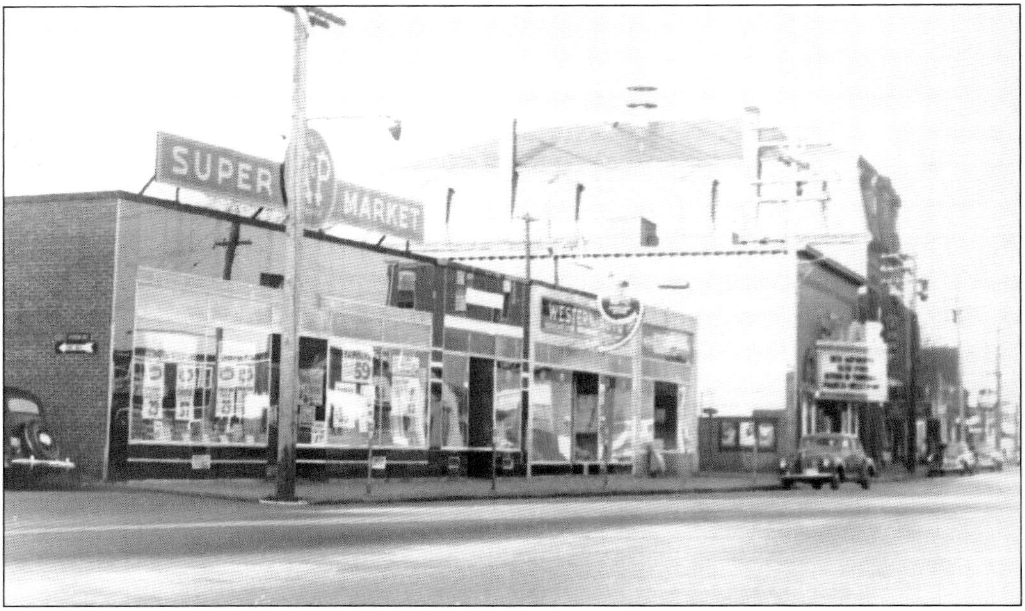

The A & P Store and the Star Theatre in the 1950s. Located at the corner of Main and Central Streets, this area is now home to the Westbrook Discount Beverage Store.

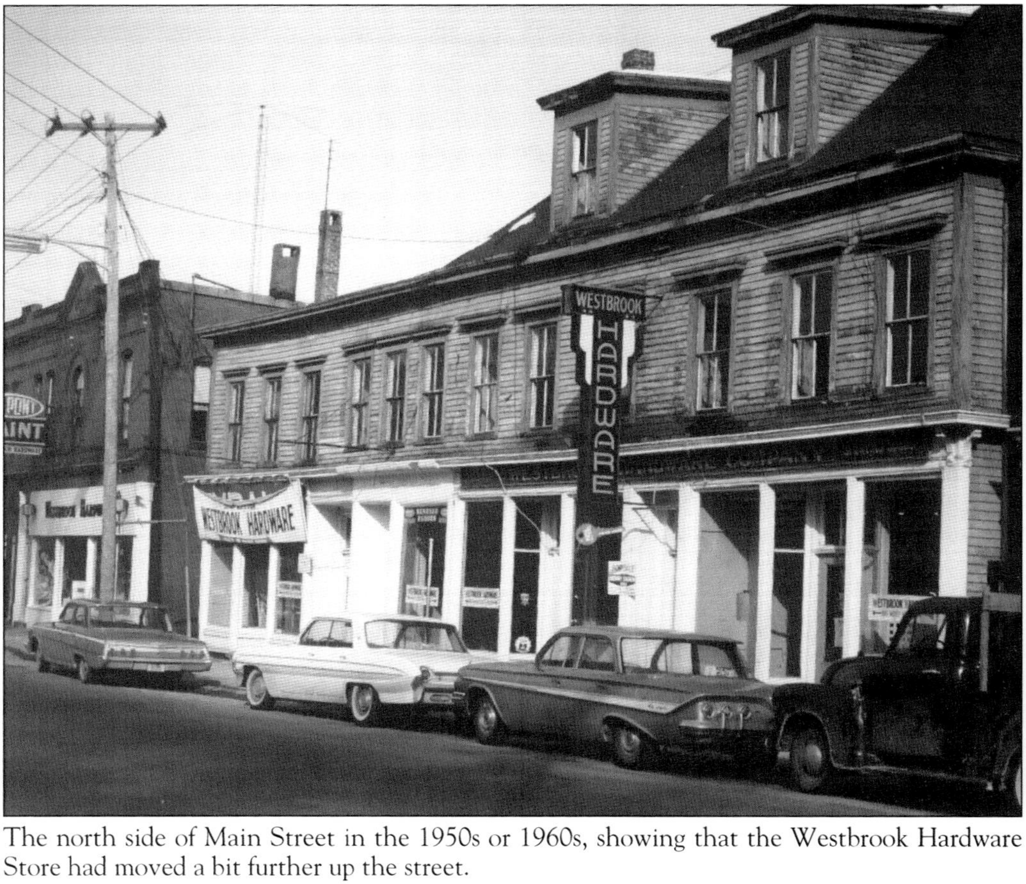

The north side of Main Street in the 1950s or 1960s, showing that the Westbrook Hardware Store had moved a bit further up the street.

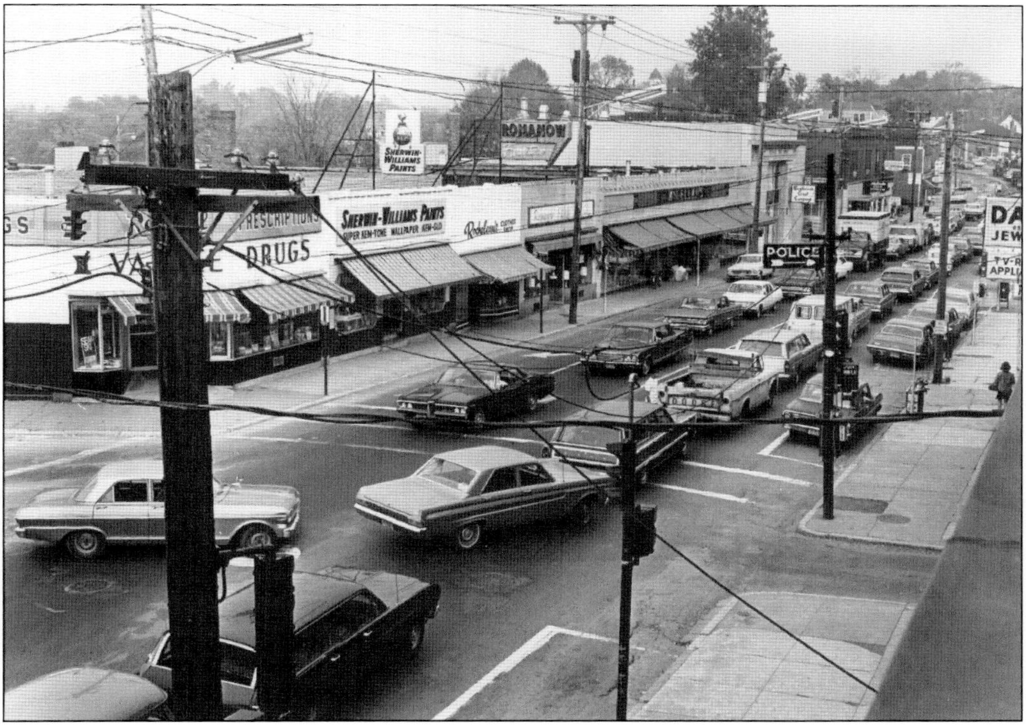

Vallee's Square, August 1969. This shot was taken before Urban Renewal.

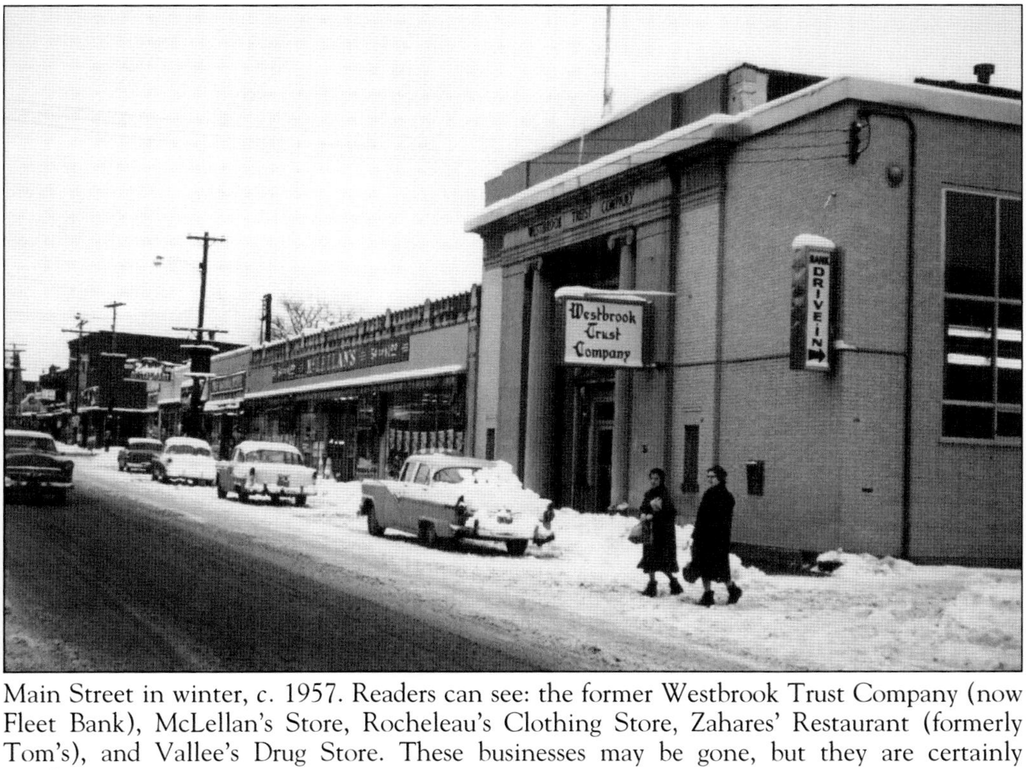

Main Street in winter, *c.* 1957. Readers can see: the former Westbrook Trust Company (now Fleet Bank), McLellan's Store, Rocheleau's Clothing Store, Zahares' Restaurant (formerly Tom's), and Vallee's Drug Store. These businesses may be gone, but they are certainly not forgotten.

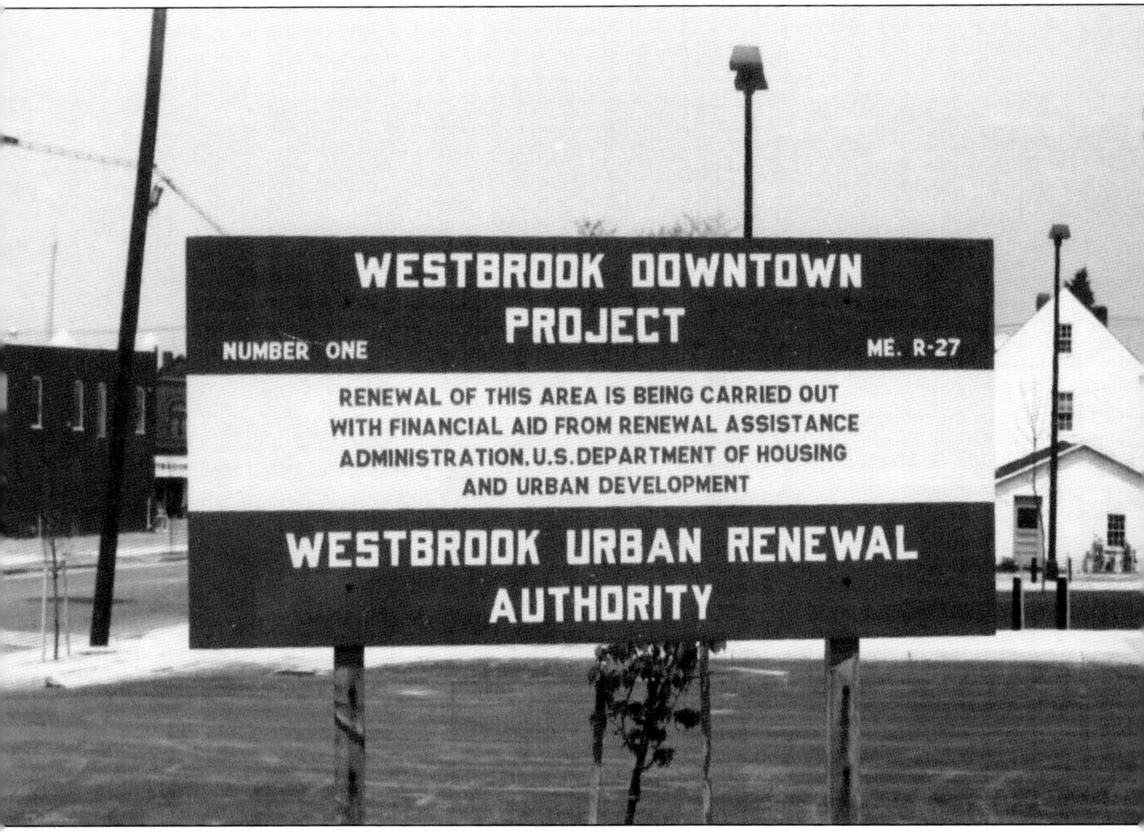
WESTBROOK DOWNTOWN PROJECT
NUMBER ONE
ME. R-27
RENEWAL OF THIS AREA IS BEING CARRIED OUT WITH FINANCIAL AID FROM RENEWAL ASSISTANCE ADMINISTRATION. U.S. DEPARTMENT OF HOUSING AND URBAN DEVELOPMENT
WESTBROOK URBAN RENEWAL AUTHORITY